NAFSA'S GUIDE TO
EDUCATION ABROAD
FOR ADVISERS AND ADMINISTRATORS

EDITED BY
WILLIAM HOFFA, JOHN PEARSON,
AND MARVIN SLIND

NAFSA: ASSOCIATION OF INTERNATIONAL EDUCATORS

NAFSA: Association of International Educators is a nonprofit membership association that provides training, information, and other education services to professionals in the field of international education exchange. Its sixty-five hundred members—from every state in the United States and more than fifty countries—make it the largest professional membership association in the world concerned with the advancement of effective international educational exchange. Members represent primarily colleges and universities but also elementary and secondary schools, public and private educational associations, exchange organizations, national and international corporations and foundations, and community organizations. Through its publications, workshops, institutional consultations, and conferences, the association serves as a source of professional training, a reference for standards of performance, and an advocate for the most effective operation of international educational exchange.

This publication can be ordered from the Publications Order Desk, NAFSA: Association of International Educators, 1875 Connecticut Ave., N.W., Suite 1000, Washington, DC 20009 USA.

Library of Congress Cataloging-in-Publication Data

NAFSA's guide to education abroad for advisers and administrators/edited
    by William Hoffa, John Pearson, and Marvin Slind

    Includes bibliographical references.
    ISBN 0-912207-62-0
    1. Foreign study—Handbooks, manuals, etc. 2. American students—Travel—Handbooks, manuals, etc. 3. College students—Travel—Handbooks, manuals, etc. 4. Faculty advisers—Handbooks, manuals, etc. 5. College administrators—Handbooks, manuals, etc.
    I. Hoffa, William. II. Pearson, John. III. Slind, Marvin.
    IV. NAFSA: Association of International Educators (Washington, D.C.)
    V. Title: Guide to education abroad for advisers and administrators.
    LB2376.N26 1992
    370.19'62—dc20   92-38037
                                                      CIP

Cover and book design by Andy Brown.

Contents

ACKNOWLEDGMENTS ... vii

FOREWORD *John Pearson and Marvin Slind* ... ix

INTRODUCTION *William Hoffa* ... xiii

ESSENTIAL ACRONYMS ... xxi

PART ONE
EDUCATION ABROAD AND
AMERICAN HIGHER EDUCATION

1 BEING A PROFESSIONAL IN THE FIELD OF EDUCATION
ABROAD *Contributors: Archer Brown and David Larsen* ... 3
- Entering the Field ... 3
- Standards of Professional Practice ... 5
- Opportunities for Professional
Development ... 8

2 THE EDUCATION-ABROAD OFFICE IN ITS CAMPUS CONTEXT
Contributors: Paul DeYoung and Paul Primak ... 17
- Institutional Structures and Values ... 18
- Institutional Policy ... 19
- Working with Others ... 22
- Getting Advice from Others: Institutional
Outreach ... 24

3 ACADEMIC CREDIT
Contributors: Eleanor Krawutschke and Kathleen Sideli ... 27
- Faculty and Administrative Commitment ... 27
- Procedures for Home-Institution-Sponsored or
Cosponsored Programs ... 29
- Programs Sponsored by Other Institutions ... 32

4 FINANCIAL AID
Contributor: Nancy Stubbs ... 39
- What Is Financial Aid? ... 39

- How Do Students Qualify for Financial
  Aid?   42
- How Is Financial Aid Awarded?   43
- What Financial Aid Can Be Used for
  Study Abroad?   43
- How Can You Help to Make Financial
  Aid Available?   45
- Additional Financial Aid Resources   46

5   THE OFFICE LIBRARY AND RESOURCE MATERIALS
*Contributors: Catherine Gamon and
Heidi Soneson*   49
- Institutional Policy and the Library   49
- Professional Goals versus
  Institutional Policies   52
- Setting Up a Resource Library   54

6   COMPUTERIZING OPERATIONS
*Contributors: James Gehlhar and
Kathleen Sideli*   59
- Assessing Needs, Goals, Support, and
  Resources   59
- Applications   64

7   PROMOTION AND PUBLICITY
Contributor: My Yarabinec   71
- Promoting Your Office and Work   71
- Promoting Education Abroad to Students   72
- Publicizing Programs   74
- Using the Media   76

PART TWO
ADVISING

8   THE DEMOGRAPHICS OF EDUCATION ABROAD
*Contributors: Stephen Cooper and
Mary Anne Grant*   83
- Four Recent Studies   84
- Basic Characteristics of U.S.
  Students Abroad   87
- Student Attitudes and Backgrounds   95

9 ADVISING PRINCIPLES AND STRATEGIES
*Contributors: Cynthia Felbeck Chalou and
Janeen Felsing* 99
• Basic Knowledge and Skills 99
• Advising Procedures and Strategies 106

10 PROMOTING STUDENT DIVERSITY
*Contributors: Margery A. Ganz, Jack Osborn, and
Paul Primak* 111
• Deciding on Priorities 112
• Advising Nontraditional Students 113
• Pragmatic and Proactive Strategies 116

11 HEALTH AND SAFETY ISSUES
Contributor: Joan Elias Gore 125
• Health Issues 126
• Personal Conduct and Safety Issues 131
• Predeparture Orientation 132
• Region Specific Information 134
• Resources 135

12 PREDEPARTURE ORIENTATION AND REENTRY
PROGRAMMING *Contributor: Ellen Summerfield* 137
• Predeparture Orientation Programs 137
• Reentry Programming 146

PART THREE
PROGRAM DEVELOPMENT AND EVALUATION

---

13 PROGRAM PLANNING, BUDGETING, AND
IMPLEMENTATION *Contributors: Jack Henderson,
Tom Roberts, Paula Spier, and Henry Weaver* 157
• Three Case Histories 158
• Critical Issues and Questions 168
• Money Matters 170

14 PROGRAM DESIGNS AND STRATEGIES
Contributors: Joseph Navari and Heidi Soneson 175
• Programs Sponsored by Your
Own Campus 175
• Programs Sponsored in Cooperation with
Others 186

15 WORK ABROAD AND INTERNATIONAL CAREERS
Contributor: William Nolting 193
  • Work versus Study Abroad: Similarities
    and Differences 194
  • Working Abroad and International
    Careers 197
  • Advising for Work Abroad 199
  • Types of Work Abroad 203

16 PROGRAM EVALUATION
*Contributors: Michael Laubscher and
  Ronald Pirog* 213
  • Program Quality 213
  • The Internal Evaluation 215
  • Evaluating External Programs 219

APPENDIXES

  Appendix 1 Study, Work, and Travel
              Abroad: A Bibliography 227

  Appendix 2 "Getting on with the Task,"
              Report of the National Task
              Force on Undergraduate
              Education Abroad, 1990 261

  Appendix 3 Penn State University's
              Program Evaluation Guide 285

  Appendix 4 NAFSA Code of Ethics, 1992 295

  Appendix 5 "How to Read Study Abroad
              Literature," by Lily von
              Klemperer, 1976 303

  CONTRIBUTORS 307

Acknowledgments

We own our gratitude to numerous colleagues who contributed their time and expertise to the production of *NAFSA's Guide to Education Abroad for Advisers and Administrators*. To begin at the beginning, we acknowledge Nancy McCormack who, almost twenty years ago, was the guiding spirit behind this book's progenitor, *The SECUSSA Sourcebook,* the outcome of a workshop held in Brattleboro, Vermont, and funded in part by the Carnegie Foundation. Nancy raised the money to support that project, organized the organizers, motivated the participants, and compiled the finished product.

Without the initiative, tenacity, and sustained efforts of Marvin Slind (University of Washington) and John Pearson (Stanford University), we would never have been embarked on such an ambitious complement to the *Sourcebook*.

At different times during the drafting process, selected readers provided immeasurable assistance and guidance:

Stephen Cooper, Louisiana State University

Paula Spier, retired from Antioch College

Nancy Stubbs, University of Colorado-Boulder

Charles Gliozzo, Michigan State University

Mary Anne Grant, International Student Exchange Program

Rodney Sangster, University of California System

Annagene Yucas, University of Pittsburgh

William Hoffa spent a long summer in 1992 editing the chapters, incorporating readers' and authors' emendations, and creating a consistent style for the manuscript. We are indebted to him for this effort.

Finally, we acknowledge the support of NAFSA's Field Service Program through a grant from the Advising, Teaching, and Specialized Programs Division of the U.S. Information Agency, which enabled NAFSA to convene a publication planning meeting in fall 1988.

Any sustained effort of this volunteer kind involves contributions from individuals too numerous to list here. They have our thanks for their support and encouragement.

—Archer Brown

Foreword

Almost twenty years have passed since the original *SECUSSA Sourcebook* was published and more than four since the plans were laid for this new publication. As Bill Hoffa makes clear in the introduction, study-abroad programmers and advisers have been fortunate that numerous publications—of an advisory and adversarial nature—have appeared during the past two decades. The time between the original *Sourcebook* and the plans for this new handbook and then between the initial call for chapters and the printed publication are significant, because study abroad experienced many changes in the years between 1975 and 1989. However, we feel that the years since 1989 have seen as many changes and might be considered the watershed years between rapid growth in overseas opportunities and a growing realization that fiscal, academic, and political conditions might be limiting this growth. If this is so, and the 1990s become a decade of change for our field, what then is the purpose of this publication?

Our view is that this publication serves as a reminder of what is basic about our profession and what is possible. We hope that this work will help newcomers to the field learn from others and give old-timers some cause for reflection. However, this work is not definitive. Given the regularity with which new issues appear—issues that might affect overseas opportunities for the rest of the decade even if they are not fully visible now—the information presented here cannot be completely up to date. The introduction seeks to redress this with a discussion of the Boren Bill, but this bill is just one of many challenges and opportunities facing the field during the next few years. While we hope that the essays included in this publication will help those in international education better conduct their work, we feel it is also necessary to look ahead and to make some predictions about future issues.

It is perhaps most appropriate to start by quoting testimony given by Sen. J. William Fulbright to the Committee on Foreign Affairs, Subcommittee on International Operations, U. S. House of Representatives, on July 9, 1992. Senator Fulbright, for so long the preeminent spokesperson for international educational exchange, commented that "the needs of Americans to understand other nations and their languages have never been greater." While we all agree, Senator Fulbright went on to say that "while it sounds impressive that seventy thousand of our students go abroad to study each year, that translates into fewer than 1 percent of U.S. undergraduates, and about 75 percent of them are studying in a few Western European countries." There are two significant elements to the senator's comments. It is a challenge to Senator Fulbright's successor—the senator who, we hope, will be to the next few decades what Senator Fulbright has been to the last few. Our hope is that this successor is Senator Boren, but this is one of the surprises that the 1990s hold for us.

The other significant aspect of the senator's talk is the number of students who study abroad. The 1990s may find that the number of students is less important than the profile of the students, the fields of study, and the destinations. In the past, this information has never been well documented. While some schools do keep excellent statistics, many don't. One challenge of the 1990s will be to perfect the collection of data and better evaluate the experiences of the students.

A similar problem is the need to further investigate the academic motives for studying overseas. How important is a program's academic content in a student's decision? Do all advisers and programmers agree? In an educational environment where home-campus distribution requirements are tightening, will we see the growth of programs that tie the overseas academic experience more and more to home-campus requirements?

It is hard to divorce academic concerns from financial ones. If NAFSA's Section on U.S. Students Abroad (SECUSSA) is to take credit for anything over the past few years it is the work performed by Nancy Stubbs, Chuck Gliozzo, Steve Cooper, Norm Peterson, and others in building into the Higher Education Act language that is more favorable to study abroad. However, this is only part of the challenge. The difficulty of funding students to go overseas is reflected in the financial climate at many institutions, a climate that might see study abroad relegated to something that is nice but not essential. Institutional frameworks of decision making, power structures, and opportunity are going to be as important in the next few years as what we achieve at the national level. A challenging prediction would be that they will become more important.

With the changing financial climate at many institutions, we are faced with deciding what services will be available to students interested in study abroad. Institutions may cut back on their programs. They may also (and there already seems to be some evidence for this) reduce advising services to students who wish to study abroad but not necessarily on their own institution's programs. The next few years will witness increasing strains on advisers in small offices as they try to cover all the bases.

Financial conditions on the home campus are a reflection of economic conditions nationally and internationally. Many SECUSSAns spoke the gospel of increased study-abroad opportunities during the 1980s, and the field experienced extraordinary growth. We can only guess—pending further inquiry—whether this result was due to our diligence, professionalism, innate charm, or to an economic climate that favored U.S. students going overseas. If it is more of the latter than we care to admit, how do we face the 1990s, which will be less favorable to students in U.S. institutions of higher education and the United States in the world market? This is not meant to suggest a reversal of the successes since 1975; the field has come too far. However, the above challenges are real, exacerbated by the world's changing political, social, and cultural climate. The 1980s were relatively calm. What will the next few years be like?

—John Pearson
—Marvin Slind

Introduction

In 1975, NAFSA published *The SECUSSA Sourcebook: A Guide for Advisors of U.S. Students Planning an Overseas Experience.* This pioneering book grew out of the professional excitement and interchange of ideas between fifty representatives from U.S. colleges and universities across the country, plus other professional educators from the Experiment/SIT, the Council on International Educational Exchange, the Institute of International Education, and the U.S. Office of Education, who had attended a December 1974 workshop held on the campus of the Experiment in International Living and the School for International Training in Brattleboro, Vermont. The workshop was sponsored by the then new NAFSA Section on U.S. Students Abroad (SECUSSA), and the costs were largely underwritten by a grant from the Carnegie Corporation of New York and Educational Programmes Abroad, Brighton, England.

In the *Sourcebook's* preface, editor Judy Frank expressed, on behalf of all those who attended the workshop and contributed their thoughts to the book's contents, hope that the book represented "the first steps toward professionalizing the field of advising U.S. students who wish an overseas experience." Denying that the *Sourcebook* contained "the final word" on advising students, she envisioned a "constant reevaluation and change" in professional training and knowledge in the years ahead. *Education Abroad* demonstrates that "constant reevaluation and change" have taken place over the past two decades, and also reveals that many of the professional concerns identified in 1975 have become perennial. The *Sourcebook* remains—for those who can find a copy—a repository of sound insight and useful advice, coupled with an inspired vision of the value of living and learning abroad. Especially noteworthy are its sections on cross-cultural training, the importance of language learning, and experiential education.

The *Sourcebook* was followed four years later by another collective effort, *Study Abroad: A Handbook for Advisers and Administrators*, also published by NAFSA. This work, to which a professional could "turn for information, points of view, practices, alternatives, suggestions and cautions," presented its counsel in outline form—unlike the *Sourcebook*, which is composed of reflective essays. Recognizing that its audience worked in diverse institutions, or in similar institutions in different phases of internationalization, the

Handbook offered numerous levels of counsel, and tried to be "descriptive rather than prescriptive."

Whereas the *Sourcebook* centered somewhat broadly on "the overseas experience," the *Handbook* gave less attention to the experiential component of living and learning overseas and centered more on study abroad, offering less pedagogy and vision. The *Handbook* acknowledged the clear historical trend during the 1960s and 1970s (which continued through the 1980s and is only just now being challenged) toward formal, academic, credit-bearing programs, sponsored directly by American colleges and universities, somewhat at the expense of other forms of international education. The *Handbook* also addressed the fact that advisers and administrators are likely to be employed by academic institutions, and that most students need credit and often financial assistance for their time abroad. The *Sourcebook* and the *Handbook*, like this volume, are concerned with the ongoing issues for advisers, administrators, and institutions: the place of overseas study in its institutional context and in American higher education; the diverse roles and responsibilities of advisers and administrators; how to evaluate programs and advise students; how to plan, implement, and promote programs; how to prepare students for their time abroad and their return; how to assess and award academic credit; and how to provide adequate financial aid—to mention just a few areas of lasting concern.

Much has changed in the field of international education since the *Sourcebook* and the *Handbook* were written; in many respects, they have become dated. The professional practice of advising and administration is now considerably more complex and demanding; student opportunities have multiplied dramatically; many more types of institutions are supporting education abroad in some form; and the national mood and economy, as well as world events, have significantly altered the climate of support for international education. What is now required of practitioners and institutions, in order to provide the best advice, services, and support that students and institutions require, is more substantial than ever before. The dimensions of the field have been greatly enlarged and its contours and terrain have become more varied. This new landscape is illustrated by the following:

• The sheer number of American undergraduates who spend time overseas as part of their studies seems to have grown during every year of the 1980s. While overall national figures now suggest that only about 2 percent of all two-year and four-year college students participate in education-abroad programs, this still amounts to an estimated total of around a hundred thousand students. At some institutions (especially private liberal arts colleges), percentages are dramatically higher, often in the 20 to 40 percent range or higher. Perhaps of even greater significance, the number of colleges and universities that have committed themselves to increasing on- and off-campus opportunities for international education has risen dramatically.

xiv

- The number of study and work opportunities available to students has increased tremendously; IIE now lists over two thousand programs taking place during the academic year and another fourteen hundred summer and short-term programs; in addition, programs are now taking place in nearly every country.

- The traditional program (a junior year of language studies, humanities, and social sciences) is still dominant, but has given way to a greater variety in program duration, student profile, and academic and preprofessional course work (from aboriginal studies to zoology).

- Encouraging and assessing education abroad and providing professional development to advisers and program administrators has become a greater part of the conferences, workshops, research activities, and publications of NAFSA, CIEE, and numerous other professional associations. As discussed in chapter 1, there are many opportunities for newcomers to receive basic training and for experienced professionals to teach. There is a growing body of scholarly studies on the impact of education abroad on students and institutions, well summarized in Henry Weaver's *Research on U.S. Students Abroad: A Bibliography with Abstracts* (NAFSA, 1989).

- Often following American patterns, other countries are now developing extensive international institution-to-institution academic exchange and internship programs for their undergraduates, especially in Europe and Japan.

- NAFSA, once the National Association of Foreign Student Advisers, then the National Association of Foreign Student Affairs, is now NAFSA: Association of International Educators—name changes that truly reflect not only the greatly enlarged scope of the association's international activities and constituencies, but also the realization that true international education must be multidirectional and global. Education-abroad professionals now see themselves as part of a complex network of international educators.

II

The field of education abroad has developed a more realistic awareness of the accomplishments required to reach the field's highest aspirations and to meet perceived national needs. At the end of the last decade, a spate of important studies and reports on international education compellingly analyzed the current U.S. situation and found it wanting. Among these documents are *Educating for Global Competence* (1988), by the CIEE Advisory Council for International Educational Exchange; *Abroad & Beyond: Patterns in American Overseas Education* (1988), by Craufurd Goodwin and Michael Nacht for IIE; *America in Transition: Report of the Task Force on International Education* (1989), from the National Governor's Association; *International Studies and the Undergraduate* (1989), by Richard Lambert of the National Foreign Language Center, for the American Council on Education;

Exchange 2000: International Leadership for the Next Century (1990), offered by The Liaison Group for International Educational Exchange; and *Getting on With the Task: Report of the National Task Force on Undergraduate Education Abroad* (NAFSA/CIEE/IIE, 1990), the complete text of which appears in the appendix).

All of these studies contain ambitious and challenging recommendations for international educators, colleges and universities, federal and state governments, U.S. foundations, and the private sector. The recommendations have enlarged the stakes and set a challenging national agenda for the entire field. The National Task Force on Undergraduate Education Abroad perhaps best summarizes the goals of the above publications when it argues that the field needs

- to make undergraduate study and other academically related experiences abroad a higher national priority, with particular reference to such specific needs as increasing financial support, greater diversity of opportunity and program participation, and the assurance of program quality
- to initiate and introduce language in existing legislation that will facilitate and expand undergraduate study abroad, develop new legislation at the state and federal levels, and explore and support nonlegislative/governmental avenues of funding
- to develop an action agenda for the exchange field and the broader higher education community and involve these constituencies in the advocacy and implementation of the Task Force's recommendations.

Because education-abroad professionals almost universally accept the recommendations contained in these studies, the question is no longer what direction the field should take at the end of the twentieth century, but how best to work together to implement these goals; to identify, tap, and recycle the requisite resources; and to set a realistic timetable and measure progress. The agreement on goals has never been clearer. However, everything we have learned since the end of World War II needs reexamining in light of our current beliefs about how a significant living and learning experience abroad can enrich and diversify the lives of students and the quality and relevance of their education. This is one of the aims of this volume. There also needs to be a new professional commitment to work within individual colleges and universities, and on a national scale, to utilize the field's accumulated professional wisdom in order to accomplish goals that a few years ago seemed idealistic.

Some preliminary successes are already apparent. The efforts of a small group of SECUSSAns, working with NAFSA, CIEE, and the Liaison Group, succeeded in having the recent reauthorization of the Higher Education Act (July 1992) state the legality of using federal financial aid for study abroad.

The language of this legislation closes previous loopholes and clarifies definitively the kind of economic assistance that students legally merit, the criteria for qualifying for such aid, and the processes of applying for and receiving it. The potential impact of this newly passed legislation is very great. Education-abroad offices will need to work even more closely than before with the financial aid offices on their campus to ensure that students receive their due.

Of potentially greater consequence was the passage in December 1991 of the National Security Education Program (NSEP). This historic legislation, initiated by Sen. David L. Boren (D-Okla.) and supported by the higher education community, established a $150 million international education trust fund that will provide (1) undergraduate scholarships for study in countries and regions of the world designated "critical"; (2) graduate fellowships in support of foreign language studies, area studies, and other international fields; and (3) grants to higher education institutions to establish, operate, and improve programs in "critical" foreign languages, area studies, or other international fields. Like the Fulbright Program in the 1940s, the National Defense Education Act of the 1950s, and the establishment of the Peace Corps in the 1960s, NSEP has the potential for making great strides in furthering the internationalization of American higher education and culture. Of special interest to international educators is NSEP's emphasis on supporting undergraduate education-abroad programming in nontraditional parts of the world, defined as areas that are culturally significant and very important to long-range American interests. NSEP also targets support for nontraditional students—those who have usually lacked the economic resources to participate in education-abroad.

This new support for education abroad from the U.S. government, as well as from many states, reflects a recognition that national self-interest is at stake in an ever more global economy and new political order. However, the rhetoric of internationalism from our political, business, and campus leaders often remains at variance with concrete achievements and unequivocal commitments. In a country that has yet to provide equal, democratic access to the best of our domestic educational system, questions of entitlement loom with regard to education abroad. In a country whose history and cultural references, especially during the current century, have been so highly Eurocentric, the reality and significance of other continents and cultures remains too often a mirage. The challenge to international educators is to build on these beginnings and to contribute our knowledge to continued advocacy and progress on our own campuses and in the national arena.

III

This book has been in the throes of creation for a number of years. Originally intended as an updated version of *The SECUSSA Sourcebook, Educa-*

on Abroad evolved into a series of essays on particular topics, each written by experts, and finally into a more unified, yet discursive and reflective guide. It attempts to provide a broad perspective on most, if not all, important issues and practices that make up the current field of education abroad. Like the *Sourcebook* and *Handbook*, its contents represent a collaborative effort on the part of many education-abroad professionals. But while the book centers on this hard-won collective wisdom, the approach is more pragmatic and suggestive than dogmatic or doctrinaire. It willingly admits that success can be achieved in a variety of ways and in a multitude of settings.

The audience includes (1) newcomers in search of an inclusive, introductory overview of the variety of professional thought and practice on advising and programming; (2) mid-level professionals whose institutional responsibilities have shifted or expanded; and (3) seasoned practitioners in need of new information, points of comparative reference, or an expanded perspective. The book avoids, as much as possible, show-and-tell particularities about specific programs and institutions, and uses case studies only when they enunciate general truths and principles. Each chapter openly acknowledges that there are a huge variety of workable approaches. The hope is that this approach will offer something of interest to nearly everyone, whatever their experience, position, or institution.

Of special note is the use of the operative term "education abroad," rather than "study abroad." While most practitioners are employed by academic institutions and most of their work concerns credit-bearing study programs for undergraduates, NAFSA has long supported a broad range of overseas educational opportunities, academic and experiential. After all, SECUSSA stands for the "Section on U.S. Students Abroad," and not, as is often assumed, the "section on U.S. students studying abroad." What might seem a semantic shift is really a recognition of the earliest and broadest principles in the field, namely support for all varieties of living and learning abroad that have genuine and lasting educational value. The term education abroad also expresses the belief that colleges and universities have an obligation to be proactive in their support of this wide range of activities.

The book is divided into three sections. The first, chapters 1 through 7, focuses on the American institutional contexts of education abroad. This section discusses professional qualifications, opportunities, and responsibilities; training and linkages with colleagues; the place of education-abroad operations within institutional structures and values; working with faculty, the registrar, and financial aid officers to define policies and procedures to ensure that students qualify for academic credit and financial aid; setting up and furnishing the advising office with the necessary materials, resources, and equipment, including computers; and the campus promotion and publicity that may be needed to sell the general idea of education abroad, as well as particular programs. The second section, chapters 8 through 12, centers on advisers and students. This section presents a national profile of students who have traditionally gone abroad to study or work, then discusses what an adviser needs to know in order to provide the best counsel and support to students; general strategies and approaches to advising; how to reach out to nontraditional education-abroad students; health and safety questions; and effective orientation strategies for preparing students for departure and return. The last section, chapters 13 through 16, centers on programming. It presents examples of how three particular programs came into being, and from these examples discusses some general principles of program planning, budgeting, and implementation; explores the academic and economic strengths and drawbacks of a range of different program models, the relative educational merits and advantages of work and study programs, and the many experiential program opportunities that now exist; and how to go about assessing quality of programs sponsored by one's own institution and those sponsored by other institutions.

—William Hoffa

Essential Acronyms

AACRAO	American Association of Collegiate Registrars and Admissions Officers
ACHA	American College Health Association
AFS	AFS/Intercultural Programs (formerly American Field Service)
AIEA	Association of International Education Administrators
AIESEC	International Association of Students in Economics and Commerce
AIFS	American Institute for Foreign Study
AIPT	Association for International Practical Training
BUTEC	British Universities Transatlantic Exchange Committee
CHE/MSA	Commission on Higher Education of the Middle States Association of Colleges and Schools
CIEE	Council on International Educational Exchange
CIES	Council for the International Exchange of Scholars
DIS	Denmark's International Study Program
EFL	English as a foreign language
ESL	English as a second language
ERASMUS	European Community Action Scheme for the Mobility of University Students
IAESTE	International Association for the Exchange of Students for Technical Experience (AIPT in the U.S.)
IIE	Institute of International Education
SAEP	Study-Abroad Evaluation Project
SECUSSA	Section on U.S. Students Abroad
SIETAR	International Society for Intercultural Training and Research
TRACE	Trans-Regional Academic Mobility and Credential Evaluation Information Network
USIA	United States Information Agency

PART ONE

Education Abroad and American Higher Education

BEING A PROFESSIONAL IN THE FIELD OF EDUCATION ABROAD
Contributors: Archer Brown and David Larsen

THE EDUCATION ABROAD OFFICE IN ITS CAMPUS CONTEXT
Contributors: Paul DeYoung and Paul Primak

ACADEMIC CREDIT
Contributors: Eleanor Krawutschke and Kathleen Sideli

FINANCIAL AID
Contributor: Nancy Stubbs

THE OFFICE LIBRARY AND RESOURCE MATERIALS
Contributors: Catherine Gamon and Heidi Soneson

COMPUTERIZING OPERATIONS
Contributors: James Gehlhar and Kathleen Sideli

PROMOTION AND PUBLICITY
Contributor: My Yarabinec

1

Being a Professional in the Field of Education Abroad

Contributors: Archer Brown and David Larsen

Entering the Field

Strictly defined, a profession is a group of people with shared expertise, standards, and goals who are employed to serve a particular and specialized social need. While professionals serve those who employ them, they are also called upon to serve the profession's ideals. Professions maintain their integrity through specialized training and certifying, enforcing performance standards, censuring those who depart from accepted practices, and defining criteria for advancement, promotion, awards, and honors. Broadly speaking, this definition would apply to physicians, lawyers, engineers, architects, and numerous other professionals. As yet, this definition does not entirely apply to the relatively new field of education-abroad advising and program administration.

Nevertheless, education-abroad advising and administration does, like other professions, have a history. The field has an evolved body of knowledge and theory, some carefully defined standards of conduct, and a bibliography of essential resources. In terms of professional development, the field contributes to the training of its members and has organized itself through meetings, publications, and communications networks to share information and perspectives and to develop a professional consensus and community.

This degree of professionalism has been developed under the broad umbrella of NAFSA: Association of International Educators—especially through the members of its Section on U.S. Students Abroad (SECUSSA)—the Council on International Educational Exchange (CIEE), and the Institute of International Education (IIE). Today, colleges and universities across the country are increasingly calling on the expertise of SECUSSAns, along with other international educators, to help them work with students, faculty, and other administrators to accomplish newly defined goals for international and intercultural learning.

Entering this field is seldom preceded by formal training in international educational exchange, though there are several master's programs in the field, such as those run by the School for International Training, Lesley College, and the American Graduate School of International Management. A host of backgrounds and experiences in areas as diverse as teaching and scholarship, international travel and study, and education administration are generally relevant. While each individual may have areas of special strength and expertise, either by virtue of his/her own background, specific training, or by personal predilection and independent learning, no one is expert in all the essential areas of this extremely diverse and demanding field. Moreover, the field is constantly expanding, and what sufficed yesterday may be insufficient to meet the challenges of tomorrow.

Because there are few formal training opportunities and the required skills and talents are so varied, the field is characterized by learning by doing. There is also a practical necessity to learn as much as possible from others involved in the profession. Practices that might be regarded as piracy in the corporate world are commonplace and encouraged in education abroad. An insight, a procedure, an information resource, an approach to a particular program developed and implemented successfully at one institution is more often than not generously shared with others. The general assumption is that when there is innovation, others in the field will hear about it and ask questions. Education-abroad advising and administration is extremely rewarding work in an arena where those questions are almost always answered in the spirit of contributing to the development of other professionals and their programs.

Many practitioners enter the field on a relatively short-term basis—at least initially—because advising or programming hit a responsive chord in their personal history, or because their institution considered advising and programming responsibilities as adjuncts to other campus assignments. Whatever their original motivation or designation, those who remain in the field tend to do so because the work is broad, diverse, and engaging and because the field is dedicated to what they see as important principles and needs in American higher education and global understanding.

Many of the skills required to be an effective education-abroad professional come from having requisite and intrinsic amounts of imagination, empathy, sensitivity, enthusiasm, and patience. Being successful without possessing such personality traits will be nearly impossible. Equally important is the ability to understand, manage, and present a budget, and to communicate with your institution's managers on their own terms. However, the challenge to every practitioner—at all levels of experience—is to build a professional knowledge base onto this personal core of conviction and integrity, so as to serve the interests and personal needs of students and institutions. Some of the professional roles you will be asked to perform need to

4

be considered.

• Advocate/Facilitator—You are likely to be the primary promoter of study, work, and travel abroad on your campus, actively pursuing and publicizing overseas opportunities and maintaining as high a profile as possible within the institution. You must create a campus environment where opportunities for international experience are viewed as feasible, desirable, and relevant in the context of undergraduate education. If you are not a leader in these areas, you are not doing your job fully.

• Liaison/Broker—You will regularly and frequently be called upon to be an information link between students, faculty, the administration, the admissions and records office, and other campus entities working to initiate and maintain orderly academic and institutional procedures. Unless your campus is unusually coherent and well organized, and unless your students are far more centered and conscientious than is usually the case, you will have to do an enormous amount of informed and politic coordination. A tremendous variety of diplomatic skills will be required.

• Educator/Consultant—Your primary work is to help each student become better informed, determine personal priorities, consider all options, make choices, develop a set of realistic expectations, and proceed through the steps and obstacles of your institutional structures. You need a global outlook and pedagogical expertise that must be shared with your colleagues on the faculty and in the administration. You are likely to know more about the particular educational benefits of living and learning abroad than anyone else on campus. Because these are hard-won insights, you are thrust into the role of educating the faculty and administration—in some instances against their will. This role requires the courage to act in support of your convictions and experience and the determination to work with others to increase high-quality opportunities for students.

A great deal of skill and knowledge is required to play all these roles successfully, as well as generous doses of tact and judgment to keep them from conflicting too much. Being in this field is seldom dull, and the variety of tasks and challenges can be truly exhilarating.

Standards of Professional Practice

As noted above, the field of international education is evolving its professionalism, including the creation of codes of behavior for individuals and institutions. NAFSA remains at work on this formalizing process. There is now an associationwide code of ethics, adopted by NAFSA's board of directors in 1989 after extensive discussions within the membership. As part of this process, SECUSSA discussed the ideal conduct of individuals working as education-abroad advisers and program administrators. In 1988 the following standards of professional practice were adopted by SECUSSA. The standards are presented verbatim:

In general professional conduct, professionals in the field:

1. In the performance of duties recognize the boundaries of their expertise, expand their expertise through consultation with colleagues, and make referrals where situations are outside their area of competence.
2. Maintain and increase their skills and knowledge through participation in professional activities, reading, research, and training programs as well as through consultation with experts in allied fields and with others in their own field.
3. Assist less-experienced members in developing their own knowledge, understanding, and skills.
4. Refrain from unjustified or unseemly criticism of fellow members, other programs, and organizations.
5. Are alert to and resist outside pressures (personal, social, organizational, financial, and political) to use their influence inappropriately, and refuse to allow considerations of self-aggrandizement or personal gain to influence their professional judgments.
6. Communicate with honesty and fairness in representing their own services and programs, as well as those of others.
7. Demonstrate cross-cultural sensitivity and respect the ambiguity and complexity inherent in cross-cultural relationships, treating differences between educational systems, value systems, and cultures nonjudgmentally.
8. Conduct themselves in a manner that is not exploitative, coercive, or sexually harassing. Sexual harassment includes sexual advances, requests for sexual favors, or any verbal or physical conduct of a sexual nature that has the effect of creating an intimidating, hostile, or offensive environment.

In advising, professionals in the field:

1. Provide complete, accurate, and current information to those seeking their assistance.
2. Advise with great care to enable students to select overseas experience (including work and travel as well as academic study) that will meet that student's academic, financial, and personal needs, including specific curricular requirements.
3. Provide ample information on choices to enable individual students to make intelligent and rational decisions.
4. Follow clearly defined criteria in selecting students for programs so as to match students appropriately with such factors as location, language level, demands on academic and personal maturity, and available curricula.
5. Strive to assure appropriate educational guidance of students bound abroad through the development of orientation and reentry

programs.
6. Maintain the confidentiality of student records and communications with students.
7. Are committed to equality of opportunity in education, and thus seek to provide information on resources for the physically handicapped and the economically disadvantaged, and other groups which are traditionally under-represented in study abroad programs.

In program administration, professionals in the field:
1. Make available complete, accurate, and current information on their programs, which clearly states institutional affiliations, all costs to participants, course work available, and arrangements for lodging, meals, and transportation.
2. Develop programs with academic rigor at least comparable to that of the home institution, with credit awarded according to standards used for course work on the home campus. They do not award credit for travel alone, and they clearly state to prospective participants the academic standards and expectations of their programs.
3. When administering programs abroad, work with the home and host institutions to assist in the proper transfer of credits for overseas study, responding rapidly to the needs of students, but with regard for the academic integrity of the institutions.
4. Develop offerings that immerse students in the cultural richness and diversity available in the locale abroad.
5. Establish budgets to permit participation by students from various economic situations, and in setting program fees, they avoid seeking institutional profit.
6. Maintain academic standards of selection when screening applicants.
7. Arrange for and make available the results of carefully designed, unbiased evaluations of their programs.
8. Select faculty and staff on the basis of educational and cultural criteria and attention to the goals of the program, with fairness and objectivity.
9. Provide adequate counseling or referral services for incoming exchange students for whom they have administrative responsibility.

As with any code of ideal behavior, human practice struggles hard to keep up, and conflicts and tensions are not improbable. No one has the time, knowledge, energy, or absolute virtue to live up to these high standards on every occasion. Compounding the challenge will be what is expected of you from your institution, which may pull you in an opposite direction. Choosing a fixed path between behavior that represents loyalty to the institution that pays your salary, and an unflinching allegiance to loftily defined but abstract and probably unenforceable professional conduct is perhaps impossible. These standards are meant to help you build into your work goals and aspirations representing the best wisdom of the field. NAFSA's 1992 Code of Ethics is reprinted as appendix 4.

Opportunities for Professional Development

A good portion of the knowledge required to serve the interests and needs of your students and your institution, as well as these standards of professional practice, will invariably come from seasoned experience, not formal training. What follows is an overview of the increasing number of opportunities for professional development in the education-abroad field.

Structured Academic Training. Although there are few specific undergraduate, graduate, or certificate programs designed to prepare anyone to be an education-abroad adviser or program administrator, there are a number of short-term, formal learning experiences that can contribute to your knowledge and skills. The following abbreviated list is representative of the types of programs currently available:

- SIETAR Summer Institute—Foundations of Intercultural Training, Georgetown University (July)
- Summer Institute for Intercultural Communication—Intercultural Communication Institute, Maryhurst College, Oregon (July)
- International Leadership Development Institute—Colorado College and the International Exchange Association, Colorado Springs (July/August)
- East-West Center Cross-Cultural Training for Educational Leaders Workshop—University of Hawaii
- Global Realities Institute—Global Realities and Education, Taos, New Mexico
- Professional Development Programs for International Educators, School for International Training—Brattleboro, Vermont (August).

(Note: the locations and dates of the above institutes may vary from year to year; current information should be obtained directly from the sponsor.)

In addition to these short-term (generally one week) programs, there are a number of training workshops conducted by individual universities, NAFSA regions, local NAFSA subgroups, and so on. Information can be found in the "Professional Opportunities" section of each issue of the *NAFSA Newsletter*, in the *Chronicle on Higher Education*, and in *Transitions Abroad* magazine.

Those interested in this type of program should also obtain a copy of NAFSA's fact sheet on "Structured In-Service Training Grants." These modest grants are available to individuals currently working in some aspect of educational exchange at a U.S. college or university, and may be applied to a training program sponsored by an accredited institution of higher education, provided the training is specifically designed for international educators. NAFSA produces an annual list of many of the training programs to which the grants may be applied.

NAFSA Field Service Sponsored Training. Through a grant from the United States Information Agency (USIA), NAFSA annually provides three types of short-term (two to three days) training for those currently working in international education at a U.S. college or university. These opportunities are overseen by the NAFSA Field Service Steering Committee.

• Individual grants are provided to basic-level participants (those relatively new to the field) and mid- to senior-level participants (three years or more of experience) to visit selected institutions in order to observe programs and procedures and confer with colleagues.

• In-service training grants are also provided for group seminars. Although eligibility requirements and funding vary for each seminar, those selected participate in in-depth training on a specific topic. In recent years, SECUSSA has sponsored an annual beginners workshop on the basics of study-abroad advising. SECUSSA has also sponsored more advanced workshops on study-abroad programming in Latin America, Eastern and Central Europe, and Asia. Individual and group opportunities tend to be offered annually and may be regionally based.

• National seminars, for which selection is competitive, are sponsored less regularly, but provide intensive training on specific, current topics of national and professional interest (e.g., managing financial aid for study abroad).

Information about all three types of short-term training programs is available on request from NAFSA.

Active Membership in Professional Organizations. There are a number of professional organizations, in addition to NAFSA, that serve individuals and/or institutions involved in education abroad. Active membership in such organizations is essential if you are to develop as a professional. Unlike scholarly associations that gather to share the results of research activities, the meetings and publications of these organizations are dedicated to networking, sharing ideas, and acquiring new skills. Most of these organizations offer ample development and leadership opportunities.

NAFSA/SECUSSA. NAFSA provides professional development opportunities for educators in international exchange; publishes the *NAFSA Newsletter, International Educator* magazine, the *Government Affairs Bulletin*, and more than a hundred professional books and papers; holds an annual conference with three thousand participants; and provides a consultation service to help institutions evaluate the strengths and weaknesses of their programs. Participation in NAFSA activities also has the benefit of bringing education-abroad professionals into contact with the full spectrum of international educational exchange. The Section on U.S. Students Abroad, one of NAFSA's five professional divisions, is interested in promoting all forms of education abroad: formal study, work, and travel. SECUSSA sponsors workshops, sessions, discussion groups, and social activities at NAFSA's annual national conference and at all twelve NAFSA regional conferences. The national and regional conferences offer basic training for newcomers. Many NAFSA publications derive from SECUSSA's professional needs and interests. In addition to this publication, SECUSSA has produced a comprehensive bibliography on education abroad. SECUSSA also sponsors SECUSS-L, an e-mail discussion list open to anyone (see chapter 6).

CIEE. Nearly 250 colleges and universities (U.S. and foreign), youth-serving agencies, and international educational programs are active institutional members of CIEE. Anyone can benefit from CIEE's information and publication services, advocacy efforts, and evaluation and consultation services. CIEE publishes a monthly newsletter, monographs, and books on education abroad. Like NAFSA, it holds an annual conference with sessions, workshops, and discussion groups devoted to a wide array of topics. Working with colleges and universities, CIEE administers consortial study-abroad programs in all parts of the world. CIEE also sells the International Student Identity Card, arranges work permits for employment in other countries, and offers a variety of other travel services.

IIE. The most inclusive annual listings of study abroad, *Academic Year Abroad* and *Vacation Study Abroad,* are published by IIE, which also conducts a bi-annual census of study-abroad activity. In addition, the Educational Associates program provides college and university members with complimentary copies of IIE publications and other services, including IIE's newsletter, *Educational Associate.*

In addition to these three long-established organizations, education-abroad practitioners can affiliate with a number of other national groups. Among these are

• The Association of International Education Administrators—for those with institution-wide positions related to international education

• The International Exchange Association—an umbrella organization for youth-serving agencies, newly merged with the Liaison Group for International Educational Exchange to form the Alliance for International Educational and Cultural Exchange

• Phi Beta Delta—a more recent, national honor society that recognizes programs for campus staff, faculty, and students involved in international education activities.

Many education-abroad professionals have also found that they have benefited by keeping their individual memberships current in groups that reflect their own particular background, interest, or avocation. These include the Fulbright Alumni Association, the International Society for Intercultural Training and Research (SIETAR), and those associations related to the teaching of foreign language, area studies, student personnel administration, and specific academic disciplines, among other categories. Many of these groups are listed and annotated in the *International Exchange Locator* (IIE for the Liaison Group, 1992) and in the *Directory of Resources for International Cultural Exchanges* published by USIA.

Education-abroad staff working on college and university campuses have access to the higher-education groups to which their institutions undoubtedly belong. These groups include the American Council on Education, American Association of State Colleges and Universities, Association of American Colleges, National Association of State Universities and Land Grant Colleges, and so on. All of these include in their research, publications, and conference activities a component on international education that in most cases, explicitly encompasses education abroad.

Almost every organization involved in international education has a regular schedule of regional meetings and conferences. Attendance at these meetings is important for the new professional, and participation on the program is essential for those who are more experienced. Meetings and conferences present opportunities to share ideas and points of view, to discuss approaches and practices, to learn about new developments and proposals, and when appropriate, to raise questions about and voice concerns for standards and practices. The forums presented by professional organizations are the best, most consistently available, and most visible means for exploring new ideas, meeting innovators and experts in the field, and sharing one's own expertise and successes with others at different professional levels.

Professional Development Abroad. Overseas travel for the education-abroad professional is essential. One must be as familiar as possible with the foreign countries and cultures in order to advise, to inform, and to design and implement useful, high-quality experiences abroad. Many professionals have lived overseas or have traveled extensively in other parts of the world. Most have participated in a foreign-study experience or have become knowledgeable about systems of higher education in other countries. All support the value of participatory learning in another culture—not merely learning about the people and the culture, but learning how people in other cultures learn.

The opportunities described below are by no means inclusive, but are illustrative of the variety of ways an individual can continue to learn from an overseas experience, even if that opportunity is not provided within the context of one's job. To take advantage of some of these, however, a fairly liberal (four-week) annual leave may be required.

11

Group Seminars and Workshops Abroad.

• Baden-Württemberg Seminar—The Baden-Württemberg Ministry of Science and Art, in cooperation with NAFSA and AACRAO, sponsors this seminar. It is held at University of Freiburg, Germany, for two weeks in November. On-site costs are covered by the seminar. Participants are elected competitively for an intensive program on the German educational system.

• Program for Administrators in International Education–Japan and Korea—This program is sponsored by the Fulbright Commission of Japan and the Council for the International Exchange of Scholars. Locations vary and the length is for one month during the summer. Program costs are covered by the sponsor. This program selects those with at least three years of professional international education experience with a U.S. college, university, or nonprofit international educational exchange organization.

• Program for U.S. Administrators in International Education–Germany—This program is sponsored by Fulbright Commission/CIES. Locations vary and the length is one month in the spring. Program costs, including airfare, are covered by the sponsor. This program selects up to twenty participants, including administrators of undergraduate programs abroad, to attend seminars on the educational, cultural, and political issues involved in exchanges with Germany.

• Fulbright-Hays Summer Seminars Abroad—These seminars are sponsored by the U.S. Office of Education. The locations vary and the length is from four to eight weeks during the summer. Costs are covered by the sponsor. Applicants must be employed full time as teachers or administrators in the humanities, social sciences, or social studies at a U.S. secondary or higher-education institution. Language requirements exist for some locations.

In any given year, other overseas seminars and workshops are offered on an occasional basis or for slightly longer periods (three to four months). Announcements of these, as well as current application information about the above programs, are usually published in the *NAFSA Newsletter*, CIEE's *Update*, IIE's newsletter for educational associates, and other professional organizations' newsletters and journals.

Overseas Opportunities Related to Study-Abroad Programs. There are a number of possibilities for participating in activities abroad that are sponsored by other institutions. The sponsors/organizers of some overseas programs that enroll students on a national basis have independent boards of advisers that are occasionally invited to visit overseas program sites. Butler University, Beaver College, Interstudy, and the American Institute for Foreign Study are among these groups. Other study-abroad sponsors periodically organize on-site visits to acquaint U.S. advisers with their programs. Denmark's International Study program (DIS) has done this very successfully for a number of years .

You can also use your summer vacation leading short-term programs abroad or serving as a resident director of summer study programs (particularly at the secondary school level). Those interested in this type of overseas (and salaried) experience should consult groups such as the Experiment in International Living, American Field Service, Youth for Understanding, or American Institute for Foreign Study.

Individual Travel Abroad. There are a number of interesting alternatives to being a tourist abroad, even within limited time constraints. There are literally hundreds of options for special interest or adult education travel currently available—and affordable. Some focus on specific interests (archaeology, bird-watching, women's issues), others on methods of travel (trekking, caravans, river boats), and still others on exotic areas of the world. No single source of information describes all these opportunities, but a good guide—which focuses on educational work, study, and travel abroad with particular reference to adult participation—is published annually in the summer issue of *Transitions Abroad*.

If you are interested in a short-term course in a foreign language—as a refresher or otherwise—there are numerous courses for foreigners. If you want to combine study in a particular subject area with a short-term experience abroad, there are good suggestions in IIE's guide and Peterson's *Learning Vacations*. Literally hundreds of voluntary service projects are conducted annually in all parts of the world. Many of the sponsoring organizations recruit individuals for assignments lasting one month or less, for which room and board and/or a small stipend is often provided. Again, *Transitions Abroad* is a good resource to track down such opportunities.

Publishing Opportunities. Publishing is one of the best ways to share good ideas—and garner some professional recognition in the process. The number of publishing opportunities in the education-abroad field is growing. The major organizations mentioned above publish newsletters, as well as other literature, with a variety of emphases and audiences. There is a constant need for good writers with fresh ideas. Most national conferences provide opportunities to submit juried papers, acceptance of which may include publication as well as presentation. These papers require careful research, considerable planning, and thoughtful writing and rewriting. Newsletters, on the other hand, will accept briefer, timely articles or reports on current developments; very often unsolicited submissions are more than welcome.

Specific-Skill Building. A wide variety of skills are called upon in education-abroad work. These range from good accounting and fiscal management practices to publication layout and design, personnel administration, international travel and tour planning, academic and student counseling, and computer literacy. Because most education-abroad professionals work on college or university campuses, they have classes and training programs—tuition free in many cases—available in related skills (e.g., management, computer technology, accounting and finance, graphic design, professional writing). Classes can be taken to fill self-identified gaps or to complement or supplement work already completed. This course work may become part of an advanced degree or certificate program that could lead to additional credentials, increased professional recognition, and promotion.

Whether you are employed by an academic institution or not, there is also ample access—in most parts of the country—to training opportunities. Community groups and service clubs frequently organize training seminars and management courses, as do various industries, management consulting and training firms, and groups with a specific training focus (e.g., Toastmasters International). If you live in an area where there are large industrial employers, you might investigate their in-service seminars and workshops. It is often possible to exchange a professional service for participation in in-house employee training programs.

Skill building can be self-taught as well. The opportunity to research and write grant proposals and to administer a grant award on behalf of a sponsoring institution or community group is a professional development activity. NAFSA makes a number of awards each year in support of local and national program proposals that contribute to the educational exchange process, including, for example, the preparation/orientation and reentry of American students studying abroad.

Internships. Internships can take a number of different forms: some are institutionalized, and others are developed individually to meet personal and professional needs. Internships frequently take the form of staff exchanges between an overseas study site and the home institution. An idea growing in popularity in recent years is that of interprogram exchange or internship. In this type of internship, an individual works in a study-abroad office or overseas program to perform a specific job for a limited period of time. The individual is expected to contribute his or her professional skills and, at the same time, to learn about the new situation and to carry that information back to the home institution. Although presenting occasional difficulties in terms of professional ethics in the area of industrial espionage, these job swaps or internship possibilities present rich opportunities for learning for all of the parties involved.

Recent moves to increase the level of professionalism within the ranks of international education and especially education abroad are resulting in opportunities for administrative staff sabbaticals, leave programs, and other accommodations. These new opportunities will provide time for employees to pursue studies or experiences that will equip them with the knowledge and experience necessary for professional growth. An effort is necessary during the coming years to share information about the potential and benefits of these programs and to encourage institutions to support interprogram internships as a development activity that will attract and help to retain the best qualified individuals.

Summary

Whether you are new to the education-abroad field, have newly expanded responsibilities, or are an old-timer simply trying to keep up with new developments, you should recognize that you are involved in a dynamic and especially demanding aspect of American higher education. Your own knowledge, skill, and talents will be tested every day. Being a professional means working hard to assimilate and embody the best that others have said and done, as well as following your own best instincts and being alert to the special needs of your own institution. There are many established networks of information and training and professional discourse. Taking advantage of these will make your work easier and more enjoyable.

2

The Education-Abroad Office in Its Campus Context

Contributors: Paul DeYoung and Paul Primak

Education abroad, as a component of American higher education, represents a diversification of the undergraduate curriculum and a broadening of liberal education. Education abroad's biggest goals—academic or experiential—are largely pedagogical. These goals stem from a seasoned conviction that students who have experienced living and learning on the social and educational terms of a foreign culture will be broadened in ways impossible to achieve on the home campus. We know education abroad generally improves returned-student classroom performance, matures students in positive ways, and makes students more likely to become contributing and empathetic citizens of the world. The value of these educational goals, in the context of the often narrowing and isolationist strains of traditional American culture, cannot be overestimated.

Whatever education abroad means philosophically or nationally for American undergraduates, and however far-flung its potential impact on students, in essence it is an institutional activity. For better or worse, it lives within the pedagogical, political, and economic realities of particular colleges and universities. More to the point, education abroad cannot and should not be owned exclusively by those who labor professionally in the fields of international education. Rather, education abroad belongs to all members of the academic community.

Education-abroad advisers and program administrators who forget or ignore this contextual truth are likely to be frustrated and ineffective. The perennial challenge is to maximize, by conscious and enlightened on-campus planning, what and how students learn beyond the U.S. campus, and to ensure that this education is understood and valued—formally or informally—as part of the American degree. The slogan that should be emblazoned over the desk of every education-abroad professional is "Think Globally, Act Locally."

The administration of education-abroad programs, however, occurs in a

17

staggering variety of organizational contexts. Some colleges are entirely new to the field, and are just tentatively finding their way. Others have in recent years made an initial institutional commitment and have established a few programs and priorities, yet know that they should be doing more, while yet others exhibit a long record and have reached what may be a real plateau of commitment and activity, or a period of stultification. Institutional settings for education-abroad activities range from an individual faculty member's office, to the single-purpose education-abroad office—be it for advising only or program administration only—to offices that advise and administer programs, to the comprehensive international education offices that serve the needs of short- and long-term foreign students and scholars, as well as American students and scholars seeking overseas opportunities.

This chapter will provide an examination of institutional variables commonly faced by education-abroad professionals. It will also review the institutional and national contexts in which education abroad operates.

Institutional Structures and Values

The services offered by the education-abroad office are usually indicated by its location on campus. The office's larger role on campus is usually defined by its placement within the institution's organizational structure. Most offices are located in one of two divisions: academic affairs or student services. Within academic affairs, the office might be an autonomous unit, part of academic advising, part of one or more academic departments (usually languages) or area studies programs, or part of the college of liberal arts. Within student services, the office might again be an autonomous unit; part of a unit overseeing all international programs (and thus aligned with services for foreign students and scholars); within the campus international center; part of the student union; or part of an office in charge of career counseling, placement, and other off-campus studies.

In small institutions, there may be no office per se, but rather a person within academic affairs or student services, or both. In this case, the person in charge of education-abroad advising and/or programming may not even work full time. This person may have a split appointment as a faculty member or staff member of a student-services unit. The demands on such a person and the need to interact effectively with all other dimensions of the campus are just as great as they would be at a larger institution.

Certain fortunate education-abroad offices—usually at larger universities with well-defined international missions and expertise—are located within a free-standing international programs office whose director reports to a senior administrator, a vice president, or provost. Should the education-abroad office be under academic affairs, the office will probably have more prestige within the institution and more support from faculty and members of the administration. If the office is under student services, the personal needs of the student may be better served as he or she prepares to enter a foreign culture, live and learn abroad, and then return to campus. However, the office within student services may be more restricted and more student-oriented at the expense of providing essential academic counseling and assurances concerning credit.

Excellent education-abroad offices are found under academic affairs and student services, yet both have drawbacks. Keep in mind that the range of services differs from one office to another, and that no single office or individual will be able to offer everything to everybody. Offices located within student services may be limited to general advising and travel services, seldom becoming involved with program development, recruitment and selection, or academic credit. The academic adviser may have advising responsibilities for language and other academic programs only, financial resources, time, and institutional pursuits precluding functioning in other areas.

Whatever the range of services offered by your office, they must be clearly defined relative to your location and the needs of your constituency. Once they are defined, you can actively seek the administration's understanding and approval that are the foundation for the office's support and funding. Once you clearly understand the administrative position of your office and its relationship with other campus offices, you begin to build a political support structure that can affirm and sustain your role.

Recognizing the characteristics, dynamics, and structures of your own organizational environment is the first step in the development—as well as the continuing viability—of your office. Understanding where your work fits within the educational framework of your institution is crucial to your success. Such contextual awareness allows your office to develop and maintain its own character, and also contributes directly to the office's ability to fulfill your institution's international goals. Since all colleges and universities change over time, it is essential that experienced education-abroad advisers and program administrators remain in tune with current institutional priorities and realities.

Institutional Policy

Education-Abroad Advisory Committee. Your best ally is likely to be an informed and supportive advisory committee. It is essential that the committee be broadly based and credible. Ideally, members should represent the institution's constituencies that are centrally involved in international education. Of primary importance are key members of the faculty who are supportive of education abroad. It is also wise to have a senior member of the faculty (ideally with current or recent membership on the curriculum committee) as the chair. Members of the administration might include the financial aid director, a business officer, the registrar, an admissions officer, and a foreign-student adviser.

19

On many campuses, administrative officers are ex officio members of the committee. They should not dominate the committee structure and their role should be confined to an advisory function. Unless it is politically untenable on your campus, try to have one to three recently returned study-abroad students on your committee. These students are true believers who can speak with authority and conviction. Lastly, you might consider reserving a seat on the committee for someone who has voiced *negative* views about the efficacy of international education.

The committee must also have a clear charge detailing its primary responsibilities and its relationship to your job and to other governance committees. These roles and relationships should be detailed in institutional by-laws. The governing document of one institution states that

> the committee shall formulate policy regarding off-campus study programs; shall review proposals for such programs from departments or divisions and shall report its findings and recommendations to the faculty. In addition, the committee shall review student proposals for participation on college approved study-abroad programs and approve or deny their applications.
>
> —Bylaws, Reed College, 1988

The roles of advisory committees at different institutions will vary considerably. Not all committees will wish to be involved in reviewing student proposals, especially on campuses where the number of student applications is large. The committee can be responsible for overseeing the application process and set approval standards. In addition, the committee can provide guidelines for the desired numbers of students participating in programs, which will assist in institutional planning for housing and admissions. Beyond its formal duties, the committee is your sounding board, your collective ombudsman, and your inner counsel. As such, the committee gives you direction, information, and the authority to act. Your voice and the committee's together can speak to and for the campus.

Setting Institutional Goals. The education-abroad advisory committee should guide the process of establishing and maintaining education-abroad programming in a manner that contributes to the institution's educational goals. Many institutions do not mention international education in their mission statement. Others mention international education, but say nothing specifically about education abroad. The committee, in order to establish its legitimacy and to guide its decision-making process, must make sure that institutional policy statements on international education are in place, and further, that education abroad is specifically mentioned as an important component of undergraduate studies.

If this is not the case, forming policy statements and having them accepted becomes the first order of business (working in conjunction with the international students and scholars office, if one exists on your campus). In formulating a statement, all elements of international education on campus must be taken into account: international students, international curriculum development, faculty exchange, on-campus international programming, and education abroad. It is in the institution's best interest that these components work together toward common educational goals. Certainly, the impact of education-abroad programming will be influenced by the integration of that experience into the students' overall education. By addressing the question of institutional policy at the outset, the committee can assist individual faculty members, as well as the institution, in placing study abroad in its proper curricular perspective.

Divisions of Labor. With institutional policy as a guide, the education-abroad administrator, working with the advisory committee and other staff, must establish working goals and priorities for the education-abroad office. The primary division of labor is likely to be between student advising and programming. In larger offices, these two functions may be done by different persons; in small offices, they both fall in the lap of a single person and must somehow be balanced.

If your institution sponsors programs of its own—or wishes to do so—a heavy portion of your work load will be taken up with program development, financing, promotion, staffing, and assessment. If your institution sponsors no programs of its own, most of your time will be spent trying to become familiar with the programs most suitable to your students and most acceptable to your faculty. With two thousand semester and year programs now listed in the IIE guides, plus fourteen hundred additional summer programs, becoming familiar with all the education-abroad options is a formidable task. More often than not, education-abroad administrators must shoulder both responsibilities.

It is always worth remembering that no education-abroad adviser or administrator starts completely from scratch, either at the beginning of a new job or the start of the academic year. Precedents are in place and activities are ongoing; administrative, faculty, and student attitudes have formed; structures and lines of authority have been established; resources and budgets have been authorized—even if by default. These are the given, and they define the current place of education abroad within the institution.

A common problem is that where things are may be at odds with your perception of where things ought to be. Conflicts may exist between institutional rhetoric and reality; between what some members of the academic community want and what seems to be immediately possible; and between national calls for increased participation in study abroad and real or imagined institutional fears, hesitations, and limits (see chapter 1). These divisions are where the study-abroad administrator necessarily lives. The question is how to resolve conflicts and how to move the institution in new directions.

Working with Others

As we move toward the end of the century, education-abroad awareness and programming on nearly every American campus is in a state of dynamic evolution. Whether you are new to the field or to your campus, or an old-timer feeling the pressures to expand and diversify, defining the academic, administrative, and financial contexts in which study abroad can best flourish at your institution is fundamental. The impact of education-abroad programming on all other sectors of the university must be anticipated. Key players in each area must be consulted and reconsulted to determine how education abroad affects existing institutional priorities and programs.

The education-abroad administrator's ongoing agenda should be to initiate, to understand, and to cultivate and maintain relationships among campus academic, administrative, and service areas. The many people who have their prime responsibilities in each sphere must remain perpetually in your activities. Where the faculty and academic administrators stand on issues such as credit validation or transfer, and residence and degree requirements will form the foundation that education-abroad offices use to administer their programs.

The registrar's office, the financial aid office, the academic advising office, and the bursar's office are also necessarily involved—as are student life (especially if it oversees such services as orientation and housing), admissions, career services, and even auxiliary service departments such as printing, student-activity centers, and the bookstore. The office or persons involved in providing services for foreign students and scholars must always be seen as an ally in the cause of internationalism. It is difficult to think of any college administrative area that is not potentially interactive with education-abroad programming.

As noted above, in order to be successful, study-abroad programs must be thoroughly integrated into the academic mission of the institution. Initiating this integration could be regarded as the primary responsibility of the education-abroad adviser, personally and professionally. The task cannot be done by one person alone, and it certainly cannot be imposed on the institution. Collaboration is crucial.

Academic Departments and Programs. It is often very helpful to consult with peer institutions on specific study-abroad program options, but you can also get good guidance at your own institution by maintaining regular liaison with other academic areas. Even though your advisory committee should contain faculty members, the committee should not have to rely on just those faculty and the departments they represent. Specific academic departments will support the programs and activities of the study-abroad office very effectively, once they see that their interests are bolstered, not threatened, by study abroad. Many faculty have studied or conducted research abroad and are likely to have strong interests in seeing their students' educations enhanced by an overseas academic experience.

Study abroad will be given more credibility by students and administration if you develop and utilize faculty interest. Working with key members of the faculty can also be critical for addressing academic policy (e.g., program structure or credit transfer). Faculty with expertise in area studies or languages can be especially helpful in addressing issues ranging from program development to student orientation. In addition to their presence on the advisory committee, faculty can be tapped for resident directorships, overseas-study scholarship committees, and other duties.

The Registrar and Academic Affairs. If your institution has one or more academic advising offices, they can often complement faculty support. Sometimes faculty members cannot answer questions students have about studying abroad, particularly about credit transfer. The academic advising or registrar's office can help educate students and faculty about the programs and the curriculum offered through your institution. Advising offices may even be willing to run a periodic information series to inform students about study-abroad opportunities (see chapter 3).

Financial Aid. Since higher education institutions must legally permit students receiving federal and institutional financial aid packages to utilize their funds to help pay for the costs of overseas study, it is important to maintain a strong communication link with key persons in the financial aid office. Financial aid regulations are complex and constantly changing. The assistance of key members of the financial aid office is crucial to staying up-to-date on developments and new regulations that have implications for students on study-abroad programs (see chapter 4).

Student Affairs. Many education-abroad offices rely heavily on student affairs offices to help publicize study-abroad programs to newly admitted students and their parents during orientation programs. Involvement in the orientation program can provide early and effective publicity—a key element in successful planning for study abroad. Many institutions have found that early information to students and parents is very effective in terms of academic and financial planning for study abroad (see chapter 7).

Foreign Student Office. On many university and college campuses, the institutional study-abroad program developed in conjunction with, or as an offshoot of, the foreign student office. The resources available through the foreign student office include access to international students for orientations on the study-abroad program, cross-cultural program expertise, overseas contacts, and occasionally, shared fiscal and personnel resources. Foreign student offices and study-abroad programs have many of the same academic aims and counseling goals. Cooperation between these two primary international components can forge a very strong and productive alliance.

Admissions. This office is usually very experienced in marketing the institution to prospective students and is very knowledgeable about curriculum, programs, and activities available at the institution. Admissions officers are always seeking incentives to offer to prospective students. With good contacts and a set of good descriptive materials, the admissions office can offer a great deal of assistance in publicizing the international program, while serving its own needs of attracting students to campus. Because admissions officers are generally experienced in producing information about the institution, they are excellent resources to assist in developing materials and a marketing plan for education-abroad programs. Working with the admissions office can help integrate the concept of study abroad and international programs into the larger image of the institution (see chapter 7).

Getting Advice from Others: Institutional Outreach

Even with the support of the aforementioned on-campus liaisons, your institution may still require additional advice, counsel, support, and perspective. There is no reason to reinvent the wheel. Your campus is not the first to wrestle with its current questions and concerns on education abroad. Others have been there and are usually willing to share their solutions and conclusions. You, your advisory committee, and your campus administration should be aware that national professional associations and organizations involved in international education can help with institutional consultations, services, resources, and programming. They can offer invaluable (and inexpensive) assistance to colleges and universities at any stage of their education-abroad program development. Primary among these are the following.

NAFSA: Association of International Educators. NAFSA is the primary professional association for all professionals working in the field of international educational exchange. Membership in NAFSA is essential for individuals and institutions seriously involved in international education. With membership comes reduced rates for conferences, a newsletter, discounted publications, and a variety of other benefits. NAFSA offers a low-cost consultation service to colleges and universities. Consultants, chosen for their expertise in specific areas of the field of international educational exchange, will visit your campus, meet with all relevant administrators, faculty, and students, and prepare a report containing specific recommendations.

Council on International Educational Exchange. Unlike NAFSA, CIEE has only an institutional membership, and is involved only in education abroad. Membership in CIEE must be applied for and approved; conducting an institutional self-study report is part of the application process. Membership provides helpful networking opportunities with other institutions, a monthly newsletter and other publications, reduced rates on many services, guidance in establishing study-abroad programs and developing consortial relationships, access to scholarships and work-abroad programs for students, and an array of travel services. In addition to its New York headquarters, CIEE has a number of overseas offices that members can use in program planning.

Institute of International Education. IIE oversees a variety of government-to-government international exchange agreements (e.g., the Fulbright program, the International Visitor program). IIE can be very helpful in program implementation, particularly in the developing world. IIE has regional offices in the United States as well in key locations overseas. Institutional membership in IIE brings with it a monthly associates' newsletter, and all major publications.

American Association of Collegiate Registrars and Admissions Officers. AACRAO is an organization whose main work concerns U.S. college and university admissions and academic transcripting. However, AACRAO has several committees concerned with international education as it affects colleges and universities. One of these committees is concerned exclusively with credit transfer questions that arise out of education-abroad programming. AACRAO holds an annual conference, which offers discussion sessions on education abroad. AACRAO and NAFSA together have published *Transcripts from Study Abroad: A Workbook* (1986). AACRAO, NAFSA, and the British Universities Transatlantic Exchange Committee (BUTEC) have published *Recording the Performance of U.S. Undergraduates at British Institutions: Guidelines Toward Standardized Reporting for Study Abroad* (1988).

Other Professional Organizations. While NAFSA, CIEE, IIE, and AACRAO are the primary membership organizations that serve the interests of institutions and education-abroad professionals, several other organizations are also beneficial. These organizations include the International Society for Intercultural Training and Research (SIETAR), which is concerned with intercultural theory and epistemology; the National Society for Internships and Experiential Education (NSIEE), which promotes hands-on learning in nonacademic environments in the United States and abroad; and the Association of International Education Administrators (AIEA). In addition, many persons involved in education abroad are active in various scholarly associations concerned with language and area studies.

Regional and National Consortia. There are a large number of consortia of like-minded and/or geographically related colleges and universities that have developed study programs around the world—often in developing countries. Some of the more prominent consortia are the Associated Colleges of the Midwest, the College Consortium for International Studies, CIEE's various Cooperative Study Centers, Denmark's International Study Program, the Great Lakes Colleges Association, the Higher Education Consortium for Urban Affairs, and the International Student Exchange Program. Joining forces makes great sense; institutional strengths often complement each other and shared costs mean more affordable programs. It is possible to join one or more of these consortia, depending on your institutional interests and qualifications. At the very least, you can learn from them how their programs were established and operate.

Summary

The contextual setting for the education-abroad office—within your college or university as well as in the broader arena of international education—must be clearly understood and continually reviewed. Regardless of your professional experience or the level of your institution's involvement in education abroad, you need a clear and up-to-date understanding of how your work relates to the college or university's educational mission. You also need to know how your position interacts with structures and priorities established by your institution's mission. You need to understand fully the broad national field of international educational exchange. Without this functional context—the microscheme of internal institutional dynamics, politics, and finances, and the macroscheme of national precedents, professional standards, and accumulated wisdom—your labors will be more difficult.

3

Academic Credit

Contributors: Eleanor Krawutschke and Kathleen Sideli

Since the education-abroad office is nominally responsible for assisting students in correlating overseas studies with home-campus studies, the office's first task is to work with the faculty—via its advisory committee or academic dean—to establish what is and what is not creditworthy. Answering this question is never easy, nor is the discussion ever final, since programs change and new programs are constantly introduced. Before the complex questions concerning program quality can be considered, a general faculty commitment to education abroad must be established, as well as an administrative commitment to create registration and recording procedures that allow study-abroad courses to be considered part of students' degree studies. (Note: Program planning and program quality issues are treated in the third section of this book.)

Faculty and Administrative Commitment

Even if your top administration is committed to education abroad, faculty attitudes can create barriers that are very hard to overcome. Faculty fears that study abroad will take away some of their best students—especially in the junior year when faculty feel students need to be concentrating on their academic major—are legitimate concerns, since students who study abroad are likely to be above-average students. Some programs abroad are not as academically rigorous (in an American sense) as home-campus studies, though many are, and the myth of laxness abroad is simply wrong or at least dated; also, some programs may be challenging and stimulating in ways that impinge on academic studies. If students return and report that they did not study long and hard, or write as many papers, or take as many tests, faculty doubts increase. It is important to clear away faculty misperceptions and to face authentic concerns about educational quality early on.

Apart from ensuring that students are advised away from programs that are academically weak, the National Task Force Report (appendix 2) suggests that the key to working with faculty is to "forge curricular connections":

> Faculty should participate in program planning, course design, and site selection, and then help fit the program into the curriculum and form part of an advisory committee to the program. Faculty can be similarly involved in programs calling for direct enrollment in foreign institutions or the design of appropriate internships. Quite naturally they will become advocates for such study-abroad experiences in their classrooms and potential future resident directors, as well as academic advisers to students returning from abroad. Most important, they will become the legitimizers of the program on campus to their more parochial colleagues, to hesitant administrators, and to doubting parents.

Gaining faculty backing for education abroad as a legitimate means of enriching and diversifying the undergraduate experience is not enough. It is crucial to make education abroad administratively feasible, and this means working closely with the people on your campus who are responsible for formally registering students for courses and recording the academic credit on their transcripts.

You need to work with the registrar and staff to develop registration and recording procedures to account for what might appear to be a hiatus in a student's studies. These procedures are especially critical for funded students when issues of academic credit and financial aid are intertwined. If students are to receive academic credit and funding—university or governmental—to study abroad, it is essential that the education-abroad office establish definitive procedures for verifying participation in overseas programs. This tracking guarantees to the administration and faculty—as well as to parents, and, when necessary, federal authorities—that the students are indeed engaged in an approved course of study, even though they are not present on campus. Such procedures not only make students' overall experiences more positive, they also help to establish study abroad as an important and integral part of undergraduate education.

In establishing procedures, the education-abroad office should follow the normal administrative structure of its institution as closely as possible. This will facilitate the processing of paperwork for all involved, especially students. It will also show that education abroad can be administered without any major deviations from established practices. However, at a university where registration and recording procedures tend to be very formal and rigid, careful negotiating may be required with key administrators to determine how the system can accommodate study abroad. In brief, registration and recording for education abroad requires enormous flexibility because of the uniqueness of sending students off campus, while still treating them, in other ways, as on-campus students.

28

To set up a workable registration and recording system, it is helpful to distinguish between earning credit by participation in a program sponsored by your own campus or by a consortium your institution belongs to, from credit earned through participation in programs sponsored by other institutions and organizations, domestic or foreign. In the first situation, students are usually able to earn credit directly from your own college or university. In the latter situation, students must, sooner or later, apply for what amounts to transfer credit. If your institution allows students to study abroad under both circumstances, two different systems must be established.

Procedures for Home-Institution-Sponsored or Cosponsored Programs

Predeparture Procedures. Before students embark on a study-abroad program, your college (or in the case of consortia, the institution administering the program) should be able to account academically for the period of time students spend overseas. Matters are facilitated considerably if your institution is able to create one or more course numbers for study-abroad programs. These course numbers will show what a student is doing during a given semester. In some institutions course numbers for study-abroad parallel home-campus course numbers—if the courses are unavailable at home, the numbers will have to be different.

Establishing course numbers may involve (1) requesting and obtaining a course designation (i.e., prefix—the department being the study-abroad unit itself—and course number for each program); and (2) having the registrar assign to a particular course a special section number every semester the program is offered (e.g., OVST M496 #7325—Overseas study in Bologna, Italy). Established course numbers assure that all future students may be officially registered in a course and section.

This procedure should allow students to maintain full-time status on your campus during the time abroad; to have their financial aid routinely disbursed; to qualify for other benefits of full-time enrollment (e.g., a senior residency requirement); and to pay program fees directly to the university bursar. With such an arrangement, your office can then decide with the administration how to make overseas payments (unless home-institution tuition is to be waived and students pay the host institution directly).

If the institution implements this type of registration and billing procedure, the education-abroad office may elect to register students collectively, rather than have them register individually. This decision turns on the personnel available and the time it takes for students to register. Because most registration occurs by semester, it might be difficult for the students to handle their own enrollment—especially in cases involving an academic year abroad. Your office may also be able to better monitor enrollment totals in its programs by processing withdrawals and additions itself.

If your office takes on this responsibility, you will need to inform other university offices (e.g., the student's school/college, financial aid office, major department) of the status of the study-abroad participant, ensuring that the student has official permission to be off campus. A computerized database can easily generate memos and lists with the necessary data. The appropriate individuals may then inform your office if the student is in sufficiently good standing to be enrolled overseas.

You may also need to accommodate students from other institutions who are accepted to participate in your programs. Some colleges and universities administering overseas programs may be able to officially register guest participants at their institution under the category of special students or nondegree candidates. These designations avoid the necessity of formally transferring guest participants to the sponsoring institution.

The education-abroad office will need to inform the bursar of any special fees that should be added to each program (e.g., insurance, excursions, airfare), and then specify which programs require separate financial arrangements with the sponsoring institutions. After students have been registered, the bursar can assess fees according to the program and bill them at the same time as on-campus students. This arrangement will allow students to receive their scholarships and other financial aid with minimal delay. Some schools may be able to disburse aid in advance with the proper documentation from the study-abroad office of the program's starting dates. There are varying models for such payments, depending on the budgetary arrangement the home institution has with its administration:

• Home-institution tuition—if it is a state-supported institution, this might be dependent on in-state or out-of-state residency, plus special study-abroad fees (e.g., insurance, housing, flights).

• Special study-abroad fee only—based on actual overseas expenses.

• Nonremittable fee only—based on per credit hour, which permits students to receive home-campus credit while actually paying the sponsoring institution the tuition and housing fees.

While Abroad. Each study-abroad program will probably have its own rules regarding on-site registration for course work abroad. You might be able to use a somewhat standardized course approval form. Once students are in residence overseas and have begun classes, the resident director can send each student's enrollment schedule to the home campus. Copies can then be disseminated to offices that need to have enrollment verified. Some institutions may require that their program director include proposed home-institution course numbers and credits for the work being completed abroad.

A number of years may be required for a program to develop a procedure of correlating equivalencies that satisfy home-campus departments.

Some institutions may demand an elaborate system for equating overseas course work (e.g., a faculty committee may be designated to study course descriptions and to make recommendations); others rely on the resident director to propose course equivalencies. The resident director may study previous credit conferrals and consult with the education-abroad adviser at the home institution. The adviser may then have to serve as liaison/mediator with on-campus faculty. In either case, you may need to verify that students have received prior permission from the home-campus departments, especially for course work in their majors.

A midyear consultation between the study-abroad office and the overseas program director allows for the adjustment of students' schedules in the second semester of study abroad. It also precludes any surprises regarding course credit once the student is abroad. Moreover, careful control of credit and course work at the midpoint of the program, whatever its duration, should allow for the smooth processing of grades when the program is completed.

Institutions should try to provide study-abroad participants with the opportunity to register in absentia for their returning semester. This means working with the registrar's office to develop policies, forms, and timetables. Procedures can be complicated, given that students study abroad for different lengths of time. In absentia registration may have to be an ongoing process. However, the development of procedures means that students are not adversely affected by studying overseas. Conversely, if students are not allowed to register from abroad—especially for courses necessary for their degree—it becomes difficult to convince others that studying abroad does not lengthen the time required to complete a degree.

Your office will usually have procedures for registering credit for overseas work and grade-transfer policies. At the termination of the program, the responsible officer at each program site must send the education-abroad office a final grade sheet listing all course work taken by students. Sometimes home-campus course equivalencies and grades (converted to the home-campus grading system) are provided as well. Other institutions rely on the transfer-credit office to make decisions about course equivalencies and grades. Some institutions may require official transcripts from the host institution as well. In cases of affiliate or sponsored programs, the office may have to involve local faculty to equate foreign study course work with home-campus courses.

Post-Program. Two issues that concern many program administrators and advisers—and especially students—are (1) the often lengthy delay between the end of classes overseas and the arrival of student performance evaluations on campus, and (2) the delay between the arrival of grade reports from abroad and the release of transcripts from the registrar. Fortunately, the advent of fax and e-mail telecommunications have speeded up the delivery of required information, often saving weeks.

A great deal of student frustration and anxiety is caused by these delays. If the interval is too protracted, students will not know what courses to take or if they will graduate on time. You should do everything possible to help speed up the process, as well as counsel students that coordinating on- and off-campus studies is complex and time-consuming. Some type of deferred-grade procedure may be necessary in order to calm nerves and expedite registration. Otherwise, the credit processing procedure is likely to entail the following steps:

1. Once the report from abroad has been received, a standardized course and grade reporting form needs to be sent to the registrar—and usually to the student, the student's on-campus school/college, and, in some cases, the student's adviser. Such a form may be designed like a transcript with the student's name, identification number, program site, and a list of all courses with American grades.

2. The registrar posts home-institution course numbers, credits, and grades on the student's official transcript. Whether or not these grades count in the GPA, or even appear on the transcript, are policy questions that should be determined well in advance of departure. This policy should be made clear to students during the advising process.

3. The registrar may keep on file the original form submitted by your office—which includes foreign course titles—in the event that the student needs it later when making applications to graduate schools or to satisfy future employers.

4. The registrar also needs to be directed by you to send official transcripts to the home institutions of all guest students. This legal document might be supplemented by any other relevant information.

5. You may wish to keep all course and grade information in a database for future reference. Lists of courses for each program can be drawn from this database. It might also serve to allow you, the registrar, and your advisory committee to gauge how foreign course work is being equated with home-campus courses, thus facilitating the annual interpretive process.

For more general information on issues relating to transcripts, consult *Transcripts from Study Abroad Programs: A Workbook*, edited by Eleanor Krawutschke and Thomas Roberts, and available from NAFSA.

Programs Sponsored by Other Institutions

Even if your institution has many programs, some students will decide to participate in programs offered by other institutions or agencies. Very restrictive policies on granting credit and/or financial aid will discourage such participation, and this is seldom fair to student needs and interests. In any case, granting direct credit is usually more complicated for students doing programs not sponsored by your college or university, so a different system of credit review and transcripting is required.

Generally, the procedure for granting credit depends on whether the student will be somehow attached to the home institution while abroad (i.e., enrolled on the home campus) or not attached (i.e., anticipating transfer credit for the overseas work). In either instance, it is important that students carefully prearrange for the credit by adhering to the procedures stipulated by your institution.

Methods of Transferring Credit for Attached Students. One option is to set up an umbrella course number, similar to that described above; this enables students to be officially registered on your campus for another institution's program. Some of the conditions of this procedure are as follows:

• Students aiming for attached status should be asked to demonstrate that the program and their own academic plans have the approval of the education-abroad office, their major department, and perhaps the academic dean and registrar (or whatever authority approves course work taken elsewhere).

• Instead of being registered for real credit hours (from which home-campus tuition fees are generated), the attached designation is usually set up for 0 credits, which may or may not translate as full-time campus enrollment for financial aid purposes. Some institutions may want to charge a small fee for this special registration.

• The education-abroad office needs to monitor students registered for 0 credits. This will assure the office of financial aid that the study-abroad program will be an integral part of the student's degree, so that standard financial aid guidelines can be followed.

• Students need to provide your office with official documentation showing that they successfully completed their program and listing course work for which they wish to receive home-campus credit.

• Your office then acts on behalf of these students to initiate the operative credit review process.

The following method is used by institutions where "0 credit hours" disqualifies students for financial aid:

• Students are enrolled (often only those who are dependent on financial aid) in twelve semester hours of equivalent home-college course work while they are abroad—or whatever is the minimum necessary to enable them to qualify as full time. Sometimes these courses have creative titles such as Foreign Study 399. Appropriate courses already in the institution's catalogue and not specifically intended for study abroad can also be utilized, (e.g., Independent Study 450).

• Students are charged regular tuition for the twelve semester hours, but their accounts are also credited for the same amount upon approval of a

33

petition for such assistance. Thus, the needy student who is already dependent on substantial financial assistance will have a $0 balance at the home institution and is not forced to pay double tuition.

• A supplementary report is drawn up by the education-abroad office showing the actual overseas courses that the student will enroll in and equivalent courses at the home campus.

• The education-abroad office receives the assessment of student performance from abroad, initiates and processes the credit evaluation, then sends the actual grades earned overseas to the appropriate on-campus departments, so that they can process change-of-grade forms for the student. The education-abroad office also sends through a no-transfer-credit evaluation form for any courses taken abroad that duplicate course work already taken. The student receives an incomplete for each home-campus equivalent course.

• The registrar should be asked to record the actual foreign course titles on the transcript next to the generic title for which the student was preregistered. Any surplus course work taken overseas is handled as transfer credit.

Transfer Credit Procedures for Nonattached Students. From the student's vantage point, being enrolled on the home campus while studying abroad is almost always preferable, because it simplifies getting academic credit. However, from an institutional point of view, this necessitates a considerable amount of administrative knowledge and effort and, consequently, expense. Institutionally, the simplest method of addressing credit questions is to handle them as transfer credit. Consequently, many U.S. colleges choose not to implement on-campus enrollment procedures, unless they are dealing with students participating in the institution's education-abroad programs. This is especially true for campuses on which the education-abroad office has only an advising function and does not administer programs.

This policy is always somewhat, and often very, problematic for students. Technically, students doing other programs are considered to have withdrawn from the institution. Whether or not a student formally enrolls in another domestic or foreign institution for a limited period of time is of no real consequence, that is, until the student applies for transfer credit. Moreover, students who are away from the home campus for an extensive period (typically, an academic year) may be required to apply for readmission. Most importantly, students considered formally withdrawn or on a leave-of-absence may also lose most or all federal, state, and institutional financial aid—unless your financial aid office is very supportive and enlightened, and unless the institution sponsoring the program can provide aid. Such institutional policies can cause students a considerable amount of distress, and they clearly hurt the cause of education abroad.

The problem can be alleviated somewhat if the home institution takes steps to assure students that even though they are off campus they will not be forgotten. Ideally, this means (1) coming up with a way to keep students on the books; (2) assuring students that course work taken in pre-approved programs will be seriously considered for transfer credit; and (3) seeing that the home financial aid office either continues to process most or all aid—or failing this, works with the sponsoring institution to draw up a consortium agreement that enables students to retain the federal monies received through your institution. This collaboration also obligates the home institution to verify that transfer credit will be forthcoming, provided student performance meets institutional standards. If your institution wishes to encourage study abroad, it needs (with your help) to develop the supportive administrative framework necessary to maintain student enrollment on campus while they are abroad. This will be even harder if students enroll directly in foreign universities.

The key to a smooth credit transfer is adequate predeparture preparation. This is when many students encounter serious difficulty. Some U.S. colleges take an extremely conservative approach, informing students that there is no way of determining whether or not they will earn transfer credit until the evaluation is undertaken after they return. Obviously, this leaves the student in a risky situation. Many students—and their parents—will not be willing to take the risk.

If this is your institutional situation and it cannot be changed, your only practical, short-range option to minimize the risk is to make available to students a listing of reasonably safe programs (i.e., those for which other students have earned transfer credit). You could also develop written guidelines to advise students about the issues and how to confront them before they depart and after they return. Making the successes of previous students known can go a long way toward giving uncertain students the assurance they need.

The following steps will help you assist students with the selection of an appropriate program and with the paperwork necessary to assure that credit will be earned—if the students do all that is required.

• Working with your advisory committee and/or the registrar, admissions office, or whatever body oversees credit transfer, design a document that requires students to summarize their foreign study plans. The document should have space for student identification data, as well as a list of potential foreign courses (perhaps equated with home-college equivalents).

• Students, with your counsel, should seek as much signed course-by-course preapproval as possible from their academic advisers and relevant departments. At this time students should also be informed about any additional requirements they will be asked to meet, such as the need to bring back copies of course syllabi, reading lists, written work, and so on.

• The signed preapproval document should then be reviewed by you and receive your final approval. Copies should be kept on file in the education-abroad office (and perhaps elsewhere), and the student should also take a copy abroad as a reminder of what was agreed upon. The preapproval form, as a sort of contract, gives the institution and students reasonable guarantees and commits each to certain responsibilities.

• You will need to maintain contact with students while they are abroad (concerning at least reentry forms and preregistration). Should a student wish to alter the study plan while abroad, he or she needs to contact your office for approval. This might entail consultation with academic departments. Appropriate notations should be made on the student's preapproval form. Many proposed changes will be the result of altered curricular offerings in the program or foreign institution, and are beyond the student's control. Others will come as interests develop and change as a result of the foreign experience. Enlightened advisers and institutions will accommodate all reasonable changes, or at least not hold students to standards that are more stringent than those that apply on the home campus.

• When the program is over, the most important item your office must receive is official proof that the foreign course work has been completed. In most cases, the student is responsible for seeing that the official transcript or similar documentation reaches you in a timely fashion. Students need to know that an official transcript is one directly issued to the home institution by a recognized institution and bears a seal or stamp. Casually typed forms with course listings do not usually qualify as official.

• If students did not file the necessary documents prior to leaving campus, the final credit transfer may take considerably longer than expected. Students may also find that they will not earn as much credit as anticipated. To prevent problems and delays, they should—as advised—bring home copies of course descriptions, syllabi, term papers, and exams, so that this information may be presented—should the need arise—to a campus department for examination.

• Awarding transfer credit for foreign study should follow the lines of granting transfer credit for work completed at other institutions within the United States. This means that there should be a department at the home college that offers equivalent course work, although matching identical courses may not be possible. Students are usually expected to earn grades that meet the minimal standards (generally, this is a grade equivalent to a C or, in some cases, a D).

• The credit granted usually appears as a block of hours posted on the home-institution's transcript, noting the foreign institution, its location, and the dates of study. Occasionally, courses will be listed. Grades are not usually computed into the student's home-college grade-point average, although a few institutions routinely do this. Generally, the transfer credit simply serves in lieu of specific on-campus requirements and counts as hours toward the degree. The back-up credit evaluation, however, will be more detailed and is likely to show the grades and specify home-college course equivalencies.

• For the record, and to advise other students, each student's file in your office should list final credit awards.

Students who have not received institutional preapproval or any assurances concerning credit nevertheless may still seek at least partial credit for bona fide overseas studies—especially if they became directly matriculated abroad. Special intensive language programs offered by language institutes, technical studies in polytechnics, research done independently, or independently arranged internships are just some of many valid educational endeavors.

Again, your institution may have a policy that absolutely forbids this sort of risky and often suspect retroactive request. Under some circumstances your institution may be willing to review all relevant documentation. The key questions are whether the learning is of high quality and would merit credit from your institution. As such, students should not be penalized for not having followed procedures exactly—especially if it was impossible to have done so in advance. Some schools may charge full tuition for such credit; others, if there is proof that tuition has been paid elsewhere, will not—with the exception perhaps of actual testing or credit review fees.

Often in these instances, individual departments conduct special testing as a means for the student to earn credit. Occasionally, this type of procedure will work with intensive foreign language programs. The home institution may arrange to test the student shortly before departure and immediately upon return and grant some credit based on the test results. In other instances, paid or gratis faculty review of research or courses is the only method that can be used. Having a special testing policy may solve a range of the problems that arise when students attend programs that appear to be academically sound but cannot produce a transcript that your institution can immediately accept.

Summary

When established campus practices concerning credit transfer are fully integrated into an education-abroad office's advising and programming, students are less likely to experience problems that can lead to loss of time, credit, or money. There are many different ways to set up and review program credit. Some apply to programs your own institution sponsors; some apply to programs sponsored by other institutions, programs, and agencies; and some apply to independent study. The key is for you to become thoroughly familiar with the policies and procedures of your own institution; to work closely with appropriate administrative personnel to formulate the fairest and most efficient means of assessing student performance; and to counsel students so that they are aware of what they need to do before, during, and following their education-abroad experience in order to maximize their chances of receiving credit.

4

Financial Aid

Contributor: Nancy Stubbs

Prohibitive costs—real or imagined—are one reason students do not consider education abroad as an option in undergraduate studies. Education-abroad programs at many state institutions do cost more than on-campus studies, and many private institutions do not allow financial aid to travel. What many students do not realize is that available financial aid resources can be used to make an overseas experience affordable. The education-abroad adviser will be increasingly called upon to provide access to affordable programs, and also to be an expert on how students can obtain internal and external financial aid. You need, at a minimum, to be able to answer the following questions:

- What is financial aid?
- How do students qualify for it?
- How is financial aid given to the student?
- Can financial aid be used for study abroad? For other forms of education abroad?
- What are the best strategies for the education-abroad adviser to help make financial aid available to students?
- Can funds be raised specifically for education-abroad students?

This chapter will consider these questions and provide basic ideas about how the education-abroad adviser can learn about financial aid, work to make it available to students, and begin fund-raising activities to develop aid specifically for education abroad.

What Is Financial Aid?

Sources of Financial Aid. Financial aid can be generally defined as any help that does not originate with the student or his or her family. Some sources for financial aid are federal and state governments; institutions of higher education; foundations; ethnic groups, clubs, religious groups, and associations; and private and public corporations.

Federal and state government financial aid for students is funded by taxpayer dollars, or sometimes by revenue-raising devices like lotteries. It is most often "need-based," meaning that the student must demonstrate financial need to qualify. Federal and state aid can also be merit-based, meaning that the student must show some special quality such as superior academic ability or exceptional skill in art or athletics. Aid can also be targeted to special groups, such as ethnic minorities, handicapped or other nontraditional students, or students entering certain professions such as teaching. Often aid targeted to a special group is also need-based, meaning that one must belong to the special group and also show financial need.

Federal financial aid is governed by Chapter IV of the Higher Education Act of 1965, which is reauthorized every five years when Congress makes what it considers necessary changes. In the last reauthorization discussions begun in 1990, a group of education-abroad professionals suggested language that would specify that using federal aid for study abroad is completely legal. This emphasis was reauthorized as part of the Higher Education Act in July 1992.

Institutional aid (any aid funded by the student's educational institution) can be based on the same eligibility requirements noted above. In addition, the student must be enrolled at the institution. This requirement often creates a barrier for study-abroad students. Many institutions, particularly private ones, are unwilling to issue institutional funds that will be spent elsewhere. As a result, students attending a private university who are heavily subsidized by institutional scholarships often cannot afford to study abroad, even if the program costs less than a year at the home campus. On more enlightened campuses, all financial aid is usable for education abroad as an entitlement of admissions and enrollment in good standing.

All other sources of aid are generally designated as private (i.e., neither governmental nor institutional). Private aid has the most diverse eligibility requirements. Unlike most governmental and institutional aid, private aid is often awarded directly to the student, who can then use the funds to attend the institution of his or her choice. There are some private sources that specify that students must attend colleges in a specific geographic region, making it difficult to use the funding while overseas.

Types of Aid. There are several types of aid:
- Grants
- Scholarships
- Loans
- Work/study or subsidized work.

Grants and scholarships are similar in that they do not require repayment. Grants are need-based and awarded to people who demonstrate that they and their families do not have the assets required to meet the institution's costs. Scholarships are generally merit-based and awarded to people who demonstrate a special ability or belong to a specific group.

While students receiving grants must often meet some minimum standard of academic progress (e.g., enrolling at least half time during the term the grant is used, maintaining a minimum grade point average), scholarship awardees must sometimes undertake specific activities. For example, an athlete is obligated to participate in a sport while receiving a scholarship. Students receiving scholarships from service clubs like Rotary International or Lion's Club might be asked to write reports about their progress or to make a certain number of appearances at local club meetings.

Loans are generally low interest or fixed interest with long repayment terms. Often the student is not required to begin repaying these loans until after graduation. Interest may also be paid by another source while the student is in school. Not all loans require the student to have a credit rating; many government loan programs are given without requiring a credit check or a cosigner. Many loan funds are self-renewing, meaning that the money repaid by former students is then lent to new students.

Loans are becoming a more important part of the standard financial aid package in higher education. This trend is producing worries on the part of many financial aid administrators. There is concern that students are borrowing too heavily and will graduate with an insupportable debt that could drive them into bankruptcy. Education-abroad advisers must consider whether borrowing heavily in order to study abroad is in the students' best interest. At the very least, the responsibility of all persons involved with students is to ensure that they understand the implications of taking out loans.

Work/study, or subsidized work, is based upon the philosophy that more students can work part time to pay for their educations if part of their salaries are subsidized by a third party. Most work/study programs are governmental, and require that a student show financial need to qualify. This type of aid can be used while studying abroad if program administrators develop an appropriate process for employing and supervising work/study students overseas. Students may work for the study-abroad program or may be placed with nonprofit or governmental agencies. These agencies may be U.S. or foreign owned. Since the extra effort and paperwork required to comply with federal or state regulations for hiring, supervising, and paying work/study students can be formidable, these opportunities may be quite limited, but it can be done.

Most students who receive financial aid for higher education receive a combination of governmental and institutional aid, though no two students are likely to receive the same package. You should become familiar with all of the kinds and sources of aid available at your institution. If you need a basic primer on federal government aid programs, ask your financial aid office for a copy of "The Student Guide" (published by the U.S. Department of Education). This booklet, which is updated every year, explains to the student and parents the types of financial aid awarded by the federal government, and also provides information on eligibility requirements, responsibilities of the student and the institution, and more.

How Do Students Qualify for Financial Aid?

Because there are different types of financial aid from different sources, the methods for qualifying for any one kind of aid differ from what is required for another. In virtually all cases, the student must fill out an application that may range from a simple request for data and an essay to a more complex request for financial information from the student and his or her family. Some applications require verification that the student has been accepted into an academic program. The application will specify all information needed to determine eligibility. To help simplify the process, most institutions use one of several standard applications that allow the student to apply for all federal, state, and institutional aid available at the home campus.

Aid available from the federal government (and from those state governments that base eligibility on federal rules and regulations) has several requirements, among which are the following:

• Students must demonstrate financial need according to set formulas. (A possible exception to this concerns certain types of student loans. The reauthorization of the Higher Education Act specifies that a pilot program will be set up to allow any student, regardless of need, to apply for a guaranteed loan. If the pilot program is judged successful, most guaranteed student loans may eventually be available to any college student.)

• Students must be enrolled at least half time in a program leading to a degree or certificate.

• Students must make satisfactory progress toward the degree or certificate during the time aid is received.

• Students must be U.S. citizens, permanent residents, or be classified in one of several immigration statuses (not F or J visa status).

• Students must have registered for the draft or be legally excused from registration.

There are several other requirements, some of which involve certifying information. In general, demonstrating eligibility for federal aid is more complex than applying for private or institutional aid. Since the majority of aid awarded to college students is either federal or state aid (at least at public institutions), many institutions find that their needs are greater than the money available. For this reason, individual institutions can set preferred filing dates, decide to leave each student with a certain amount of unmet needs (an amount of need purposely not covered by financial aid), or devise other strategies for spreading the aid dollars among the eligible students.

Procedures to verify information given on the application are also a routine part of the financial aid process. Verification may require that students who have already left for a study-abroad program provide documents or explanations. The process can also change the amount of award after students are abroad, causing the need for much communication and even changed plans if the award is greatly reduced.

How Is Financial Aid Awarded?

Once the student qualifies for aid, how is it delivered? In the case of federal, state, and institutional aid, the campus takes possession of the funds and disburses them to students at appropriate times, generally at the beginning of each term. Private scholarships may or may not be disbursed through the campus. If a condition of receiving a private scholarship is that the student be enrolled in school, most donors will send the check to the campus to be disbursed when classes begin.

Once a student begins classes, most federal, state, and institutional aid is disbursed by the bursar's office by applying the aid to the student's bill. The major exception to this is Stafford and SLS (Supplemental Loan for Students) loans from the federal government. These loans, and sometimes the federal Perkins Loans, are disbursed in check form directly to the student, who must sign a promissory note and endorse the check. New methods for disbursing loans, including electronic transfers to the student's college, are being developed. These new methods may help reduce current problems in getting loan proceeds to a student who is abroad. The 1992 reauthorization of the Higher Education Act allows students studying abroad to use powers of attorney to have loan checks signed. This welcome change eliminates the need to have government checks sent all over the world (and back!) to get the proper endorsement. Students receiving need-based federal and state aid are not allowed to receive aid that exceeds their budgeted cost of education. If a student receives a private scholarship, financial aid administrators need to know so they can—when appropriate—reduce need-based aid so the student is not getting more than the budget allows.

Private scholarships may be disbursed in check form or may be applied directly to the student's bill if the donor sends a check payable to the home institution. Once a student's tuition and fees are subtracted, any remaining balance is distributed to the student in a refund check. This system is the most efficient and accountable way to disburse aid to a student on the home campus. In the case of study-abroad students, the normal system can cause delays and difficulties. You have to be prepared to help students arrange to receive aid disbursed through the home campus, and often have to help explain why payments may be late.

What Financial Aid Can Be Used for Study Abroad?

Using federal financial aid for study abroad is perfectly legal, as long as the student is eligible and the campus disbursing the aid has ensured that the student is properly enrolled and will receive credit. Most state aid, since it is awarded using federal rules and regulations, can also be used by qualified study-abroad students. Some financial aid offices still resist awarding federal or state aid to eligible students. There are a variety of reasons for this opposition, including the lack of sufficient institutional monies, the extra work involved in giving aid to students away from the home campus, and the feeling that study abroad is a frill.

Some financial aid officers are faced with the problem of needing to retain federal funding exclusively for use on the home campus. Even many public universities are now tuition-driven, meaning that they must take in a certain amount of revenue from tuition and fees each year to survive financially. Many institutions feel they cannot afford to give aid to students who will spend the money elsewhere. As an education-abroad adviser, you will need to find sufficient support for overseas study in order to overcome these arguments. Since the law mandates equal access to aid for all qualified students, denying aid to a student who is receiving credit on an overseas program could be hard to explain to federal or state auditors. Audits by the Department of Education are conducted at all institutions that award federal aid. If an audit finds too many instances of wrongdoing on a campus, the federal government can restrict or even refuse to grant appropriations of aid. Ensuring that financial aid awards meet the requirements of the federal (and state) government is in the best interests of the institution.

Several years ago, a ruling from the U.S. Department of Education stated that student loans could be given to students who engage in study abroad that is directly applicable to their degree or certificate. Many financial aid administrators took this to mean that students could use financial aid only if all courses taken overseas applied to the student's degree requirements. This argument lacks merit for the simple reason that a student can take electives at the home institution that have nothing to do with specific degree requirements and still qualify for financial aid.

Institutional and private aid may or may not be available for study abroad, depending on the eligibility standards. This is a real problem for students who attend private institutions where substantial scholarships are awarded from the school's endowment funds. All institutional and private aid should be made equally available—especially at private institutions—for overseas study, as long as students are participating in legitimate and approved programs and receiving credit toward their degrees. To deny this support to students with financial need while more affluent fellow students participate in study abroad is to sacrifice the principle of equal access to all academic opportunities.

While some arguments appear to justify denying full financial aid to students studying abroad, it is not in the institution's financial or academic interests to take this position. The responsibility of convincing others at your institution of the many advantages of providing adequate financial support for education abroad lies on your shoulders. You will need to educate financial aid administrators and develop proper standards and controls to ensure that aid is properly awarded, disbursed, and tracked. Education-abroad administrators can and must be involved in this process, both to help students get aid and to help the financial aid officers fulfill their legal obligations.

How Can You Help to Make Financial Aid Available?

The answer to this question is summarized in the following words: knowledge, communication, and cooperation. A knowledge of the financial aid available on the campus and the requirements for eligibility is necessary to understand how it might be used by study-abroad students. Communication with several offices, including financial aid, the registrar, the bursar, and academic departments, is needed to coordinate special policies and procedures for awarding aid. Cooperation among the above offices is required to properly award aid, to verify its use, and to avoid violating federal and state law. You must also be a determined and resourceful activist, lobbyist, and outspoken proponent for using current funds and for finding new funds. Without your active leadership, nothing new is likely to happen.

Where do you begin? First, you need to accept the fact that using financial aid for study abroad will probably involve more work for you and your office, as well as for several other administrative offices on the campus—at least initially. The extra work results from needing to create new procedures, including the following:

• Who decides if the study-abroad program provides credit that will be accepted by the home institution? (See chapter 3.)

• How are study-abroad students identified and rostered on the campus giving the aid? (An important question, since many state loan agencies that monitor the use of student loans now have direct access to campus computer records.)

• Who determines the budget for a study-abroad program? (The 1992 reauthorization of the Higher Education Act allows the cost of study abroad to be used to determine how much aid a student should receive. This means that students attending low-cost public institutions can qualify for more aid if the cost of study abroad is higher.)

• Who notifies the financial aid office if the student withdraws?

• Who monitors academic progress and records grades and hours once the program is finished?

• What should be done if the grades are not received from abroad before the beginning of the next academic term (an important point when monitoring satisfactory academic progress)?

• How does the student get his or her aid?

• Who communicates with the student and/or parents if there are problems with financial aid while the student is away?

• How does the student get aid applications for the next academic period? Should application deadlines be extended for study-abroad students?

• How will payment schedules be altered to allow study-abroad students to receive their financial aid before paying?

• How must computer systems be altered to allow for the special needs of study-abroad students ?

• Who is going to pay for all of this and do the extra work?

Answering these questions will take time, concentration, and good communication with the appropriate departments. An invaluable discussion of these and other problems can be found in NAFSA's *Financial Aid for Study Abroad: A Manual for Advisers and Administrators* (1989). This book covers strategies for meeting the special needs of study-abroad students, models for working with faculty and administrators, and a more detailed explanation of financial aid.

The questions outlined above can be even more complex when the student wishes to study in a program sponsored by another institution. There is a way to contract out part of a student's education. Consortial or contractual agreements allow students studying for a limited time at another college or university to use federal aid. While a contractual agreement will solve some of the problems mentioned above, the agreement will also require another layer of procedure. Once again, knowledge, careful communication, and cooperation are needed to create a viable system that can handle the student's and the institution's needs.

One of the best resources for establishing these new procedures is networking. Contact other institutions and see how they have solved similar problems. Call nearby institutions that run study-abroad programs. Contact NAFSA or CIEE for a list of institutions with big education-abroad programs, or go to regional or national NAFSA or CIEE conferences and meet colleagues. Be aware that each campus has an individual system. Even the best advice will have to be molded around your institution's policies.

Additional Financial Aid Resources

There is a national dearth of scholarships and grants aimed specifically at undergraduates who wish to study abroad. This lack of alternative funding has limited participation in education abroad largely to those who can afford it through parental and/or institutional support. There are numerous examples of students who cannot qualify for need-based financial aid but who also cannot find an extra $1,000 to $4,000 needed to participate in the study-abroad program that most meets their academic needs.

There is some recent good news for study-abroad students and administrators in the National Security Education Act (NSEA), which Congress passed late in 1991 (PL 102-183). This bill recognizes the need to have more college graduates understand the world and its languages if the United States is to compete in a global economy. Funding for NSEA comes from the U.S. Defense Department budget. Some NSEA funding will provide scholarships for undergraduates who study abroad in areas of the world considered critical to the long-range diplomatic, economic, and other interests of the United States. This is the first time the federal government has provided scholarships specifically for undergraduate education abroad. The bill indicates heightened interest from the U.S. government for ensuring that more college students have an education that is international in scope. Whether NSEA presages further forms of financial support remains to be seen. The actual number of students who will benefit from NSEA—in relation to the national need—is yet to be determined, and competition will be stiff. Since sources of extra funding are limited, the education-abroad office must consider two primary alternative strategies: (1) attempting to develop or find study-abroad programs whose costs are approximately the same as costs at the home campus, and (2) developing special funding sources.

Affordable Programs. Try to build a modest library of funding books that include scholarships for undergraduate study abroad. Many of the basic international funding books include a few entries for undergraduates. Listings of these books can be found in NAFSA's "Work, Study, and Travel Abroad: A Bibliography" and in the appendixes of *Financial Aid for Study Abroad*. Make these available to students in the study-abroad office, or perhaps ask the campus library to stock them in the reference section.

Most college students have seen advertisements for scholarship search companies that claim there are millions of dollars of unused scholarship funds available through private organizations. Most often, these scholarships are targeted to students with specific backgrounds, such as ethnic or religious groups, children of veterans, descendants of immigrants from specific countries, people majoring in specific subjects, and so on. While the study-abroad adviser should be cautious about encouraging students to use commercial search services, some students will be able to find private scholarships that can be used abroad. Most financial aid offices or campus libraries have resource books that list these types of scholarships. Encourage students to do their own research for scholarships that fit their particular background or field of study.

Many cities have branches of international friendship organizations, such as Alliance Française, Goethe Clubs, the Dante Alighieri Society, or the League of United Latin American Citizens. These organizations are affiliated with certain countries; if a local chapter exists, see if it offers scholarships or loans to students planning to study in that country. Many have modest programs that aid students who are going abroad.

Some of the large international service organizations, such as Rotary International, have scholarships for students who are engaged in study or research abroad. The Rotary Scholarship is a well-known example of support for undergraduates and graduates going abroad. Contact the local branch of this and other service clubs to see how students can apply for the scholarships. Ask those local branches if they would consider creating a special award for local high school graduates who wish to study abroad.

The CIEE offers travel scholarships, known as Bowman Scholarships, for students engaged in study or research in Third World countries, where the cost of round-trip transportation is often very high. In 1991, the CIEE Education-Abroad Scholarship for Minority Students was established. Funds are raised through contributions from members and foundation grants, with awards made on the basis of financial need and merit.

Fundraising. You should also consider direct fundraising to create a pool of scholarship funds specifically designated for education abroad. Begin by contacting the campus development office to see if such an appeal can be worked into an annual fund drive—perhaps even targeting alumni who have studied abroad. Working with the development office allows the education-abroad office to get expert advice about how to raise money. The fundraising will also help provide access to mailing lists, postage, the alumni magazine or newsletter, and the local community. Your pitch should be that academically qualified and interested students at your institution should not be denied the educational and career advantages of an overseas experience because they lack money—which may be no more than the difference between home-campus and overseas costs.

Some education-abroad offices have been successful in setting up program budgets in a way that generates some funding for students on financial aid. Others charge an administrative fee or surcharge to all students studying abroad, some or all of which is put into scholarship funds. At the University of Texas, the education-abroad office worked with the student government to add a nominal amount to normal student fees, thereby generating a large pool of money to support overseas study. These are just some of many ideas worth trying.

Summary

The lack of adequate funding for education abroad ought not to be a problem—apart from the national problem about how to guarantee equal access for all students to all of American higher education. The most important duty of the education-abroad administrator is to make study abroad a viable alternative. Through knowledge, communication, and networking, regular and alternate sources of financial aid can be found. The time involved may seem daunting, but the rewards to students make the effort worthwhile.

5

The Office Library and Resource Materials

Contributors: Catherine Gamon and Heidi Soneson

An important question for all education-abroad advisers and administrators is how to design, organize, and supply the office with resources that are requisite for its particular mission. Answering this question involves the following variables: (1) your campus location, (2) the physical space, (3) the budget, (4) your institution's commitment to education abroad, (5) the office's location in your institution's administrative structure, and (6) the academic interests and needs of your students. In general, the books and other materials should reflect institutional history and values.

Institutional Policy and the Library

By definition, a good resource library contains the materials needed for the defined range of programming supported by your institution. Even advisers with ample budgets, time, and space will make conscious choices about materials, rather than ordering everything and then considering how to use it all. In smaller offices, the issues are even more pointed. Consider at the outset (and review annually) the function and scope of your advising services and/or program administration, because this will influence the resources you make available to students and the resources you need to perform your job effectively. The following are some essential questions to answer before setting up your library:

• Does the office advise on your institution's own programs only? Other institutions' programs only? Or both?

• Does the office provide information on credit-bearing academic programs only? Does it provide information on short-term work opportunities and other experiential programs overseas? Do students expect to find information on how they might travel independently?

• Does the office only do student advising, or is it also responsible for setting up and administering your institution's own programs? Or consortium programs? Are these programs run exclusively by your office or in conjunction with academic departments or area studies programs?

• Is the office responsible for awarding academic credit? If so, for your institution's programs only, or for any programs? What is its relation to the academic dean's office? To the registrar's office? To the financial aid office?

• Is the office the only office on campus involved in international education or is it part of an inclusive international programs office? If it is independent, does it share resources and work closely with the office that provides services to foreign students and scholars? With the international center?

• Is the office responsible for providing predeparture orientations? Contact with students while abroad? Reentry programming?

• To what extent are students traditional undergraduates, wishing a general language and culture experience abroad ? To what extent do they have specialized curricular or preprofessional interests and needs? What are their language abilities?

• Will the office serve graduating seniors and graduate students? Faculty members? Staff? Is there any expectation, formal or informal, for assisting family members of students, faculty, or staff? Community people with no direct affiliation to the institution? Will the office be working with U.S. students only, or with foreign students wishing to go abroad as well?

Policy/Resource Trade-offs. The answers to these fundamental questions should provide some guidance as to the amount and type of resources you need. If the office has a very narrow scope (e.g., you advise only for your own three programs in England, France, and Spain; your institution does not allow financial aid to travel; your office has no role in the awarding of credit, and does not assist students who want to work abroad) obviously your resources can be limited in breadth. If your office advises students on your own programs in all parts of the world, on affiliated programs, and on programs offered by other institutions and agencies; if it has a voice in matters of credit; if students come seeking information about work and travel abroad; if you must work closely with the financial aid office; if you are responsible for orientation and reentry; and if you have adequate space and budget, then your office should have an extensive range of materials on hand.

Most offices are between these extremes, and need to make conscious choices about resources. You may wish to be all things to all people, but neither available space, budget, nor time will allow. Not having exactly the right book or pamphlet on hand for every single student may be regrettable, but it is not much of a problem if your campus has other resources. What is in your library will depend on what else is available in other campus units offering international educational services. You have done your job if you can direct the search.

If the international student office has an extensive library of materials on countries and regions where American students may be interested in studying, there may be no need to duplicate these resources. If the career center stocks material that would guide students seeking international internships, there may be no reason for the same resources to be on your shelves. If there is a campus travel agency that sells the Eurail Pass and helps students find good low-cost airfares and accommodations, then your library may not need to carry this information. On the other hand, if your campus is big and students are just as likely to seek help in one office as another, the best solution may be to have as much information available in as many locations as possible.

Professional Bibliographic Needs. While the bulk of your resources will be available to anyone, you will need to determine what resources you—as a professional—need in order to have the background information to assist others. Beyond basic NAFSA, IIE, and CIEE reference guides and training manuals, you will want to keep abreast of new developments in the field through subscriptions to professional newsletters and magazines, such as the *NAFSA Newsletter*, and CIEE's *Update*. You will probably need to have copies of IIE's *Academic Year Abroad* and *Vacation Study Abroad,* catalogs of the most popular study-abroad programs, and volumes on the history, development, and professional practice of international educational exchange. You should become familiar with all publications available from NAFSA, CIEE, IIE, AACRAO, SIETAR, and Intercultural Press. In addition, you may wish to have a variety of reference materials on cross-cultural theory and training (see chapter 12).

Making Choices. Institutional policies may limit student choice by (1) restricting student access to information about programs; (2) allowing participation only in approved programs; (3) allowing only institutional funds, including financial aid, to be applied to home-institution programs; and (4) denying academic credit to students doing other programs. If any of these are true on your campus, compiling a large library on an array of programs may be a fruitless exercise.

No education-abroad office is obliged to provide information on all programs available to students. The supermarket approach makes sense only if all program options are open to all students. Even at institutions that actively encourage participation in a large variety of programs—its own and others, academic and experiential, on all continents—there are always some reasons for limiting materials (e.g., to focus student attention or to conserve space). Your library should concentrate on materials that best serve the general needs of students from your institution, and should feature programs, locations, and opportunities chosen through work with your advisory committee, with returned student evaluations, and with colleagues in similar settings.

51

Your initial selection of materials will represent a stage in the counseling process without necessarily excluding information about other choices. However inclusive or exclusive your approach, you must represent the distillation of institutional thought and must provide the very best professional guidance. If your library presents information only on a limited number of pre-approved programs, you should be ready to defend your selection.

Professional Goals versus Institutional Policies

National Goals. Advisers are often caught between their loyalties to their institution and their broader desire to serve the expressed interests of individual students. This conflict has implications concerning the availability of library resources and related counseling. When institutional policy limits students to a few approved programs, the library materials are limited to these programs as well. What do you do when these programs do not serve the needs and interests of certain students? Do you make information on other programs available? Some advisers express a strong desire to provide complete and accurate information about all education-abroad opportunities, regardless of institutional policy. If you are one these advisers, you need to be a strong advocate of expanding overseas opportunities on your campus. Advisers have a professional obligation to work with the faculty and administration to broaden the institution's vision of education abroad, especially by recognizing that traditional models of study abroad do not serve all interests or needs. To quote again from the report of the National Task Force on Undergraduate Education Abroad:

> For students who are older, of minority background, employed (46% of full-time students under 25 are employed at least part-time), disabled, or have limited funds, study abroad often is not perceived to be an option. The needs of such students are mostly ignored by the more typical study-abroad models and structures.... Undergraduate interest in work experiences abroad is increasing rapidly and certainly at a faster rate than study-abroad program participation.... Internships, various types of cooperative education arrangements, voluntary service and independent study/research projects are among approaches which could generate academic credit or be academically or professionally relevant to degree programs at the home institution.

Serving the needs of such students requires an inclusive vision of education abroad, and the policies and resources needed to support it.

Academic versus Experiential. Often, institutions distinguish between the value of academic and experiential programs. It is important to stress that academic and experiential are not—however precisely defined—mutually exclusive. These terms vary with time and from institution to institution. Even carefully controlled branch-campus programs abroad have an important experiential dimension just by taking place in a foreign culture. Conversely, an internship or a teaching project is often as intellectually and interculturally stimulating as a classroom experience on the campus of a major foreign university. Still, a fundamental question remains as to the degree of emphasis your institution is willing to place on education-abroad programs that are not academic in the traditional sense.

The degree of institutional support that now exists for domestic work programs, internships, fieldwork, public service, and independent study is usually a good guide to how the institution will support educational activities abroad. Even if your institution has not taken a proactive stance on experiential education, you are likely to see many students expressing an interest. Unless there is another office on campus that provides counseling and information, and if students believe that such experiences will prepare them for careers and for life—at least as well as, if not better than, a classroom experience—your library needs to be ready (see chapter 15).

Expanding Destinations. Increasingly, advisers are assuming responsibility for diversifying educational opportunities. Some 80 to 85 percent of the American undergraduates who study abroad go to western Europe. Current faculty strengths and institutional interests may only reinforce these traditional patterns. Student interest in studying or working in other regions is growing slowly. There is a lot of established preference on the part of students, faculty, and parents, and changing established practice will not be easy. Complicating the matter is the fact that programs in developing countries are more difficult to establish and maintain.

NAFSA and CIEE have encouraged more programming in Asia, Africa, Latin America, Oceania, and other nontraditional locations. One of the main emphases of the new National Security Education Program is getting more students to critical areas (broadly defined as those regions and cultures that have traditionally attracted few students but are seen to be in the U.S. national interest). Information on programs in western Europe is more abundant than information on opportunities in the developing world, but such information is available. (For example, CIEE's *Guide to Educational Programs in the Third World* describes more than two hundred study, volunteer, and work programs.) A dramatic and effective way to challenge students to consider nontraditional locations is to provide ample and attractive materials on these locations.

Working with your language and/or area studies programs is a good way to augment existing resources and generate interest in specific geographical areas. Certain areas, whether emphasized in the home-campus curriculum or not, capture students' interest and imagination because of current political or social developments.

53

Financial and Access Issues. Should an education-abroad library only contain information on programs within the economic reach of the average student? This is an important and troubling question. Most students finance education abroad from the same resources that pay for their domestic studies. Sensitivity to program costs is important when collecting and displaying information.

A sensible solution is to balance your library with information on appealing programs at a range of costs, perhaps concentrating on programs that most students can best afford. You should also be taking a proactive stance in lobbying for the fullest possible use of financial aid funds for study abroad, as well as collecting information on scholarships, fellowships, and grants available to students (see chapter 4).

Setting Up a Resource Library

Organizing Space and Materials. The space available for the education-abroad library is of paramount concern. A full-scale, multimedia resource library requires extensive space, not only for the bibliographical materials, but also for computers, copy machines, typewriters, printers, fax machines, and the furniture and equipment for performing a range of various administrative and clerical functions. Space is necessary for students to sit down and pore over materials; a presentation area for small meetings is very important; and some private space for advising students is essential. Ideally, all libraries would have enough space to meet all these needs—and be located conveniently in the middle of campus. However, this ideal set-up is rarely the norm, and most advisers have less space than they need. While it is possible to operate in a room that serves as your office and as a repository of materials, the minimum standard is two rooms: one for materials and one for individual counseling. If a third is available, this room can function as a general reception area staffed by an assistant, secretary, or peer counselor who also helps direct students to the information.

How you classify materials is very important. Even a small collection of books and brochures needs to be carefully organized. Most libraries divide program materials into files that are either country- or region-specific. Each of these files is then subdivided into categories such as study, work, travel, funding, and general (dealing with more than one category). While initially it may seem most expeditious to place program brochures in files or boxes, materials soon become mangled and out of order. You may have to invent an elaborate but clear system involving the use of detailed classification systems. Many primary materials may need to be placed in three-ring binders. Once you have a system, you will need a way of explaining it; if you are the only one who understands its logic, it is of no use .

The bulk of program brochures is likely to arrive unsolicited and free, but many valuable items will not. You will need to place your name on certain mailing lists and research and order new materials. You will need to decide how to spend your budget wisely, since you probably cannot buy everything. Also, weeding out superseded materials takes vigilance, but if not done periodically, the library will no longer be useful. It is essential to consider the time, staffing, and procedures involved in periodically editing and updating library resources.

Types of Material. The following is a generic grouping of the types of materials a well-stocked education-abroad library is likely to contain.

Institutional Policy Information. You might want to produce your own materials to give an overview of the resources; to explain institutional policies on program selection and approval, credit, financial aid, and other essential concerns; and to clarify the advising process and application procedures for your and/or other programs. This can be done on single information sheets or can be summarized in a handbook. Other information sheets can be developed to summarize opportunities in certain geographical areas, for students in particular academic disciplines, for minority students, for students with disabilities, or for certain categories of pursuits (e.g., summer work abroad). Many of your colleagues will have extensive collections of such materials and will be glad to share copies.

Scholarship, Fellowship, and Grant Information. This information comes in many forms: pamphlets, fliers, chapters of books, and complete reference volumes. Screening can help identify false leads and blind alleys, as well as those support schemes not available to undergraduates.

Reference Books. Beyond the IIE's *Academic Year Abroad* and *Vacation Study Abroad*, there are few bound volumes giving anything close to an overview of the full range of study-abroad programs now available to undergraduates—and the IIE volumes list many programs open only to sponsoring institution students. CIEE's *Whole World Handbook* has the advantage of listing study-, work-, and travel-abroad programs, but the disadvantage of listing only those programs sponsored by CIEE member institutions.

Program Brochures and Catalogs. Your office will most likely be flooded with promotional brochures. Many will be well designed, with seductive prose, sophisticated graphics, and photographs. The best will detail with candor what the program is and what it is not, what it offers and what it does not. What you keep for your library and what you throw away will depend on considerations enumerated above. For most students, seeing a range of opportunities and program pitches is a useful exercise that aids in making a final selection.

Program Evaluations. Many advisers place copies of evaluations completed by recent participants alongside program brochures. An alternative is to arrange evaluations by country (and often, within this, by city or region). Evaluations are an invaluable resource as long as students respect the confidentiality of past participants (see chapter 16), and are aware that every student is likely to have a different experience.

Magazines. From time to time, interesting magazine articles appear that support education abroad or highlight the culture or politics of a particular country. It is helpful to place such features in the files with program brochures and country information. *Transitions Abroad* magazine, which appears six times a year, is a unique compendium of information and perspectives on study, work, travel, and living abroad. Many articles are written by students or other program participants, and each issue contains new ideas and solid leads on how to obtain more information; there is also a resource guide series. This is a magazine students actually read, so it is worth subscribing to it, as well as excerpting and filing some of the articles separately. NAFSA's semi-annual *International Educator*, while not devoted exclusively to education abroad, also contains valuable features.

Videos, Films, Slides. Your library may include a set of slides, photos, or films taken by past program participants. In addition, more and more programs are making brief videos available. IIE also has a good general video called "Planning for Study Abroad." Not all such products are equally appealing or effective, but at their best, images of living and learning abroad, coupled with honest responses (given on site) from program participants, can have a great impact on students.

Foreign University Catalogs. Many foreign university catalogs are now being mailed to American education-abroad offices; some are also available on microfiche, which saves file space but requires a special reader. These catalogs give the full curriculum and help students get preapproval for courses.

Self-Advising Programs. Various attempts are now being made to produce interactive computer programs to take students through the early stages of selecting the right program. Ideally, the computer programs will allow the counseling process to begin at a higher level (see chapter 6).

Knowledgebases. Education-abroad libraries are on the brink of making available—through electronic communications—an absolutely staggering amount of information from sources throughout the country and around the world. IIE put its information on all programs on a database that was to be annually updatable, but the project has been shelved due to insufficient interest among subscribers. This development and others, when and if they mature, will alter the nature and function of the education-abroad library (see chapter 6).

A Basic Library. The bibliography found in appendix 1 of this book is a modification of the most recent SECUSSA bibliography, "Study, Work, and Travel Abroad," published by NAFSA (1989). It consists of three major sections:

- A selection of basic reference materials for the education-abroad adviser, divided into various subcategories

• Items considered to be essential to advisers or to a basic resource library (marked with an asterisk)

• A list of organizations and publishers that can furnish advisers with the publications listed in the bibliography as well as publication lists and/or free information on study-, work-, and travel-abroad.

This bibliography is not designed as a comprehensive list of all materials available in each category. It identifies and briefly describes reference materials that are currently used by study-abroad advisers and provide sufficient breadth and depth to serve as basic and useful works. It does not evaluate the resources.

While every attempt has been made to verify the accuracy of the information in the appendix at the time of publication, addresses, telephone numbers, and prices are subject to change. Also, new and revised publications become available on a continuous basis.

6

Computerizing Operations

Contributors: James Gehlhar and Kathleen Sideli

Computer technology has revolutionized using, storing, and sharing information. Even the smallest education-abroad office can benefit from computers, which years ago ceased to be the preserve of the complex, wealthy university with graduate programs in science, engineering, and technology. Computers no longer require highly technical knowledge to operate effectively, though you will need to train yourself and your staff to get the most out of the investment.

Large offices, with their many constituencies, complicated communications needs, and limited staff, cannot accomplish their many tasks efficiently without the assistance of computers. One- or two-person offices can also run more efficiently with the aid of computers. The purpose of this chapter is (1) to guide advisers and administrators to the hardware they need—and do not need—and (2) to illustrate the types of software and how they can be used in the education-abroad office.

Assessing Needs, Goals, Support, and Resources

Advice about computers and software is easily dated by rapid advances in technology. Office computers are becoming cheaper and more powerful. Experts now predict that the capacity of today's mainframe will be the capacity of the personal computer six years later. This means that deciding what equipment you need is a complex matter.

The basic desktop PC (personal computer) has become increasingly powerful, with more applications than even dreamed of a decade ago. Laptop computers can now perform most of the tasks previously limited to desktops. The miniaturization continues with amazingly versatile and powerful notebook PCs with built-in modems for telecommunications. Slate computers recognize handwriting and format it into print, and scanners can now copy almost any text or graphic and convert it into computerese. Local area networks (LANs) are becoming more popular and flexible. Student-accessed computer bulletin boards are becoming increasingly common and present the education-abroad office with new opportunities to promote its services to students—without those students entering the office.

Database applications offer exciting possibilities. Simple relational databases enable you to enter and retrieve data in a large variety of configurations. Increasing access to large national knowledgebases, which store huge amounts of data, allows users to locate and access even more data. Desktop publishing, picture transmissions, and speech-input computers are also developing at a fast pace.

Before looking through computer catalogs and visiting showrooms, examine your office, determine your needs, and gain some understanding of the larger issues involved in purchasing computer equipment.

Budget. The real cost of computerization is always more than the price tag on the hardware. Software has to be purchased; often computer furniture has to be purchased; staff have to be trained; and the computer will often need service and, eventually, extra memory. The estimated cost of the average PC is not $2,000, but nearer $15,000—an estimate you may or may not wish to reveal to your dean.

Building your office's computing capacity by increments over a period of years, rather than investing in a complete system all at once, is a good idea. Do not begin with older systems that are already out of production. In addition to an item's price, consider its convenience factor. The more expensive versions of some equipment and some software programs may cut your labor costs significantly because they are quicker or can accomplish more with a single command.

Start-Up Training. Be cautious about galloping technology and the proverbial bells and whistles. You do not want recent innovations to pass you by, but you also do not want to invest in something irrelevant to your skills and needs. Concentrate on how you want to do business, and then choose equipment that allows you to accomplish your work most efficiently. Once you have decided upon the system, you should immediately begin preparing your staff to use it.

Courses taken before the equipment arrives can instill enthusiasm and set appropriate expectations, but you need to be realistic about the time required to get your computer configured and your databases set up. Your office will not be computerized in a single week or month. The real question is how much training and how much commitment will be required. Any computer class you take will be to your advantage. If time, money, and ambition are limited, you should opt for simple, user-friendly technology.

Building on What Exists. What already exists on your campus will be a major factor in your decision making. Most campuses find it advantageous to sign contracts with software and hardware firms. These contracts usually give the institution price advantages, but they may also stipulate that no competing brands may be used on campus. Check with your campus computing center (or its equivalent) and determine what brands and models are available at special prices—and which are specifically excluded. Try to discover what equipment or software your institution actively supports through the availability of knowledgeable staff or service contracts. Buying bargain computers or software programs for which no local service is available is a very poor investment. You also need to consider what, if any, computer equipment will be shared with the international-students office; its requirements and priorities will have to be taken into account.

Microcomputer versus Terminal Work Station. Work-station terminals have no computing capacity of their own, but instead depend upon mainframe or other computers elsewhere. Most travel agents and bank tellers have such work stations. The advantage of these terminals is an automatic link to most, if not all, the computing capacities and data storage on campus, probably good support services and training, and immediate compatibility. However, when the mainframe is down, so are all the terminals in your office. You may also get locked into programs and applications designed for scientific or scholastic purposes, which may not apply to your needs.

The alternative is a stand-alone PC that has its own computing ability. Stand-alone computers are preferable because they provide more flexibility at little difference in cost and, if needed, can be connected to a mainframe. However, making stand-alones practical involves purchasing hardware and software that are absolutely right for your office, and on learning to take advantage of their capacities.

Apple versus IBM. The world of microcomputing remains divided on which of these two monolithic systems is better for the office. However, the divide is narrowing. Files can now be shared easily among the various Apple models. IBM and compatible models also readily share files. However, sharing files between these two types of computers requires that you purchase one of many available conversion programs or "translators."

Local Area Networks. It is now possible to have an internal network that links individual offices to a larger central computer that acts as a file server. On a LAN, printers and PCs work through the phone lines, and IBMs and Macintoshes can be integrated onto the same network. Any move toward a LAN should be thoroughly investigated with the university computer center and communications office in order to answer some of the following questions: Is your current equipment adequate? What will be the complete cost of a LAN? What do you want from a LAN? How much trouble is involved in maintaining a LAN?

Color versus Monochrome Screens. Until recently, Apple offered largely monochrome screens, whereas IBM and its compatibles offered more choices. Color screens are more expensive than monochromes, but perform a wide variety of functions that would otherwise be difficult. Modern, high-resolution color screens are easier to read than the older variety.

Expanded Memory. Computer programs are getting larger, which means that they occupy more memory. Consult the computer center on campus to ensure that your computer has sufficient memory to accommodate future developments. When purchasing any new computer equipment, you should always investigate the possibility of future upgrades in memory. Education-abroad offices tend to have little money for replacement of computers, so it pays to think ahead and get advice.

Printers. There are choices galore. Important considerations are the per-page cost, the quality of printing (e.g., whether you want impact printing or laser printing), print style, the speed of printing, and the amount of noise the printer produces. Printing multicopy form sets obviously requires an impact printer.

Modems. Modems are devices that allow you to connect your computer via telephone either directly to other modem-equipped computers or, via the university electronic mail "gateways" to which campus personnel can connect free of charge, into the global "internet" of e-mail users.

The word "modem" is an acronym for "modulate-demodulate," or the process by which the modem changes digital computer signals into the analog signals carried by most telephone lines. Your PC will require a modem to access electronic mail if your PC uses a telephone connection to link to another computer or e-mail system. E-mail can be accessed without a modem via a LAN or by a direct link to the university mainframe computer.

If you wish to purchase a modem, there are a variety of models from which to choose, depending on your computer brand and model, the speed, and other qualities you desire. Modems may either be "internal" (fitting inside your computer and not requiring extra space or a separate power supply) or external (sitting on top of or alongside your computer). One advantage of an external modem is that it displays a variety of signal messages to enable you to check its operation.

The speed and sophistication of modems has increased dramatically in recent years, in parallel with their decline in price. Most advisers purchasing new modems should select a 9600 or 14,400 bps model with built-in data compression and error-checking features. Such modems, widely available for a few hundred dollars, enable you to connect at very high speeds over ordinary phone lines to other modem-equipped computers around the world. Modems increasingly also provide, for only a modest extra cost, both send and receive telefax capability directly from your microcomputer, and often voice-mail capability as well, thus possibly eliminating the need for separate stand-alone fax machines or telephone answering machines in a well-computerized international office.

Software Compatibility. As with hardware, your software programs should be capable of talking with each other. There will be many occasions when you would like to send a personalized form letter to a list generated from a database, or would like to pull a financial table from a spreadsheet to use in a newsletter. These tasks can be easily accomplished if your software programs are compatible. You should assess your software needs as soon as possible and standardize the software purchases in your office. Your colleagues may have their favorite software, but preferences should not lead to a wide variety of programs. Find out which software programs are supported by your computer center, and encourage everyone to learn how to use them. Discuss purchases of new software from the point of view of the whole office, rather than the preference of one staff member. Discussions will pay off in the end when all staff are comfortable on a select number of programs.

Portability. This is the age of laptop and notebook computers. People who travel find laptops very useful, as do people who take their work home. As noted above, laptops and notebooks and their software should be compatible with the software used in the office.

Maintenance and Service. You need to be familiar with what can go wrong with computers and be prepared to deal with problems. The more sophisticated the equipment, the more technical the expertise that will be required. You should build safety nets into your budget and administration. If possible, you should designate someone within your office as a trouble shooter, and make sure that his or her job description reflects this additional burden. Otherwise, you need to call in more sophisticated technicians. If they exist on campus, the costs may be minimal. The costs of outside service can be high.

Computer Furniture. Unless your office's existing furniture accommodates your new computer equipment perfectly, be prepared to invest in desks and chairs made specifically for computers. The new equipment must be comfortable to use or it will not be used.

Data Security. Protection from accidental loss and theft are important concerns. For each important file, you should make a back-up file that must be updated each time the original is changed. You may purchase devices that automatically produce a second copy of your files, and you may instruct

63

many software programs to produce the necessary back-up. There are also ways of protecting your data from unauthorized eyes. Some computers actually have locks and keys that prevent unapproved use, and many programs provide for a series of security passwords before allowing access.

Additional Counsel. General advice and specific, practical assistance with your computer concerns are available from MicroSIG, NAFSA's "microcomputer special-interest group." MicroSIG can help you learn what others with interests similar to yours have found to be successful in their offices and develop new solutions to data-processing problems. It can also help in selecting, purchasing, or setting up equipment and in learning how to use electronic mail, desktop publishing, databasing, and other common computer applications.

MicroSIG has provided a diverse menu of computer literacy training for the NAFSA membership since 1985. The bulk of its activity has been in five areas: (1) administering the Inter-L electronic forum as a communications medium and training vehicle for international educators; (2) sponsoring sessions to be presented at NAFSA national conferences; (3) presenting sessions and distributing resource materials at NAFSA regional conferences; (4) publishing the MicroSIG Newsletter; and (5) drafting "layered training outlines" to be used in local, regional, or sectional NAFSA computer training workshops.

These outlines, layered to the needs of beginning, intermediate, and experienced users, are available in electronic form from the Inter-L archives (see Telecommunications below), or in print versions from MicroSIG liaisons with NAFSA's 11 regions. Outlines are currently available on the following topics: electronic mail, telematics, desktop publishing for the international office, database applications in international programs operations, word-processing for the international educator, and general design principles for computer training workshops.

MicroSIG also publishes and distributes to all its paid subscribers a regular newsletter, *Microcomputers in the International Office*. Each issue contains articles on Inter-L, papers on issues and health considerations for computer users, guidelines for using specific software applications in international offices, and instructions on how to obtain further help with computer-related questions. The newsletter is an important print supplement to the continual electronic supply of training information relayed via Inter-L.

Information on MicroSIG may be obtained from Jim Graham, 4301 Terry Lake Road, Fort Collins, Colorado 80524, tel. 303.493.0207, e-mail JGraham@lamar.colostate.edu.

APPLICATIONS

Of the many computer applications currently in use in advanced and well-equipped education-abroad offices, at least some will be useful to your office. Sufficient computer expertise for all of the following applications is likely to be available on your campus.

Word Processing. Word processing is used for correspondence, brochures and information sheets, mailing labels, and mass mailings that use address databases.

Spreadsheets. The flow of information in and out of an education-abroad office is constant, and the need to take stock often vital. A spreadsheet program can make organizing and tracking this information easy. Common spreadsheet functions include line budgets and graphic representations. In each case, a number of variables (e.g., enrollments, exchange rates, GPAs, fees) can be automatically recalculated using a computerized spreadsheet. In budgeting, for instance, a program such as Lotus 1-2-3 can automatically update costs expressed in dollars against the latest exchange rates of foreign currencies. The effect of increases or decreases in enrollment on a preestablished budget can be instantly revealed. Any office that uses roughly similar budget categories year after year will quickly discover the benefits of using spreadsheets. Year-to-year comparisons of budgets are easy to grasp when information is presented in pie charts, line graphs, or other graphic devices supported by all popular spreadsheet programs.

Databases. Relational database programs allow you to organize data in a variety of ways, then retrieve it in different configurations. This means that new data need be entered only once, creating a resource that can be accessed repeatedly in a variety of ways. You can create a database that includes personal and academic information for each applicant to a study-abroad program. This information can later be sorted (reorganized) by year, last name, major, GPA, home address, zip code, birthday, and so on. For example, you have stored information on applicants for your program in Madrid. You can now ask the program to give you the average grade-point average of the applicants, a breakdown of academic departments supplying students, or the number of juniors in the program. Participant names and addresses can also be extracted and merged with a standard letter on a word-processing system.

The first step involved in setting up a database is deciding what categories, or "fields," of information will be important, and the maximum number of characters there might be in each field. Figure 1 is an example of a student record after the fields have been established but before data has been entered.

Entering the information requires basic computer skills. A good software package will prompt you at every step and alert you if there has been an error. Retrieving information from a database is no more complicated than

FIGURE 1. SAMPLE STUDENT RECORD

programs [ ]	zip_2 [ ]
year [ ]	phone_2 [ ]
survey [ ]	pres_lang [ ]
res [ ]	other_lang [ ]
last name [ ]	university [ ]
first name [ ]	class [ ]
middle name[ ]	major [ ]
ss [ ]	school [ ]
sex [ ] title []	interv_day [ ]
birthday [ ]	test_score [ ]
citizen [ ]	status [ ]
address _1 [ ]	address_3 [ ]
city_1 [ ]	city_3 [ ]
state_1 [ ]	state_3 [ ]
zip_1 [ ]	zip_3 [ ]
phone_1 [ ]	phone_3 [ ]
parents [ ]	average [ ]
city_2 [ ]	credits [ ]
state_2 [ ]	

typing. Database programs allow a request to include an unlimited number of fields in a single report.

Some uses for a database of student records follow.

• Participant lists or rosters. Databases could include lists of students (local and permanent addresses, and telephone numbers), resident directors (social security numbers, majors, birthdays, passport numbers, etc.), registrars/bursars (names, social security numbers, program, number of credits), selection committee, news bureaus (name, program, year, hometown—sorted by zip code)

• Letters. A relational database should allow for a letter-writing feature, making it possible to send a form letter to a select group within the database. Such letters, like those announcing an applicant's acceptance to a program, could be personalized according to the fields (e.g., name of student, address, specific program, dates of program, etc.). This function was previously the exclusive domain of word processing, but it is now a common feature of many databases.

• Labels. Current database programs allow you to print labels in a variety of formats.

• File tabs. Since most offices tend to keep paper files, using the database to print the tabs saves a lot of needless typing. You can print on either the standard rolls of dry adhesive-backed tabs or self-sticking tractor-feed tabs.

• Interview charts. Charts can be prepared on each applicant and given to the committees that conduct interviewing. Fields could include interview day and time, name, class standing, major, GPA, current language course, and past language courses. These charts can be organized chronologically by interview time, with sufficient space between entries to allow note taking.

• Statistics. A database can supply a range of statistical information. Determining where to concentrate promotional efforts would be one use of this data. For the database to be effective, information needs to be entered in a consistent fashion (e.g., students' majors should always be abbreviated the same way to facilitate alphabetization). Information that might be useful to a study-abroad office includes how students found out about the programs; student majors (to be used in recruiting efforts by helping an office decide where to target advertising); and student GPAs before and after overseas studies.

In addition to a student database, an education-abroad office that is responsible for providing grade reports for participants can maintain a course and grade database. These databases, when related to each other, can report the final results of each student and create course equivalency lists for the resident director and students at each program site, so they can see how course work has been accepted at the home university in the past.

Expert Systems. Interactive computer technology—the mainstay of most computer games and self-learning programs can—theoretically—assist you and your students in the advising process. Most students are comfortable being guided through the process of ever more refined selection that animates the automatic teller machines at banks and at library computer terminals. Setting up a database with program information that can be accessed by location, GPA eligibility, calendar, language, curriculum, accommodations, costs, and so on, and controlled by student preferences is technically possible. Once the student has entered his or her needs, interests, and qualifications and responded to programmed follow-up questions, a list of suitable education-abroad programs will be suggested by the computer.

To date, no fully satisfying interactive program has been developed in our field, despite numerous attempts by experienced advisers and IIE. Some of the reasons behind this failure are the complexity of the relationship among the student, the adviser, and the institution; the lack of national terminology and standards; and the abundance of programs.

Even those working on such programs agree that computer-assisted advising should never replace personal counseling. At best, computer programs can get students through some early questions, give them some basic guidelines, and prepare them and you for further discussions. Some institutions have been successful in setting up databases of student experiences and program evaluations, which can be accessed by other students; but paper files can also be used for this purpose. Campuswide and public bulletin boards are also being used to announce deadlines, visits by program representatives, new programs, and so on.

Desktop Publishing and Graphics. Anyone with a PC and some design sense can produce surprisingly attractive documents with desktop publishing software and a laser printer. After the initial outlay for the program and the appropriate printer, publications can be produced on desktop for a fraction of the cost of traditional typesetting and design. Current software programs are versatile and permit frequent editing and design changes. There are also graphics programs specially designed to produce large banners, attractive announcements, and fliers. These programs offer a variety of type styles, enabling you to produce simple images or eye-catching displays. The combination of hardware and software needed for desktop publishing may be beyond the reach of small offices, but costs are coming down.

Telecommunications. The electronic resource with which advisers are perhaps most familiar is Inter-L, the organization-wide e-mail forum run by MicroSIG. More than 1,000 NAFSA members in more than 450 institutions on 4 continents currently subscribe.

Inter-L provides a variety of information services to international educators. At its basic level, it is an instant forum for soliciting help with obscure questions of credentials equivalence, specialized study abroad opportunities, or the myriad other questions that daily confront international personnel. It is also a rapid and cost-effective vehicle for distributing general information, such as NAFSA's "Weekly Updates," to the membership. Further, it is an on-line library, with materials available instantly, 24 hours a day. Such materials include the NAFSANet and NAFSAFax directories, OSEAS database directory, and complete U.S. State Department travel advisories.

The addresses of all current Inter-L subscribers can be obtained by sending the command "Review Inter-L" to Listserv@VTVM2. An alphabetized institutional listing of international educators (including many who are not currently Inter-L subscribers) can be obtained with the command "Get NAFSANet Directory" sent to Listserv@VTVM2. This electronic directory, as well as its companion NAFSAFax Directory, both updated monthly, have been particularly helpful in maintaining individual communications within the highly mobile NAFSA membership.

Yet Inter-L is only one of over 2,500 different "listserv" forums, each serving a different specialized audience, and all freely available on the internet. The news and reference resources available through these other listservers are often invaluable to international educators, even if we are not their primary audience.

Following the impetus of Inter-L, SECUSSA decided in 1991 to establish its own electronic forum. SECUSS-L is a mechanism for sharing knowledge, information, and perspectives about overseas educational opportunities with other professionals in the field. It is primarily intended to be of use to advisers, program administrators, and other international educators involved in study- and work-abroad programming originating on U.S. college and university campuses or done in conjunction with overseas educational institutions. SECUSS-L is the only U.S.-based electronic forum dedicated solely to the discussion of the issues of education abroad for U.S. students.

The goals of SECUSS-L are

• To provide notices of all local, regional, and national meetings and conferences of interest to study-abroad advisers and program administrators. These notices begin with dates, places, themes, fees, and so on; continue with program descriptions; and conclude with assessments and summaries.

• To offer succinct summaries of new articles, books, essays, and other writings on education.

• To carry out brief surveys of trends, opinions, perspectives, when a national sample is needed quickly.

• To give brief announcements—so that interested parties can seek further information on their own—of new study- and work-abroad programs, or of significant new developments in established programs. No advertising, promotion, or special pleading is allowed.

• To function as an essential link on the Emergency Communications Network in times of global crises, and to provide current and accurate information from overseas and across the country.

• To raise and discuss broad, national issues and problems concerning education abroad, internationalizing the campus, gaining cross-cultural competence, and so on.

• To provide a forum for asking questions and receiving counsel and perspective from more experienced and/or informed colleagues.

• To review and update information on the educational systems in countries where American undergraduates wish to study—changes that often affect education-abroad opportunities.

• To list job openings in the field.

Regardless of your professional affiliation or personal interests, there will be a number of lists beyond Inter-L from which you could freely benefit. The message "List Global" sent to any listserver will produce in your e-mailbox a list of the names and descriptions of all 3,000-plus lists. The message "SUB (listname) (your name)" sent to any listserver would then subscribe you to a list, at no charge or obligation. Access to the wealth of electronic information is as simple as this.

Another resource currently under development is NAFSA's own ANSWER knowledgebase, a computer-accessed information system that will contain information relevant to all interests within the NAFSA organization.

ANSWER will contain bibliographies, articles, references, records, travel advisories, surveys, and a host of other useful data.

Summary

Computer technology can help the education-abroad office operate more efficiently and more professionally, enabling you and your staff to devote more time to advising and program development, and less to mundane paperwork and record keeping. Your initial investment of resources and patience (while your office adapts to new systems and resources) will be amply repaid by the innumerable long-range benefits.

7

Promotion and Publicity

Contributor: My Yarabinec

Convincing more students, faculty, administrators, parents, legislators, foundations, corporations, and the American public to support increased overseas opportunities is a political task. The value of overseas programs must be sold to many potential constituencies through persuasive and compelling arguments, and such efforts can be assisted by some basic marketing principles. There are three simple rules to successful promotion: variety, repetition, and appropriateness.

Repetition and variety go hand in hand. The first ad or brochure a student sees may not be effective, and a repetitious message with no variety will be dull and useless. A repeated message in a variety of formats is more likely to get a student's attention and help the message get memorized. The student who passes your poster, then reads an article in the campus newspaper, then picks up a free bookmark promoting your office, and the student who sees a well-designed flier, then receives a brochure at student orientation, then hears a classroom presentation are more apt to realize the possibilities of overseas education.

Before defining what is appropriate publicity, you must clearly identify your audience. Advertising a study-abroad program to students who do not qualify, cannot afford the cost, or are not free to go when the program is offered is of little good. Focus your advertising on particular groups of students (e.g., science majors, minority students, classics students, or fraternity or sorority members). You also need to ensure that your message reaches the faculty and parents who support the students. If your advertising is not geared to a particular audience, you will be engaged in a frustrating and wasteful exercise.

Promoting Your Office and Work

Few professionals in education abroad have a business background; consequently, commercial sales techniques are often alien. Also, other aspects of your job—counseling students, developing programs, working with the faculty—may seem more important and enjoyable. You may also possess the lingering suspicion that selling educational experiences is inappropriate. However, as a relatively new, often misunderstood, and still somewhat invisible part of undergraduate education, the field of education abroad needs to build support in every way possible, on and off campus.

Most people are aware of the publicity required to ensure that a campus event is well attended or a worthwhile social cause is supported. Kiosks and bulletin boards crammed with fliers and posters and ample ads and notices in the school newspapers are common sights on every campus. Making the campus community aware of your office and services may represent a huge challenge, but you need to devise a conscious strategy to advertise your programs and to promote your services.

It can be counterproductive to promote education abroad to students before securing the broad support of the faculty and administration. Gaining such support should be the first goal of your publicity efforts. If you have the support but education abroad has low visibility and participation levels, your challenge is to reach students with the message that education abroad exists and is possible. If your campus has many programs and a long history of involvement in international education, then you may need to broaden and diversify programming into new academic and geographical areas, and to attract students from a wider spectrum of the student body.

If your office is part of a larger entity—academic advising, student affairs, career services, or international programs—you may need to differentiate your services from those around you. A higher profile will increase awareness of your services, remove misunderstandings about your purpose, and also make it easier for supporters, volunteers, money, and contributions to find you. A higher profile will also draw the attention of campus administrators. If the education-abroad office receives positive and regular media coverage, the office will be noticed by the administrators who weigh allocations of budget, personnel, space, and other resources.

Promoting Education Abroad to Students

You cannot begin to advise students until they have demonstrated an interest in studying or working abroad, and then come into your office to look at materials and seek your counsel. Your challenge is to get students to this exploratory point.

College Promotional Materials. Increasingly, high-school students are looking for education-abroad opportunities as part of their college education. It is imperative that your institution's opportunities be a prominent part of any promotional materials sent to potential students. You should work with the admissions office to ensure that education abroad is promoted in an engaging fashion in print, photos, and graphics, and that admissions counselors stress these opportunities at college fairs and in interviews with students. If you have developed a general flier or poster (see below), they should be on display in the admissions office.

Freshman Orientation. Working with students and academic affairs, you should prepare a presentation that will urge students to begin thinking about how to include a study or work program in their undergraduate education. This is a good chance to distribute materials and to invite students to your office. Using some enthusiastic and articulate returned students as part of your office's presentation can be especially effective.

The College Catalog. The education-abroad opportunities and the services of your office should be prominently featured in any academic/student services catalog your campus publishes. This information should explain how to include overseas studies in the degree and feature your own programs, as well as the range of other programs available. Policies and procedures also need to be spelled out. If your institution offers financial aid for study abroad, this should be made clear. In addition, departmental entries might indicate study-abroad opportunities for majors, and the index should be cross-referenced to facilitate locating opportunities by country and language.

Fliers and Posters. Promoting education abroad will be much easier if your office can produce a general-information flier. This flier needs to be attractive (though not necessarily expensive); the language needs to be straightforward; and good graphics are essential. Developing an eye-catching poster for general use on campus is also a good way to call attention to your office and its services—the poster should highlight the excitement of studying or working overseas. Such a poster can also be used to advertise general meetings and meetings about particular programs, if blank space is left at the bottom. It might also mention related products or services offered by your office (e.g., international student ID cards, rail passes, youth hostel cards, books, etc.).

General Information Meetings. Most experienced advisers and administrators agree that there is a great value to hosting general information sessions or open houses for students exploring overseas opportunities. How you set up and publicize this meeting depends on the size of your campus, the facilities available, what help you can get from others, and a number of other variables. Most meetings are held at the beginning of each semester or quarter. On some campuses meetings occur monthly; on others, weekly. Having supportive faculty, key administrators, recently returned students, and peer-counselors participate will help create interest and enthusiasm. While your own remarks will stress the academic and personal values of education abroad, as well as institutional policies, your goal might be to encourage students to come to your office and begin exploring their options.

Education-Abroad Fairs. In recent years, many campuses have begun annual study-abroad fairs as a very effective way of publicizing education abroad to large numbers of students. The basic idea is to bring together in one large room—during an afternoon, evening, or for an entire day—representatives and/or past participants of many different study and work programs, so interested students can ask questions and get further information. While such an event serves the interests of promoting particular programs to students, it also boosts the idea of overseas study and highlights the varieties of options. Though fairs are aimed at students, they also provide opportunities for faculty and administrators to get to know programs and to realize the diversity and quality of current national programming. Some of the bigger fairs include information on international work and travel. Others are conducted in conjunction with international student organizations and celebrate global diversity.

Organizing and operating a successful fair is a major undertaking. It requires careful long-term planning, good timing and publicity, and the need to oversee a multitude of logistical details. You will need a great deal of help from your staff and from other offices. Just deciding whom to invite and how to arrange for their practical needs is a major chore. But the cumulative impact of a well-attended fair can be powerful and long lasting. A fair—compared with most other means—can bring an extensive amount of information to a large number of students economically and efficiently. It will certainly boost the profile of your office. Very useful advice on how to put on a successful fair can be found in Joan Gore's pamphlet, "Organizing Successful Study Abroad Fairs" (AIFS Advisers' Guide No. #3).

Piggybacking. If you have kept abreast of other events on campus, you may be able to piggyback your education-abroad message to other international activities. For example, if international students give presentations in courses that focus on their home country, they could be encouraged to end with an invitation to study overseas. Similarly, if there is a foreign film series on campus, general brochures about your office could be left at the entrance to the auditorium.

All of the promotional opportunities listed above can greatly bolster the image of education abroad on your campus. Ideally, these opportunities will prepare students to begin the advising process. Promoting particular program opportunities requires another set of strategies.

Publicizing Programs

Getting the right students interested in the right programs is one of the major challenges facing education-abroad advisers. But it is perhaps even more difficult to get the attention of a particular group of students once you have identified an overseas program that might interest them. In order to reach these students, a targeted promotion needs to be defined and carried out.

A targeted approach involves identifying a group of students who you think are appropriate for a specific overseas program, and then devising a publicity campaign aimed at the group. Some examples are a campaign devised to attract English literature and history majors to an exchange program with an Irish university; a campaign directed at Latin American studies, public policy, or social work students (and those with African American or Hispanic backgrounds) to interest them in an established program in the Dominican Republic that has good course work in urban studies and economic development and offers a social service agency internship; and a campaign directed at architecture and art history students to attract them to a program in Denmark that focuses on contemporary Scandinavian design. Each of these programs must be marketed in a way that will attract the desired audience. Your promotional tools include:

- Program posters, brochures, and other such objects distributed in areas frequented by the targeted students, including departmental libraries and hallways
- Outreach to academic advisers in relevant subjects (visits, mailings, and program materials)
- Articles in department newsletters
- Advertisements in periodicals such as *Transitions Abroad* and the *NAFSA Newsletter*
- Classroom presentations
- Special mailings and meetings for students who have declared relevant majors.

In addition to promotional efforts to students with particular academic interests, you can design campaigns directed at students seeking (1) programs in particular geographic regions (e.g., Africa, eastern Europe, or the Third World); (2) programs that are highly experiential or service-oriented or require a lot of independent research, rather than spending time in the classroom; (3) programs that are not in English-speaking countries but offer a curriculum in English and the opportunity to learn the language and live with families; (4) programs that are equipped to accept students with physical or learning disabilities; and (5) perhaps even good programs that do not require a very high GPA for admission. Since the profile of students who have traditionally studied abroad (see chapter 8) is so narrow, it is very important to promote overseas opportunities to the nontraditional study-abroad student. Your publicity should make this vast majority of students reconsider education abroad, and make them aware that your office is ready and eager to talk with them.

Using the Media

Every campus has its own forms of communication, such as the campus newspaper, radio station, and video channel. While the campus-centered focus of these media seems to exclude concerns with faraway places, there are many ways to get the media's attention, and ultimately the attention of students. Since student media often have a commercial base, paying for ads in the newspaper to boost your office or programs is one option. Make your press releases appealing to student editors and encourage follow-up features. You might also host a reception for reporters from the paper.

As advantageous as these tactics are, most study-abroad offices do not have large discretionary budgets for advertising and hospitality. Another approach involves increasing personal contacts with editors, writers, and media managers. Why not meet with the faculty adviser and editors of the campus newspaper, go over articles, make follow-up calls, or encourage students to submit articles about their experiences? When you begin to see announcements and features appearing, always remember to thank the newspaper. It is also surprising how often a specially invited reporter actually comes to events and programs. Always remember that outreach from you and your office should always be cooperative and collegial.

The Campus Newspaper. The campus newspaper may appear daily, several times a week, or weekly, so knowing deadlines and timing your message for optimum impact is often tricky. In addition, you should be familiar with the various columns and announcements that appear regularly.

Feature Articles. Features are desirable because they usually provide an implicit pitch for the value of education abroad, in addition to adding a human-interest element, whether through participant interviews or personal accounts. Such articles also remind all readers, including faculty and administrators, of the benefits of your office. You can often be proactive in suggesting tie-ins between planned feature topics and your programs. For example, most campus newspapers perennially run articles about love and dating for their edition on or near Valentine's Day. A possible tie-in could be how a student feels about the differences in dating practices in his or her host country while overseas on one of your programs. Tie-ins and suggested story topics should always promote education abroad in general and your office in particular.

The Calendar Section. Most campus newspapers provide a regular opportunity for disseminating information in a calendar section. Find out the requirements and deadlines and submit as many announcements as possible. Take advantage of this free service to announce meetings to discuss your programs, deadlines for applications, visits by representatives from other programs, fairs, and other international events. The calendar section can also help your office identify events that attract students who might be interested in an overseas experience. For example, you might consider distributing pamphlets or fliers at a Japanese art exhibition or guest lecture on international business.

Letters to the Editor. Letters can be written by you, your office, or returned students in response to some related matter. Make sure that students identify themselves as alumni of your programs. A letter need not be explicitly about overseas study or a particular foreign country. For example, an article about the business school could inspire a follow-up letter suggesting that study abroad will help make Americans culturally and linguistically more successful in pursuing careers in international business.

Personal Columns. Since students often read these, an occasional, cleverly worded message in the personal column section of your campus newspaper may attract more curiosity and attendance at an event than a more expensive advertisement. For example, "Darling, he suspects! Meet me at the Study Abroad Information Meeting, Next Wednesday, 7:30 p.m., in McLaren Hall. Turtledove."

Other Campus Publications. Do not overlook opportunities to get out your message in all campus publications. Do not be shy. Internationalism is hot, and your office can be a pivotal rallying point. These publications might include
- Faculty and staff newsletters
- Department newsletters
- Alumni magazines and newsletters
- Any publications put out by your campus international center
- All admissions brochures.

Other Media Possibilities. The campus radio station may run public service announcements. Student-accessed electronic bulletin boards are becoming increasingly common and can provide a very receptive audience. Advertising in periodicals that reach students likely to be receptive to education abroad should also be considered if your budget permits.

Points to Keep in Mind When Using Campus Media. Avoid confusing and blank terms as well as abbreviations, acronyms, and jargon. What may seem clear to you may be confusing to others. Make it as easy as possible for the writer or media contact to understand your point. You should be readily available, responding quickly with additional material and offering to identify students for the article, and be understanding when your articles do not get published. Always be certain that announcements and articles include details about where to get more information. Your chances of having your article published and published accurately will be enhanced if you use the following tools:
- Press Release. These should be provided for every suggested story to

ensure that key information is included in the final version. Always remember to include who, what, where, when, why, and where to turn for more information. Try to limit the release to one page and always be sure to include a contact name and phone number of a person who will actually be available; reporters will not call back again and again.

• Press Kit. This should include a cover letter (highlighting the essential elements of the story), the press release, an information brochure (if any), all pertinent information, and your business card.

• Photos. These can be submitted with the press kit or sent separately along with a caption. Photos with captions will provide further interaction with the writers and editors. If you need the picture, make sure you arrange to have it returned.

• Follow Up. Give feedback to the media. Thank them for covering your meeting or printing your story.

Other Methods for Promotion on Campus. While using the campus media may be one of the best ways to launch your message, there are a number of other means that serve the same purpose. Examples include
   • Display cases
   • Fliers on campus bulletin boards
   • Banners
   • Information booths
   • Classroom presentations
   • Videos on loan at the library
   • Representation at campus festivals and activities
   • Photography exhibits
   • Bookmarks, printed with your message.

Community Media. Members of a campus community do not live in a vacuum. They watch, listen, read, and notice what is conveyed to them by the local media. Utilizing the local media can be especially effective in smaller communities, and should not be overlooked as a worthwhile promotion tool in urban environments. One advantage of dealing with community media is that, as professionals, these media representatives are more stable than their student counterparts. This stability allows you to develop personal relationships with the hope of seeing more return for your publicity efforts. Initially, you should approach the local media with basic news stories, such as an article honoring students chosen for a particular study-abroad program, rather than tie-in coverage ideas. When approaching the community media, it is even more important to use the standard tools of press releases, press kits, and so on. All earlier suggestions made regarding the campus media also apply to the community media. In addition, do not be afraid of sending your news often; the local media are always looking for filler. The return is that your message is presented to a larger audience.

There are also occasions when the media will come seeking you, as when there is civil unrest in a country where students from your campus are studying. These occasions cannot be anticipated, but they are certainly likely to happen given the increasing number of students studying and working overseas in an increasing number of countries. You should be prepared in case of such an event. Remember that anything you say to the media will be taken as an official statement representing your institution. Therefore, be prudent and work in cooperation with your campus public information office and other appropriate authorities. Remain pleasant and fair at all times in your dealings with the media. Do not promise more than you can give and consider carefully the confidentiality of your information. Staying calm in times of overseas crises and responding professionally to campus and media requests for information can do wonders for the reputation of your office.

Summary

Most likely your office will be responsible for bringing good programs into being, advising students about the plethora of opportunities that exist abroad, and using your imagination and persuasion to publicize and promote these opportunities to your students, faculty, administration, and local community. Appropriating some of the methods of sound marketing and advertising can work to your advantage. This is not a matter of employing public relations hype or slick promotional gimmicks. Good and effective promotion involves knowing your market and knowing the best range of programs for your market, then using a variety of convincing strategies to sell your programs and services.

PART TWO

Advising

THE DEMOGRAPHICS OF EDUCATION ABROAD
Contributors: Stephen Cooper and Mary Anne Grant

ADVISING PRINCIPLES AND STRATEGIES
Contributors: Cynthia Felbeck Chalou and Janeen Felsing

PROMOTING STUDENT DIVERSITY
Contributors: Margery A. Ganz, Jack Osborn, and Paul Primak

HEALTH AND SAFETY ISSUES
Contributor: Joan Elias Gore

PREDEPARTURE AND REENTRY ORIENTATION PROGRAMMING
Contributor: Ellen Summerfield

8

The Demographics of Education Abroad

Contributors: Stephen Cooper and Mary Anne Grant

Education-abroad advisers and program administrators require accurate information about why U.S. students go overseas, how they make choices, where they go, and what they study. Considerable data exist on foreign students in the United States, but until recently little research has been done on U.S. students abroad. The extant studies suggest a reasonably coherent profile of U.S. students enrolled in study-abroad programs, but they provide little information about students who engage in other forms of education while they are overseas. We clearly need more research on U.S. students abroad and their impact on U.S. higher education at the individual, institutional, and national levels.

Only a handful of colleges and universities fully understand the range of international activities undertaken by their students. Although most institutions maintain records on those who study abroad and on programs they sponsor, fewer keep accurate records on students who take part in programs sponsored by other institutions and agencies. Fewer still know how many of their students participate in serious educational activities abroad that may not result in the award of academic credit. Such information is vital if we are to formulate a rationale for carrying out the recommendations of the National Task Force, which include achieving a more diverse body of students studying abroad and more varied geographical destinations, program types, and financial support.

Anyone who has advised students who are considering an educational foray overseas, or traveled abroad with them, or talked with them after their return home, knows readily that student motivations are often complex and that the value of their studies derives only partly from their formal academic program overseas. This is not to say that instruction abroad is inferior—though this is a common perception at home—but rather that living and learning beyond the reaches of American culture have a holistic pedagogical value not attainable on their home campuses. Yet academic gain per se is what justifies studying abroad to most faculty and administrators.

In part, the relative absence of information on U.S. students abroad can be linked to the decentralization of many campuses. But the lack of information also comes from having no clear institutional rationale for wanting and needing such information. Many academic educators are unwilling to admit that genuine learning can take place beyond the American classroom. As a rule, campuses that send significant numbers of students abroad, whether for academic or cultural experiences, tend to keep more complete records than those institutions sending marginal numbers.

But as "internationalizing the campus" becomes an increasingly serious institutional goal, education-abroad activities are sure to be more fully recognized and documented on more campuses. Moreover, administration and the faculty will expect education-abroad advisers and/or administrators to possess accurate information not only on your own students and programs but also on how they compare with those from other similar institutions. The information contained in this chapter should help you put your own institutional activity in a national context.

Four Recent Studies

Taken together, the following studies represent important steps in obtaining a clearer national understanding of who is venturing abroad on academic programs, where they come from, what they seek, and how they fare.

Open Doors. For many years the Institute of International Education (IIE) has conducted an annual census on international students and scholars studying and doing research on U.S. campuses. These data—covering overall numbers, national origins, sources of financial support, fields of study, enrollments, and rates of growth at virtually all accredited colleges and universities—have been published in a volume called *Open Doors*. Only in recent years has IIE sought similar kinds of data on U.S. students abroad, using various methods to gather this information. First, it contacted foreign institutions of higher education, requesting data on the numbers of American students enrolled. Then, concluding that most American students were enrolled in branch-campus programs and not at foreign institutions, it surveyed the directors of American university-sponsored programs on their enrollments. Neither method proved satisfactory.

A more varied approach was then taken to measure activity during the 1985–86, 1987–88, and 1989–90 academic years. *Open Doors* developed a questionnaire to be filled out by the office on campus best able to furnish accurate data. The results are included in the *Open Doors* volumes for these years. These data, the most comprehensive information available on U.S. study abroad, should prove highly useful to all education-abroad advisers and administrators. The information has been drawn on heavily for this chapter.[1]

There remain a number of limits to the IIE studies. As noted, IIE counts only study-abroad students—those who receive academic credit from their home institution for the successful completion of an academic program abroad. As IIE admits, this results in a "conservative picture of study-abroad activity." In addition, the institutional response rate has never been as high as it should be because of continuing uncertainty on the part of numerous institutions over how to count students studying abroad through programs sponsored by other institutions and agencies, American and foreign. Thus, many institutions that other indicators suggest are sending students abroad, often in significant numbers, do not return the questionnaires and are therefore not counted. In other cases, students appear to have been counted twice, once by their home college and again by the institution sponsoring their study-abroad program. Nor do all institutions seem to be able to answer all questions. Only 58 percent of responding institutions in the latest survey, for instance, provided data on their students' field of study.

Council on International Educational Exchange (CIEE) ISIC Questionnaires. From 1983 to 1986, CIEE sent out questionnaires with its application forms for the International Student Identity Card (ISIC). The assumption was that few students venture abroad without first purchasing this card. Researcher Jolene Koester analyzed thousands of responses, which yielded significant information from U.S. student travelers about who they were and why they planned to go abroad. Her findings were published as *A Profile of the U.S. Student Abroad—1984 and 1985, a CIEE Occasional Paper.*[2]

Unlike the IIE surveys, which count those who study abroad for academic credit and include only college students, this CIEE study counted students who were engaged in a broad spectrum of education-abroad activities: U.S programs, direct enrollment, independent study, work, internships, as well as family-stays, travel, and recreation. It also sampled responses from large numbers of high-school students. The result is an interesting documentation of student backgrounds, attitudes, concerns, and goals, gathered as they anticipated their stint abroad. Yet the limits of the study are that such self-reported facts, intentions, and reflections do not necessarily describe what these students actually did or what they learned.

The Study-Abroad Evaluation Project (SAEP). In 1982 several researchers undertook the first major longitudinal study on the impact of study abroad on participants. Several hundred students from four universities provided data through questionnaires, and some were interviewed by telephone. The results of this research were published in the book entitled

Study Abroad: The Experience of American Undergraduates; an abridged version was recently published as a CIEE Occasional Paper, edited by Barbara Burn and Elinor Barber.[3]

The special value of what became known as SAEP is that its sophisticated methodology allows a comparison of U.S. students in western Europe with students remaining in the United States. Revealing information is provided on how students who study abroad differ from those who do not; what changes through the experience abroad and what does not; how much these changes may be attributed to programs and countries and how much is individual; and what the long-term effects of the experience abroad might be. Nevertheless, the study is admittedly limited in scope because so few programs, countries, and students were surveyed.

In the International Interest (1992). This study examines much less data but is nevertheless national in its scope and implications. It surveys the international activities of fifty "small, selective, independent colleges dedicated to liberal education" (sometimes referred to as "the International 50"), demonstrating conclusively the great national divide that exists between what is possible at affluent private institutions (those with large endowments, an internationalized faculty and curriculum, and ample financial aid) and what is possible at larger, more academically complex institutions—especially those supported by public funding and enrolling students from more diverse socioeconomic backgrounds. The study found that a significant exposure to internationalism at the undergraduate level produces strong postgraduate results in international commerce, service, and scholarship.[4] Graduates of these few colleges, plus a few others like them (which accounted for just 1.8 percent of all baccalaureate degrees awarded nationwide in 1988):

- Make up 10.4 percent of the enrollment at graduate schools of international affairs;
- Have received 9.1 percent of the Ph.D.s awarded in all international fields, and 11.4 percent of the Ph.D.s in European history, 15.5 percent of those in Russian, and 20.4 percent of those in Japanese;
- Represent more than 10 percent of the United States' ambassadors and 9 percent of the nation's foreign service officers;
- Are three times more likely to have majored in foreign languages or area studies than their peers at the nation's major research universities and 5.3 times more likely than are all college graduates nationally;
- Enter into the Peace Corps in proportions 2.5 times greater than their peers at all colleges and universities; and
- Are four times more likely than lawyers to specialize in international law than might be expected by their numbers.[5]

The report argues that these impressive contributions to international studies, diplomacy, and other fields stem from the common values and attitudes of liberal education, which challenge parochialism and encourage students to be open to change, acquire effective communication skills, learn foreign languages, and see ideas in their full complexity. It also illustrates, albeit indirectly, two other important points: (1) the majority of other small, private colleges have not made this commitment to internationalization or achieved these results; and (2) the resources required to bring these results about are far beyond those now available to many private and most public universities.

In sum, much can be learned from the studies and statistics we now have, though they are far from exhaustive. The profiles that follow—examining numbers of students and schools, program types, destinations, fields of study, academic rank, length of stay, and gender—are particularly beholden to these four particular studies. Other points of reference come from data on foreign students in the United States and patterns of practice that have long been evident.[6]

Basic Characteristics of U.S. Students Abroad

Overall Numbers. Although a few U.S. colleges have had study-abroad programs since the early twentieth century, it was not until the 1950s and 1960s that students were being sent abroad in significant numbers.[7] In its earliest years, study abroad was largely limited to students from private colleges and universities. This has changed over the last two decades, with a notable increase in college students interested in study, travel, and work abroad. While the percentage of students from private institutions who study abroad is much higher than the percentage from public institutions, the overall absolute numbers may be roughly comparable.

• 1985–86: 709 institutions (65.2 percent of those polled) reported they had students studying and earning credit abroad. Overall, about 48,000 students were abroad.

• 1987–88: 804 institutions (59 percent of those polled) reported they had students abroad earning credit. Overall, the number rose to more than 62,000.

• 1989–90: 905 institutions (78 percent of those polled) reported students from their institution were studying abroad and earning credit. Overall, the number again rose, to nearly 71,000.[8]

Based on these figures for the years 1985–90, 21 percent more institutions (from 709 to 905) awarded credit for study abroad, and student participation increased 32 percent. Further, most observers believe enrollments have continued upward (though perhaps at a more moderate rate) since 1990.

In spite of these rates of growth, however, these figures suggest (when they are seen as a percentage of total enrollments in the broad spectrum of American undergraduate education) that study abroad remains a rather marginal activity, something undertaken by about only 2 percent of all students prior to graduation—4 percent if two-year colleges (that furnish only 6 percent of the total study-abroad population, while they enroll more than half of all American undergraduates) are excluded.

A cursory look at the most obvious subdivisions of the data also shows only negligible to very limited activity at most two-year and small four-year public institutions; the figures are only somewhat better for major public universities. At the other extreme, well-endowed private, liberal arts colleges are frequently sending abroad 20–40 percent of each graduating class, and some send even more. Major private universities do not achieve the numbers of their smaller counterparts, but many are in the 6–10 percent range. Only one research university, for instance, sent as many students abroad as did the average college in the select International 50 grouping, and only four sent as many of their undergraduates abroad as did three-fourths of the private colleges in this grouping. At the other extreme, it is clear that many U.S institutions are sending very negligible numbers of students abroad. However, interesting and noteworthy campus-to-campus exceptions exist at all levels.

As noted, these figures are for participants in credit-bearing study programs. According to recent estimates from CIEE leaders and experienced NAFSA members, another ten thousand American undergraduates work abroad each year or engage in some other form of experiential education (for example, teaching, volunteering, doing research, and so forth). If one adds these students to the IIE figures for 1989–90, updates them to 1992–93, and factors in those perhaps not counted, the most liberal extrapolation places the total number of American undergraduates engaged in some form of education abroad annually at perhaps something less than one hundred thousand.[9]

Duration of Stay. From the 1940s through the 1960s junior year abroad was the widely accepted term for what we now call study abroad. Then the dominant pattern was to study overseas during one's entire junior year—usually languages and literature, culture, history, art, and politics. Because this was done almost exclusively by students (most of whom were female) majoring in one of these areas, all courses counted toward the major and a full year's worth of credit was guaranteed. Over the past two decades, the trend has been away from year-long programs and toward programs of a semester or less.

As the IIE 1989–90 data show (see table 1), fewer than a fifth of U.S. students studying abroad now do so for a full academic year—though the absolute numbers of students may have remained constant. The largest percent-

TABLE 1
U.S. STUDENTS ABROAD 1989–90

Duration of Stay	Students (%)
Calendar year	0.7
Academic year	15.9
Summer	33.9
Semester	35.2
Quarter	6.4
Other	7.9

Source: IIE

age of students now participates in semester programs, but these are spread over the sophomore, junior, and even senior years. Programs of shorter duration, from a few weeks to an academic quarter, seem to be the fastest-growing sector. Students who go abroad for language immersion are more likely to spend a year; students with minimal or no language skills typically spend a semester or less.

Many observers view this pervasive shift toward shorter and shorter stays abroad as regrettable. They point out that the educational impact of a year-long program (ideally a full-immersion, language-based program involving traditional course work at a foreign university), where the student has the time to develop interests and make friends, is much greater than that gained from a shorter program. There is also some evidence that American students shy away from the longer programs because they may feel threatened socially or academically by a whole year abroad, worry about the separation from friends and loved ones, or be reluctant to put aside other campus pursuits for this long.

There is no doubt, however, that more and more students are having an educational experience abroad prior to graduation because of the abundance of short programs. United States institutions now offer more than two thousand programs for the full academic year and fourteen hundred summer programs, as demonstrated by the 1992–93 editions of IIE's *Academic Year Abroad* and *Vacation Study Abroad* volumes.[10] Most students in these shorter programs simply do not have the academic flexibility or the money (many need to work during the school year, and most during the summer) to do anything else. In addition, there is mounting evidence that the right kind of short program for the right kind of prepared student can have a tremendous impact.

Data are scarce on the numbers of American undergraduates now studying for degrees at foreign institutions of higher education. Indeed, foreign-degree studies are not normally seen as a species of study abroad. Usually study-abroad programs are supposed to be done as part of the American baccalaureate degree. Again, it should be noted that the majority of the nearly 400,000 foreign students studying in the United States are seeking American undergraduate or graduate degrees. This sharp contrast is due in part to the less specialized nature of the American B.A. and the greater liberality of American institutions in accepting transfer credit compared with their foreign counterparts. Interestingly, the ERASMUS program in Europe is now moving closer to adopting many American practices with regard to short-term study programs in other countries, and the consequent acceptance of transfer credit.

Gender. IIE, CIEE, and SAEP data agree that most U.S. students studying abroad—nearly two out of three—are women (again, the figures for incoming foreign students are just the reverse). There are several explanations for this imbalance, though few valid justifications.

First, study abroad has traditionally been associated with foreign-language study and the liberal arts, and women have tended to dominate enrollments in these fields. Study-abroad programs are not nearly as numerous in engineering, business, agriculture, and the technical sciences—traditionally male-dominated fields. Presumably, when more women study engineering and more men major in French, things will change.

Second, but much more conjectural, the imbalance reflects American cultural values. Societal and parental expectations in the United States have traditionally inculcated young men to pursue "serious," career-oriented degrees while young women are encouraged to "cultivate" themselves and/or prepare for marriage. Given the prevalence of such sexism, and the notion that a study-abroad experience is a somehow frivolous, we can see why more women than men have traditionally studied abroad. But because these assumptions are changing, this gender imbalance may soon even out.

Program Sponsorship. IIE defines a program as either a group of students studying in a foreign setting or just one or two students participating in a bilateral exchange. Accordingly, 82.1 percent of the students covered in the IIE survey enrolled in programs identified as "sponsored by U.S. institutions of higher education and consortia"; 10.3 percent were listed as directly enrolled in a foreign institution (often, perhaps, as part of an exchange agreement); and 7.6 percent had "other" kinds of enrollment. Though this breakdown is perhaps not as dramatic as these figures suggest—given that many institutions keep insufficient records on students enrolled in programs sponsored by other institutions—it remains clear that most U.S. students study abroad through programs or arrangements made by their own schools.

There are academic and economic reasons for this pattern. First, American institutions want to maintain as much control as they can over academic quality and, by extension, the integrity of their degree. Such ownership ensures faculty and administrative support and builds student interest and momentum from year to year. In addition, owning one's own programs (even though they entail capital expenses) helps to control costs directly and avoid what is known as "tuition flow" to other institutions. Such programs can also be used as recruiting devices for on-campus study. In addition, institutional linkages, of which a study-abroad program may be only a part, often provide opportunities for faculty research, the recruitment of foreign students and scholars, and joint projects.

Two other reasons merit consideration: earning credit and using financial aid. Students are more likely to realize full-credit transfer for study abroad and can more easily obtain and use their financial-aid packages when they participate in study-abroad programs through their home institutions. Direct enrollment abroad and study through other programs have tended to make both more difficult, though this is changing.

Academic Level. U.S. students go overseas for study mainly as undergraduates. IIE data show only about 6 percent are graduate students. Of the undergraduates, most are juniors, with only a few freshmen or sophomores. Only about 6 percent are in two-year degree programs. Few graduate students study overseas. It is too expensive. Most of them have to borrow or work while in graduate school—many of them by teaching or assisting with research on fellowships at the home university. Unlike American universities, overseas institutions are not generous with such awards to foreign students. Further, in contrast to the curricular breadth of much American undergraduate education, American graduate degrees demand highly specialized training, so anything taken abroad would have to be highly congruent. Nevertheless, it seems likely that graduate study abroad—especially course work toward a joint international degree—will be a growing phenomenon in the coming decades.

Destinations. IIE data show that over three-fourths of all American students continue to choose to study in western Europe (see table 2), with about 30 percent of all students going to the United Kingdom alone. Of the ten most popular countries, almost all are European. Mexico, Israel, China, and Japan are modestly popular countries, but pale beside the European destinations. Interestingly, the countries popular among U.S. students stand in almost diametrical opposition to the countries that send students to the United States. Relatively few western European students, for instance, come to the United States for study, while relatively few Americans choose China, Hong Kong, Taiwan, Korea, or Indonesia.[11]

The popularity of western Europe, including the United Kingdom, can be explained in several ways:

There is history and long-standing precedent. Since U.S. students began academic sojourns abroad, beginning in the nineteenth century, they have mainly gone to western Europe—at first for theological training, then for graduate research, and more recently for undergraduate study. It has become an American academic tradition.[12]

Second, language study remains a mainstay of study abroad, and the languages of western Europe—French, Italian, Spanish, and German—are the ones most commonly taught in American high schools and colleges. These preferences are still not seriously threatened by the advent of other language instruction, such as Russian, Chinese, and Japanese. The one exception may be that more and more students with Spanish-language competency are looking toward Latin America.

Students without foreign-language proficiency, or who do not wish to pursue language study (and this is, alas, the case with most American undergraduates), have been increasingly welcomed over the past decade in England, Scotland, Wales, or Ireland, as well as now in Australia and New Zealand. In addition, numerous European programs that are taught in English have recently appeared, in part because of developments in the European Community, including ERASMUS. Studying in English has opened up curricular possibilities, so students of business, engineering, science, and many other fields can now take courses of high academic quality and receive credit toward their major.

Ethnicity seems to continue to affect students' choices somewhat, and this appeal has continued to work in favor of European destinations, given that most Americans are of European descent (at least those who have been in the United States long enough to become economically established).

TABLE 2

REGIONS HOSTING U.S. STUDY-ABROAD STUDENTS, 1985/86–1989/90

Host Region	Study-Abroad Students		
	1985/86 (%)	1987/88 (%)	1989/90 (%)
Africa	1.1	1.2	1.3
Asia	5.4	6.1	5.0
Europe	79.6	75.4	76.7
Latin America	7.0	9.2	9.4
Middle East	4.0	4.7	2.7
North America	0.9	1.4	0.8
Oceania	0.9	1.2	1.9
Multiple Regions	1.0	0.8	2.2

Source: IIE

Media attention, as well as tourism, may also make Europe an attractive study destination. Conversely, newspaper and television coverage of political unrest, violence, poverty, or other forms of social instability in such areas as Central America, parts of the Middle East, and India has probably inhibited student flows to these areas. And U.S. news coverage of Africa, for example, focuses either on famine or civil unrest, certainly deterring traffic to that continent. In considering media effects, it is important to remember that parental attitudes influence the country choices of many students.[13] It is also perfectly true that if stable and well-regarded education infrastructures are not in place, as is true of many Third World countries, students will continue to spurn such destinations. Cost may be another factor. It is somewhat cheaper to travel to western Europe than to most other regions of the world.

Finally, we should not ignore the impact of simple peer pressure and campus precedent. U.S. students going abroad to study have very often been persuaded to do so by friends who are past program participants. Also, U.S. students frequently go abroad with their friends or in groups. In short, whatever the adviser or faculty says, groups of individuals, however socially bound, influence each other's decisions. Students going overseas on their own, on a program nobody else from their college has done, are in a minority. Students, and their parents, seem greatly swayed by the prospect of studying abroad with a professor from their own campus on a program run by their own institution. To the degree that its curriculum is Eurocentered, Europe becomes the likely destination.

Field of Study. Most U.S. students pursuing overseas study have majors in the humanities or the social sciences (see table 3). These particular fields of study have traditionally supported cultural inquiry and are often tied to foreign-language requirements.

Most American students believe they should receive at least some credit in their major to justify study abroad. In contrast to their foreign counterparts, American students use their study-abroad program as time for academic exploration outside their major. So the IIE figures do not necessarily show the full range of curricular studies undertaken by American students abroad. Koester's research confirms that most of them are seeking to expand and diversify their studies and outlooks through the program; further, they believe they were really able to achieve this. At the same time, such broad aims tend to be more attainable for traditional liberal arts students than for those in other areas.

More than 10 percent of the students surveyed in the IIE studies were business majors. This reflects the growing number of students who chose to major in this field during the 1980s, perhaps also reflecting their growing awareness that business means *international* business. As interest in international trade expands and the federal government continues its support of

TABLE 3
U.S. STUDY-ABROAD STUDENTS

Fields of Study	1985–86 (%)	1987–88 (%)	1989–90 (%)
Agriculture	1.0	0.8	0.4
Business/management	10.9	11.1	10.9
Education	4.1	4.1	4.6
Engineering	1.6	1.4	1.3
Fine and applied arts	6.9	6.4	6.1
Foreign language	16.7	14.8	12.5
Health sciences	1.7	1.4	1.1
Humanities	7.8	11.0	11.9
Liberal arts	18.2	20.9	19.9
Mathematics and computer sciences	1.3	1.2	0.8
Physical/life sciences	3.8	2.5	3.7
Social studies	13.7	14.0	16.6
Undeclared	4.2	3.8	3.4
Other	8.2	6.8	6.8

Source: IIE

program development, this may be the fastest-growing group of students in study-abroad programs.[14] Many business students are encouraged by their schools to pursue nonbusiness studies while abroad so they can broaden their knowledge of history, language, and culture—although they cannot receive credit toward their major. Other schools take the opposite view: studying international business from a non-American perspective is the primary reason for studying abroad.

The relatively tiny number of science, engineering, and agriculture students studying abroad seems due primarily to curricular restraints and requirements. Because of rigid course prerequisites and sequencing, students in these fields cannot usually substitute course work taken elsewhere for those offered on the home campus. Additionally, their studies seldom touch on world issues, history, and culture; language study is seldom required. Going abroad means falling behind, and falling behind means entailing more costs to complete the degree. Further, because the United States was thought until recently to excel in science and engineering teaching and resources, students and departmental advisers alike may see little value to study abroad. Conversely, foreign students head for the United States expressly to study engineering, business, and science—almost completely the opposite pattern.[15]

Student Attitudes and Backgrounds

Beyond the basic characteristics of the U.S. student abroad revealed by the IIE surveys, the CIEE questionnaire and the SAEP provide some supplementary information on the attitudes and background of U.S. students who have studied (and worked) abroad in recent years. These findings might be regarded more tentatively than those based on the IIE data, since there is an element of subjectivity in the student responses sampled. Nevertheless, it becomes clear that the U.S. student abroad is unusual in some respects, and these merit attention and further exploration.

Family Background. Participants in year-long programs are largely the sons and daughters of college-educated parents. In addition, almost a third of the students responding to the CIEE surveys reported their parents were proficient in a second language and/or had lived overseas. They also reported that their families had been a major influence on their decision to go abroad.[18] As one would expect, study-abroad students from the International 50 colleges typically come from families in which both parents have college degrees, have traveled abroad, and speak foreign languages.[16]

Prior Travel Abroad. The CIEE questionnaires reveal that more than half of the respondents had traveled overseas before.[17] This may have been with their families, on an exchange program, or as tourists with friends. Obviously, this prior travel was a formative and positive experience. Advisers and program administrators recruiting students for overseas study can readily identify a pool of potential participants by locating such students on campus. However, this approach is akin to "preaching to the converted" and misses the larger challenge of making education abroad appeal to less well-traveled and privileged students.

Motivation and Goals. Aside from the influence of family and friends, why do U.S. students elect time abroad? Viewed academically, language learning and cultural exploration are powerful motivators. Preparation for an international career is another. Travel opportunities stimulate a great many students. Other motivational factors emerge in the discussion of other profile characteristics, below.[18]

International Orientation. A predictable and important characteristic of U.S. students abroad is their pronounced global outlook. Those students with previous international travel reported increased interest in international affairs, and students planning study abroad express more interest than those who remain on campus. The SAEP, focusing on students in year-long programs, also discovered that study-abroad participants held more positive attitudes toward their selected overseas country and less favorable images of U.S. foreign policy and cultural life than similar students who remained on campus. The SAEP students going abroad were also more interested and active in cultural and international activities before their sojourn than their peers.[19]

Financial Resources. A good deal of misery and myth surrounds the question of how students fund their programs abroad. It is typically thought (outside our field) that those who go on programs abroad represent only the affluent. Although the picture is incomplete, evidence suggests that study-abroad students draw from a variety of sources, including personal savings, scholarships and loans, and family support. The key variable, however, is less family background than the availability of financial aid. Thus, students from any background who attend colleges with liberal financial aid policies study abroad in good numbers. One reason for the growing popularity of overseas work programs may be that they help reduce the cost of an overseas experience. At the same time, students who need to work during the summer—and these are by far the majority—cannot participate in most summer work programs, even if their earnings would cover their expenses; they need to earn money for the next academic year.

Students in year-long programs tend to rely slightly more heavily on parental contributions, possibly because students who remain on campus have more opportunities to work than those abroad.[20] This finding has significance for study-abroad advisers and program administrators. Highly motivated students can prove resourceful in putting together the funds needed for study abroad. Further, as more U.S. colleges and universities make financial aid available to study-abroad participants, more will participate.

Academic Ability. Study-abroad students, especially those in academic year programs, exhibit above-average scholastic performance and consider themselves strong academically.[21] This is not surprising: most programs require a B or better average for admission. It might be useful to know the extent to which academically average students desire study abroad experiences and what could be done to accommodate them. To do otherwise perpetuates a limitation of opportunities for overseas international experiences to the academic elite. Could average students benefit from study abroad? Should overseas study for U.S. students expand to include them?

Career Orientation. Significant numbers of study-abroad participants expect to have international dimensions in their future careers, and hope that time abroad will enhance their marketability. U.S. students in higher education show marked career orientations, and those going abroad more often than not link their vocational goals in some way to their international academic experiences.[22] As demonstrated by the report, *In the International Interest,* these are realistic expectations. This has obvious implications for recruiting business majors, but it also suggests the potential for students who are planning other vocational pursuits to consider the global applications of their fields and their potential international career involvement.

Summary

The above profile of students now engaged in some form of education abroad—mainly participation in a formal study program—is based on the best available data and experience. Many more students undoubtedly fit this very profile, but, for a variety of reasons, have chosen not to travel abroad as part of their undergraduate studies or have been discouraged by circumstances and a lack of support.

As the National Task Force has pointed out, the profile of U.S. students abroad will remain fixed in type and numbers until there is a "national mandate," expressed through the endeavors of U.S colleges and universities, to recruit a more diverse body of students who can consider such opportunities; provide a greater array of program types, including nonacademic education; diversify study destinations; integrate study-abroad programs more fully into the curriculum; and provide the resources to support such expansion and diversification. The challenge to the education-abroad adviser and administrator is to exert a leadership role in this mission.

Notes

1. Marianthi Zikopoulos, ed., *Open Doors, 1988–89: Report on International Educational Exchange.* (New York: Institute of International Education, 1989); also see Marianthi Zikopoulos, ed., *U.S. Students Abroad: Statistics on Study Abroad, 1985–86.* (New York: Institute of International Education, 1988).

2. Jolene Koester, *A Profile of the U.S. Student Abroad.* (New York: Council on International Educational Exchange, 1985); and Jolene Koester, *A Profile of the U.S. Student Abroad—1984 and 1985.* (New York: Council on International Educational Exchange, 1987).

3. Elinor G. Barber and Barbara B. Burn, eds., "Study Abroad: The Experience of American Undergraduates in Western Europe and in the United States," 1990. An abridged version was published by Greenwood Press, Inc. (Westport, Conn.) in 1990, with the following coauthors: Jerry S. Carlson, Barbara B. Burn, John Useem, and David Yachimowicz.

4. David C. Engerman and Parker G. Marden, *In the International Interest: The Contributions and Needs of America's International Liberal Arts Colleges.* (Beloit, Wisc.: Beloit College, June 1991).

5. Ibid., Executive Summary, *i–ii.*

6. We are grateful to Marianthi Zikopoulos, IIE, for supplying additional

data and for permission to use the tables that appear in this chapter.

7. Richard D. Lambert, "Study Abroad: Where We Are, Where We Should Be." Paper delivered at the Forty-first Annual Conference on International Educational Exchange (New York: Council on International Educational Exchange, 1989) 13.

8. These figures are taken from IIE, *Open Doors,* passim., for the appropriate years.

9. John E. Bowman, "Educating American Undergraduates Abroad: The Development of Study-Abroad Programs by American Colleges and Universities," CIEE Occasional Paper no. 24. (New York: Council on International Educational Exchange, Nov. 1987), 13–16.

10. IIE, *Academic Year Abroad, 1992–93,* and *Vacation Study Abroad, 1992.* (New York: Institute of International Education, 1992).

11. "Highlights of the 1988–89 International Student Census," *IIE Educational Associate* (Dec. 1989–Jan. 1990), 3.

12. Bowman, "Educating American Undergraduates Abroad," 13–16.

13. "More Americans Travel Abroad," *Campus Update* 11, no. 10 (Nov. 1989): 1.

14. "U.S. Department of Education Centers for International Education," *NCISPA Newsletter* 12, no. 2 (Jan. 1990): 7–9.

15. Koester, *Profile* (1985), 14

16. Barber and Burn, eds. "Study Abroad," 9; Koester, *Profile* (1987), 14; Koester, *Profile* (1985), 17, and (1987), 18–19.

17. Koester, *Profile* (1987), 13.

18. Barber and Burn, eds. "Study Abroad," 13–14; Koester, *Profile* (1985), 11, 13.

19. Koester, *Profile* (1985), 19; Barber and Burn, eds., "Study Abroad," 11–13, 16.

20. Koester, *Profile* (1985), 16, and (1987), 17.

21. Barber and Burn, eds., "Study Abroad," 11.

22. Koester, *Profile* (1985), 13; Barber and Burn, eds., "Study Abroad," 15.

9

Advising Principles and Strategies

Contributors: Cynthia Felbeck Chalou and Janeen Felsing

As we saw in part 1 of this book, advisers have few formal means of learning everything they need in order to counsel students on education-abroad opportunities. Advisers nevertheless need to possess the following skills and experience:

• A complete and objective knowledge of the range of academic and experiential programs available to American undergraduates—not just programs sponsored by his or her own institution

• A firm grasp of institutional academic policies so that education abroad can be integrated into degree studies; this includes program approval, admissions standards, graduation requirements, credit transfer, financial aid, and so forth.

• Strong interpersonal counseling skills and advising techniques, based on familiarity with undergraduate student needs and knowledge of development theory.

• A seasoned awareness of current cross-cultural theory and an ability to prepare students and others for the challenges of living and learning abroad and for reentering American society and resuming their studies.

Basic Knowledge and Skills

Knowledge of Education-Abroad Programs. Education-abroad advisers need to know about the full range of credit-bearing education-abroad programs now available—both those sponsored by their own institution and those sponsored by other institutions and agencies, both academic and experiential. This means being familiar with hundreds of diverse programs in operation all over the world. With the nearly two thousand existing programs offered during the academic year, plus almost as many summer and short-term programs, this seems an especially daunting proposition.

In point of fact, a good portion of the programs listed in the IIE guides are open only to students from sponsoring institutions; some are open to others only on an occasional basis, when spaces remain; while many are not available every semester or year. A careful reading of the eligibility requirements in each listing of the IIE volumes will elicit this information. Potential programs may also be discovered via the brochures, catalogs, fliers, and posters that are mailed out by sponsoring organizations and agencies, often in great abundance. The simple fact that these materials are being mailed to your office demonstrates their openness to qualified students.

Most of these materials contain solid and factual information. But you still need to be an especially critical reader, and your advisees will almost always need your help in interpreting this sort of literature. Lily von Klemperer's "How to Read Study Abroad Literature" (1976) offers sound advice on reading program literature. This indispensable guide is reprinted in the annual editions of IIE's *Academic Year Abroad* and appears as appendix 5 of this volume.

Unless your institution is well off the beaten track or has an especially restrictive policy that prevents your students from participating in outside programs, program representatives will probably visit you during the year. These visits represent an invaluable opportunity for you, your faculty, and students to learn about new programs or to update information on ongoing programs. From these visits and from the program materials, you should be in a position to answer at least the following questions:

• Is this program worthy of transfer credit at my institution? Is it operated by an accredited degree-granting institution or by an agency from which my institution has agreed to accept transfer credit? Does it satisfy all the criteria my institution has established for study-abroad programs? Will it accept students who may not receive credit from my institution? How many students might be interested even if credit is not possible?

• What are the program's entrance requirements and course offerings? What students are most suitable? What GPA, course work, and foreign-language proficiency are required? Are courses taken directly at a foreign university or are students taught separately?

• Can students interact with the host culture? Is significant field experience required, or are internships an option? How are students housed? In apartments with other Americans? In residence halls with other foreign students? In residence halls with native students? With families in a genuine homestay, or in a boarding arrangement?

• What administrative support is provided, both in the United States and abroad? Is there an office in the United States that facilitates admission and provides predeparture information, or should students be prepared to complete applications in the foreign language and send them abroad? Is a resident director on site, or are students expected to be mature and experienced enough to cope on their own?

• What are the *inclusive* costs, and can my students afford them? Does the program offer scholarships or work/study options for which students might be eligible? Can student loans or tuition scholarship be applied to program costs?

If key information about these programs is vague, misleading, or missing, you should request that it be supplied or clarified. It is appropriate to ask for course descriptions, program evaluations, and names and addresses of previous participants; advisers can either encourage students to obtain them or can request them directly. Contacting study-abroad advisers at other institutions is also a good way to learn about an unfamiliar program. The point of these actions is not to find the "perfect" program (be suspicious of evaluation reports that fail to report problems), but, rather, to ensure that a particular program meets your institutional standards and is appropriate for a particular student.

In addition, as an education-abroad adviser, you also need to understand the panorama of experiential programs—internships, work, service learning, teaching. Students are increasingly drawn to such opportunities as they grow to understand their educational relevance and value. Such programs often make education abroad possible for students who cannot afford it. Students who see traditional study abroad as cloistered and limiting may well be open to a more indigenous experience, one lived in closer contact with the native language and culture (see chapter 15).

Knowledge of Institutional Policies. Colleges and universities with a tradition of education abroad have evolved either restrictive or open policies on program participation. Obviously, these are relative terms, and pure examples of each are rare. Most institutional policies are generally restrictive in some ways and open in others. The key is to understand the rationale behind your own institution's policies, and to challenge and alter those policies when, in your professional judgment, changes should be made that would benefit both students and the institution.

Restrictive policies make it impossible, or nearly so, for students to enroll in programs sponsored by other institutions and/or any programs not formally approved. All unapproved programs arc thus deemed off-limits. If this is the case at your institution, you obviously need to be familiar with all facets of your own and other approved programs. But as a professional you must learn as much as possible about any program that might interest students at your institution. Programs change over time, and new programs come into being. So it is important to stay current. It is always useful to have the most informed and all-encompassing context for discussing the pluses and minuses of any particular program. Lastly, you will surely have students whose best interests may be served by "unapproved" programs. If you have some sort of petition process to handle such instances, your ability to help them receive permission to participate may depend on your intimate knowledge of the strengths of these programs.

There are many legitimate (and a number of questionable) reasons to limit student choice. Program decisions can be based on the valid assumption that some programs are better than others, and that the institution has more wisdom and experience in such matters than do individual students. If this is the case at your institution, it is imperative that the review process be open and thorough. Some institutions have transfer-credit restrictions that make it difficult to transfer significant amounts of credit, including study-abroad credit. Yet when nonacademic criteria are used to prevent students from choosing certain programs—for example, as a means of filling home-campus programs—educational legitimacy often gives way to expediency. As an international educator, you should challenge policies based solely, or primarily, on economic considerations.

Institutions with open policies permit their students to select from a wide array of study-abroad program offerings. This approach rests on one or all of the following assumptions: (1) all accredited U.S. and foreign institutions sponsoring programs can be counted on to ensure quality; (2) the most important task of the education-abroad adviser is to help students choose the program best suited to their particular goals, needs, interests, academic preparation, and financial circumstances; or (3) there is no such thing as a perfect program, only a perfect match between the right student and the right program.

Proponents of this approach argue that, ultimately, it is the student who must take responsibility for making a success of his or her international experience. They point to instances in which students have had excellent learning experiences on mediocre programs—and vice versa—to prove their point. If this is the approach of your institution, then obviously it is in the students' best interest (and your own) for you to become familiar with as many programs as possible—though, given the wide array of choices, this is an enormous task.

Other academic policy questions include the following:

• What is the process for transferring credit from overseas studies to the home transcript? If the program is not your own, is an academic transcript required from a foreign and/or U.S. degree-granting institution?

• What is the role of the student's academic adviser, especially in relation to your role? Who has the final say on program approval and participation?

• What constitutes an introductory course versus an upper-division course? Who approves credit for general education requirements? For major requirements? Is this done by the registrar? By a faculty committee? By your office?

• Are grades received abroad included in the domestic GPA? If not, are grades at least recorded somewhere on the transcript? Or are all courses listed as pass/fail?

• How do students present their work when they return to campus?

What system is in place for adjudicating student appeals on course credits?

• Can students do independent study abroad? Can credit be granted for internships or other nonclassroom education?

The key is to know enough about academic decision-making procedures and collegiate/departmental requirements to establish realistic expectations and provide the kind of information both students and their faculty advisers need in order to make informed and judicious decisions.

The education-abroad adviser also needs to be familiar with a whole range of student-support services and policies. Foremost among these is a grasp of federal and institutional financial aid policies, as you will need to serve as a liaison with campus financial aid personnel. You will probably need to elicit information about students' financial resources (scholarships, grants, loans, income from part-time work) and to know if these resources can be applied toward the cost of the study-abroad program the student has selected. Financial aid officers may ask you for a budget detailing expenses of the program as well as verification that the program has been approved for transfer credit. Students need to be made aware of penalties if they withdraw from the program, or if they drop to less than full-time credit. Students also count on advisers to tell them about on-campus scholarships for which they might be eligible (see chapter 4).

You will also need to be aware of general campus policies that pertain to students who leave the campus for periods of time and then return. In some cases, they will be considered continuing students who simply happen to be away from the campus; in others, they may be seen as having formally "withdrawn" from the institution, even though it is clear that they will return in good standing. In any case, this means working with student affairs personnel to learn about medical services and insurance; leaves of absence and readmission; preregistration procedures and timetables; campus-housing applications and processes; codes of social conduct and disciplinary practice; and other similar matters.

Student Development Theory. Your work as an adviser will certainly require you to give considerable thought to the intellectual and psychological development of undergraduates. Advisers who have had professional training in student counseling have found that various student development theories provide excellent background for understanding the complex adviser/student relationship. Further, a conceptual understanding of how a suddenly changed social and mental environment may affect students is essential if you are to understand fully what is likely to be on their minds before, during, and after their time abroad. Here are several theories that might be useful:

• According to Ender, Winston, and Miller, the following conditions or principles are essential in the developmental academic-advising process:

Advising is a continuous process with an accumulation of personal contacts that have a synergistic effect. It must therefore concern itself with quality-of-life issues; the adviser's responsibility includes attention to the student's total experience in the institution. Advising is goal related; it requires the establishment of a caring relationship, which the adviser has the primary responsibility for initiating. Good academic advising is also intrusive. Whether they like it or not, advisers serve as role models for the students with whom they have contact. Advising is a focal point for the integration of academic and student life. Advisers are in the unique position of being able to encourage students to utilize the full range of resources, services, and learning opportunities available within the institution.

• According to Arthur Chickering's theory of college student development, students from puberty until age twenty face identity issues that require them to experiment with roles and life-styles; to make choices and experience the consequences; and to identify their talents, experience meaningful achievement, and find meaning in their lives. Going abroad gives them additional opportunities to experiment and grow by this inductive process of trial and error.

• Delworth and Hanson also note that these identity issues can be exceedingly well addressed by an education-abroad experience. They find that students are concerned with finding and integrating an adult philosophy of life, morality, and values—to grope with the questions "What am I to believe? Am I to accept my heritage, or do I have to decide what I am really going to stand for?" Advisers who are aware of this developmental need can discuss with students the variety of ways they can use their foreign experiences to explore these identity issues.

• D. H. Blocher identifies seven ingredients for growth in a learning environment: involvement, challenge, support, structure, feedback, application, and integration. Students differ widely in their need for each of these elements, and advisers and students will want to discuss them during the process of selecting the right program. For example, some students will prefer the security of a more structured branch-campus program, while others will be drawn to the challenge of becoming more independent, for instance via direct enrollment in a foreign institution and living on their own.

• William Perry's theory, developed through observing generations of Harvard students mature and then published as *Forms of Intellectual and Ethical Development: A Scheme,* stresses that growth comes in stages, each of which helps the student reach a deeper realization that there are no "right" answers, and yet that all answers are not equal in value. An education-abroad experience, according to an application of Perry's thinking, provides a quantum leap forward, helping students to assess and evaluate positions of knowledge, become comfortable with ambiguity, tolerant of cultural differences, and aware of cultural paradigms. This leads to an appreciation of cultural and social relativism, without concluding that everything in the world is relative.

Cross-cultural Theory and Skills. Although learning about another culture is the most obvious objective of foreign study, learning to learn *in* another culture is an equally valid objective. An adviser's responsibility therefore does not end with helping students select a program. Students must also be prepared for living and learning in cultures that are different, often dramatically so, from the one in which they were raised. Your job—though one usually shared with others, including the on-site resident director—is to help students prepare to approach culture as a medium—an unconscious conditioning agent that influences almost all perceptions and values.

Cross-cultural understanding has been studied and written about for many years by anthropologists and behavioral psychologists, as well as by many travelers, observers, and other experts. A huge amount of literature on the topic exists, some of which should be in your education-abroad, or at least campus, library. Education abroad is not something to be entered into lightly, nor, conversely, be hedged about with caveats. Approaches to cross-cultural understanding are easily divided into "culture general" and "culture specific" concerns.

Culture General. Certain predictable phenomena are encountered by everyone who enters a new culture: first, there is a period of disorientation and discomfort, which lasts until the signals and clues of living in that culture become understood. The adjustment cycle often follows predictable patterns—typically, initial elation and excitement, followed by confusion and discomfort, which often leads to depression, anger, and hostility. As surroundings become more familiar, communicative ability improves and new friendships are made. The cycle is complete when these feelings change to acceptance and appreciation of the new culture.

The degree to which different students experience what we have come to call *culture shock* is likely to vary significantly, depending on the degree of cultural difference they encounter (less in England, more in Zambia), the support mechanisms in place abroad, the type of program (less in an "island" program; more in a full immersion program), and many other variables, including personality. The person who has difficulty coping with difference, change, and uncertainty at home will most likely have more difficulty making cross-cultural adjustments abroad.

Wherever they are headed and however long their stay, all students can benefit from a discussion of "culture general" issues. The challenge is to expose them to what might happen and how they might feel while encouraging them to view both their discomfort and the adjustment to another culture as part of the ongoing challenge of living and learning abroad.

Powerful and effective group simulation games, such as "Bafa Bafa," are particularly effective in raising awareness of what "culture" is and how one is likely to think and feel, especially at first, in a culture different from one's own.

Advisers should also be ready to work with students who suffer from what is called *reentry culture shock,* especially as this common phenomenon occurs on campus, not across the ocean, following a positive experience abroad and an apparently happy return. Reentry adjustments are especially troublesome in being unexpected; at their worst, they can affect student academic performance and social life.

Culture Specific. Whereas culture-general preparation can be done with all students together, regardless of where they are heading, culture-specific orientation advising can be effective only when the focus is on a single country or region. You will, of course, want to encourage students to gain as much culture-specific information as possible before they depart. This includes using the library to read about geography and climate, as well as national and regional history, culture, politics, and economics.

You will also need to present basic information about customs and manners, day-to-day mores, and popular beliefs in each country. Because this vital information may not be found in books, this is a good opportunity to invite foreign students from the particular countries where your students are heading, faculty members who have visited these countries recently, and newly returned students, to the various country-focused, small-group sessions you organize.

A full discussion on orientation and reentry counseling is to be found in chapter 12. Discussions of such cross-cultural concepts as "attribution theory," "cognitive dissonance," and "selective perception" can be found in articles and books by such respected authors as Gary Althen, Milton Bennett, Richard Brislin, John Condon, Neal Grove, Robert Kohls, and Josef Mestenhauser. Consult the bibliography in the appendix of this book.

Advising Procedures and Strategies

The following section will discuss particular advising strategies being successfully used on many campuses, based on the principles outlined above. These include initial intake procedures, one-on-one advising, and alternative strategies.

One-on-One Counseling. The advising process begins at the front door, with a welcoming staff and an appropriate environment. An up-to-date education-abroad library and orientation to its use, as suggested above, are essential if students are to understand that selecting a program is an interactive process, and that they will ultimately be asked to make their own informed decisions. Whether students are greeted by a study-abroad adviser, a secretary, a student assistant, or an interactive computer program, these initial exchanges are aimed at explaining basic procedures and eliciting some introductory information on both sides. Students should be encouraged to read through the introductory materials you have prepared, begin to explore the range of possibilities open to them, and schedule an appointment with you for the next stage.

Initial Advising Session. In the initial contacts, it is important to establish an open and honest relationship. You should find out a little about the student: year in school, major, academic background, previous travel, language competency, occupational interest, time of year planned for going abroad, possible length of stay, tentative thoughts on study versus travel or other experience abroad, financial resources, and parental attitude. This information is fundamental to enable you to assist a student in defining his or her personal abilities, goals, and perceptions. Always ask: "What are your reasons for wanting to go abroad?" This question will help guide the student in exploring these issues. At this initial stage, some students will have a clear idea of what they hope to accomplish, while others will not—they simply want to experience another culture and are open to a variety of possibilities.

The general principle is that it is best to go abroad primarily for a unique learning experience. It is never wise to go only to get away from problems existing in the home situation. Students should be informed that, while a change of location may at first seem to relieve some personal pressures, the problems may be considerably increased by anxieties caused by loss of the security of being in a familiar setting and the need for adjustment to a foreign culture, educational system, and social environment.

The student should be reminded that a study-abroad experience requires careful planning. Most advisers recommend four to twelve months for planning. Longer lead times are needed for longer programs. Time is needed to initiate discussion with the student's academic adviser or department head to learn about the policy for granting credit for study abroad. Together, they should determine what effect study abroad might have on credit toward the degree, time of graduation, and advantage in the job market after graduation.

Following this discussion and the clarification of the student's goals, you should begin to give information on a wide range of opportunities abroad. These options should be introduced and discussed at some length to acquaint the student with the various choices available. The student should be encouraged to spend time in the education-abroad library skimming information on study possibilities, beginning with those administered by the home campus or consortia in which it participates. You are responsible for recommending good—which means appropriate for this particular student—programs and indicating apprehensions concerning less sound choices when the student requests such information. You should also encourage certain students to consider nontraditional study sites.

107

Directed Research. To further assist the student in independent predeparture research, the adviser should recommend specific reference books where information about the foreign institutions and educational systems from program sponsors can be gathered. Resources in the main campus library, foreign government information services in New York City, cultural offices of embassies in Washington, D.C., and consulates in other major cities also may have useful information about the educational systems, institutions, and programs, and also about the life and culture of different countries. The more the student knows about the foreign country, culture, and the educational system and its expectations, the better he or she can cope with it once there.

Follow-up Advising Sessions. Consideration of program costs and available ways of meeting them should begin with early talks with parents and the financial aid office. Costs of programs should be checked, being sure that all items of expense are included. Some program literature may indicate what the program charge covers but omit such essentials as lunches or weekend meals, health and accident insurance, and transportation. Note that almost all study-abroad students spend substantially more on elective travel than they expect.

Students should be referred to persons whose knowledge about a particular area of the world is more current and extensive than your own. These resources include international students and members of the community, visiting scholars, U.S. students and faculty returned from abroad, and returned Peace Corps volunteers.

Most students need encouragement. If language proficiency is not adequate, intensive study should be started. Or, if the student cannot afford a study-abroad program but is skilled in a language and reasonably self-sufficient, you might encourage the student to undertake independent study or consider working abroad. In this way the student will be able to pursue options most suited to his or her capabilities and financial resources.

After a student has carefully reviewed the options, you should provide assistance with making the final selections and submitting applications in a proper and timely manner. The student should probably be encouraged to apply to more than one program unless there is reasonable certainty of acceptance by the first choice.

Advice should be provided on institutional policies and procedures pertaining to:

- The payment of tuition and/or program fees
- Refunds, if the student does not go or withdraws before the program is completed
- Prior approval for courses taken abroad, if required at your institution
- Submitting records of study completed abroad for evaluation and credit
- Registration and housing upon return

• Independent study or direct enrollment.

Throughout the entire advising process, you should supply suggestions and guidelines that assist the student in further defining personal goals, in addition to supplying the information discussed above. When you do not know an answer, either find the information requested or recommend a person or address to contact for information. Keeping records of the names, addresses, qualifications, and interests of students will enable you to call or write a student when new information comes in, to keep in touch with him or her through a newsletter while abroad, or to contact the student upon return. Copies of applications, prior credit-approval forms, letters of recommendation, and transcripts will also need to be kept in some cases, but be aware of regulations concerning confidentiality of student records.

Alternative and Supplemental Strategies. One-on-one counseling is the best way to share your knowledge and experience with students and to help them reach responsible decisions. But the time demands on both advisers and students often make it difficult to devote the energy and concentration these discussions deserve. But time with the study-abroad adviser is only part of the process. Students should also be examining the written materials you have prepared for your library—essential information on such topics as institutional policies and procedures, program evaluations, required travel documents, using the library, low-cost airfares, predeparture readings, summer jobs abroad, and so forth. Advisers can use other resources as well to make more efficient use of limited time and to add to the effectiveness of the advising process. Some of these are:

General Meetings. Most experienced education-abroad offices either begin each term with a large general-information meeting for students who are considering education abroad, or hold such meetings periodically. Such meetings need to be fully promoted to everyone, and it is sometimes helpful to have key deans and faculty present, as well as returned students. If attendance is good and you have prepared a lively overview of institutional policies, the options that exist abroad, and how to approach and use your office, meetings can result in lots of enthusiasm and the prospect of beginning personal advising at a higher level.

Small Group Advising. It is also useful to arrange meetings for smaller groups of students interested in: (1) your own programs; (2) program types (e.g., language-immersion programs or programs with internships); (3) particular countries or regions; or (4) programs geared to specific majors (e.g., engineering, business, music, nutrition, etc.). A group session may take a little longer than talking with one individual, but it will take much less time than successive individual interviews. These sessions can also include returned students, faculty who have interests in these areas, or visiting program representatives.

Referral to Colleagues. You may not need to answer all questions—especially the most technical ones—when others on campus either know more than you do or have the authority to make decisions in certain areas such as credit transfer, financial aid, billing procedures, and the like. In short, take advantage of your campus network; remember that others are also there to assist students. Referring students to others not only saves time but also lets students know that support for education abroad is institutionwide. Referrals to faculty members involved with particular programs should also be common.

Peer Advising. With proper training, returned education-abroad students can serve as effective advisers. The training might include discussions on what they considered important in their experience, what information and counseling they themselves had (or did not have but needed), how to reach more students, and especially on how everybody's experience abroad is in many ways unique, yet with common elements. Clearly, you must be judicious in your selection of peer advisers because some students are incapable of generalizing about their experience to make it relevant to others, while others are capable of spreading all sorts of misinformation. You need to be able to distinguish students who simply "had a good time" from those who seem to have grown and matured. Interesting and committed students who have made the most of their opportunities abroad and who have a real desire to use what they have learned to assist others can be very effective adjuncts in the advisory process.

Summary

There are many types of successful advising. What works for one person may not work for another; what worked this year may not work next year. What is clear is that advising is a very complex and dynamic interpersonal process that cannot be reduced to easy formulas or universal answers. Nevertheless, the relations between you and your students will be enriched and deepened the more you know about your institution, program options, student maturation, and cross-cultural training. Putting your knowledge to work to benefit both your institution and its students is then a matter of having the time, energy, and concern to carry out the strategies you have planned.

10

Promoting Student Diversity

Contributors: Margery A. Ganz, Jack Osborn, and Paul Primak

Chapter 8 profiled U.S. students now studying abroad. It showed that students outside of the affluent mainstream have not participated significantly in education abroad. Indeed, this paucity of nontraditional students (at least in proportion to their numbers in American colleges and universities) is conspicuous. CIEE's Advisory Council for International Educational Exchange observed in *Educating for Global Competence*:

> Students who study abroad are from a narrow spectrum of the total population. They are predominantly white females from highly educated professional families, majoring in the social sciences or humanities. They are high achievers and risk-takers. Many have had earlier overseas travel or international experience. Whether by their own choice or lack of encouragement to do so, there are fewer men, members of minority groups, students from nonprofessional and less-educated families, and fewer students from science, education, or business among undergraduates who study abroad.

Another study, "Report of the National Task Force on Undergraduate Education Abroad" (1990), (appendix 2) points out that:

> Efforts to expand the number of undergraduates who study abroad must address the lack of diversity among them.... Even though minority enrollments in American colleges and universities increased overall to eight percent of all four-year college students, minority participation in study abroad has increased little, representing only a tiny fraction of all undergraduate study abroad students.

"Getting on with the task" means that proactive efforts are required of every adviser and program administrator. Although real obstacles do exist, especially curricular and economic ones, part of the problem is the perpetuation of individual and institutional assumptions. Such assumptions clearly

111

limit what does and does not happen. One important barrier to study abroad is the widespread misconception of families, students, and their institutions that study abroad is not an achievable goal. Making such an experience for such students "an achievable goal" therefore remains your primary challenge. How you address these "misconceptions," however, depends not only on available resources and precedents but also on your imagination, energy, and priorities.

How far does your commitment to promoting international educational exchange extend? The convenient and traditional commitment inspires advisers to promote opportunities only to students with sufficient resources and backgrounds to take advantage of all that is available. After all, one of the strengths of education abroad is that it continues to attract self-motivated and adventurous students who usually do not need to be told that international living and learning is worthwhile, but just require some assistance to work out their will. Further, only a fraction of undergraduates who could be participating in overseas programs actually do so. Because everyone agrees on the need to expand numbers overall, there is plenty to be said for concentrating one's efforts on this huge group of traditional students.

But beyond the national goal of encouraging more students to have a significant international experience abroad prior to commencement, what are our obligations to push beyond traditional norms, to include a wider cross-section of the undergraduate student population—including those from more diverse racial and ethnic backgrounds, older students, male students, students with physical disabilities, and those majoring in business, science, technology, education, and the arts? What, in short, is your, and your institution's, answer to the entitlement question: if education abroad is as important as we believe and say it is, how can we possibly defend making it available only to certain categories of students?

Deciding on Priorities

As noted above, the typical student who studies abroad is not difficult to categorize. On a national scale, only about 2 percent of all approximately thirteen million undergraduates participate in some sort of education-abroad program. It would be sensible to infer that those who remain on campus represent by far the dominant U.S. tradition, rather than—as it seems to us in the field—the other way around. But, since goals in the field of education abroad are to increase numbers and diversity nationally, our focus must be on identifying types of students who do not traditionally participate in education abroad—at least in proportion to their numbers in the U.S. undergraduate population. Once identified, these students must be given viable opportunities. Some subgroupings of such students would include:

- Those majoring in subject areas *other* than the humanities and social sciences, such as business, science, technology, nursing, engineering, architecture, music, art, education, agriculture, and so forth.

• Those attending community colleges, technical colleges, and other two-year degree-granting institutions, which now account for more than half the total undergraduate population.

• Male students, who now make up slightly less than half of all enrollments.

• Part-time and older students (over twenty-five years old), now constituting a third of all U.S. undergraduates.

• Those with "minority" backgrounds, as defined by their racial and/or ethnic heritage: African, Hispanic, Asian, native American, and so forth.

• Those with physical and/or learning disabilities.

Students in most of these categories—especially older, minority, community college, part-time—are not likely to have the funds even to consider education abroad as an available option, much less an "achievable goal."

As the Task Force Report pointed out, different types of programs are needed to suit the needs and interests of different types of students. Diversifying programs means appealing to more diverse participants:

> In expanding study abroad to encompass 10 percent of all undergraduates and diversify both participants and destinations, merely replicating and multiplying current program models is unrealistic and inappropriate.... The needs of [nontraditional students] are mostly ignored by the more typical study abroad models and structures. The Task Force cannot prescribe the new models.... These must be developed pragmatically by individual institutions, consortia, or other appropriate organizations. However, features to consider include more short-terms stays, flexible language requirements, "no-fee swapping" of students between U.S. and foreign institutions, and built-in work or service components that reduce costs.

Such variations on expanding program models as a means of opening up education-abroad opportunities to a new range of undergraduates will be discussed in part 3 of this book. Expanding the curricular relevance of study-abroad and experiential programs will also be discussed in these chapters, as will reasons why colleges and universities need to do more to promote them as options. But most study-abroad programs are perfectly suited to many nontraditional students. The question is how to develop an advising emphasis that will capture their attention and answer their special needs.

Advising Nontraditional Students

It is the rare institution that has not made efforts in recent decades to open itself up to new kinds of students. As a consequence, most colleges and universities have achieved a far more diverse student body. But whether your institution is a small, private rural college, a midsized public university located in a town, or a large, urban "multiversity," the nontraditional students—whether constituting a minority or majority of the total enrollment—probably do not participate equally in education-abroad opportunities.

There are a number of exceptions to this general truth, institutions that through good leadership and dedication have overcome many inhibitors to education abroad. Some large public universities, such as the universities of Massachusetts, Minnesota, California, and Kansas, as well as Michigan State University, have good affirmative action policies and send 5–10 percent of their undergraduates abroad, many through direct-exchange arrangements with foreign universities. Some private colleges, such as Kalamazoo, Middlebury, Bates, and Dartmouth, can show that minority students, with full financial aid, study abroad in percentages proportional to their numbers on campus. Others, such as Spelman and Scripps, have had unusual success in developing superior support services for nontraditional students.

Spelman College, the oldest African American women's college in the United States, has been sending its students overseas since 1957. But in the last five years, under the presidential leadership of Johnnetta Cole, numbers have increased dramatically. Approximately half of those students who go abroad study in full academic year programs; about 25 percent are premed majors. Some Spelman students come from families able to make the financial commitment (which can be as much as double the cost of a domestic year), but most have to work hard to come up with the money.

Scripps College is a small, private liberal arts college for women in Southern California. It enrolls about six hundred students, 21 percent with minority backgrounds—about half of them Hispanic. The "typical" Hispanic Scripps student comes from a family, most often from the Los Angeles area, that speaks Spanish at home. She is usually the first member of her family to attend college and may well be the primary English-language spokesperson for the family. Many such students have to balance their studies with their responsibilities as a resource person for other family members. In spite of very extensive support services, the attrition among Hispanic students is higher than for white students. Still, out of the about eighty-five Scripps students who studied abroad in 1989–90, 13 percent were nonwhite and 5 percent were Hispanic.

The Spelman example may not be fully applicable to many other historically black colleges and universities, nor may the Scripps example be fully applicable to public institutions with large percentages of Hispanic students. But much of what each school has accomplished merits close inspection.

With special counsel and experience, advisers can learn how to counsel students with physical disabilities. A survey conducted in 1984 by Mobility International USA (MIUSA) revealed that only 1 percent of all participants in international educational exchange in 1983 had physical disabilities, while 71 percent of the organizations responding to the survey indicated that they had not enrolled a single disabled student in their programs. That same year the *Statistical Abstract of the United States* showed that 14.4 percent of the U.S. population was disabled. This is a glaring lack of proportional representation and represents a challenge to study-abroad advisers.

The MIUSA survey also examined a number of current professional perceptions regarding disabled students and education-abroad programs. When asked why they might not be providing opportunities for disabled students in their programs, colleges responded that they (1) could not find host families for disabled students, (2) encountered negative attitudes on the part of staff here and overseas, and (3) felt they could not provide what they saw as extra assistance needed by the disabled participants.

These findings suggest that education-abroad advisers need more information and training about disabled students. The first task is for advisers to realize that barriers to participation in programs abroad, for most disabled students are more psychological than physical. These barriers are evident in the skepticism of administrators both at home and abroad and in the publicity we produce for our programs. In other words, limits are imposed on the disabled student before the question, "Can I study abroad?", is even broached.

Perhaps the most significant barrier is the overseas program administrator who assumes that he or she must make the program site completely accessible and provide special services at the expense of activities and materials for other program participants. An MIUSA official illustrates the situation well:

> An important distinction is in the use of the word *accessible*. Perhaps some of your hesitation ... is in thinking that if you accept a disabled person, your program must be able to meet their needs in every way.... Most people with disabilities are very well aware that the world is not "accessible." ... A problem that might seem insurmountable might be something

> that they cope with regularly, and for which they have a developed a simple coping method.

To meet these needs, Mobility International offers a host of services that colleges and universities are encouraged to utilize. These include:
- Information for host families being recruited for disabled participants
- A checklist of individual needs for disabled students
- Special training for staff

115

The 1991 Americans with Disabilities Act defines what institutions *must* provide for students with learning or physical limitations. Because it mandates certain actions, the Act may well have legal implications for the education-abroad office, just as it does for your institution as a whole. Therefore, advisers and administrators should consult with university counsel, and with those responsible for campus services to disabled students, about any liabilities to which the education-abroad office may be exposed under the Act and its still evolving regulations. Fortunately, there is no shortage of published information explicating the act; the office of the university counsel or the university personnel office should be able to direct you to appropriate resources.[1]

For many minority and handicapped students, just enrolling in college is a tremendous step, graduating from college is a dream, and going overseas to study is often unimaginable. There is a special urgency today to work toward eliminating racial, ethnic, and other attitudinal barriers to all the richnesses of higher education. By taking affirming actions, you can show students who have faced discrimination (and are likely to face it again) that you and your institution are truly committed to helping them in every way possible.

Traditional ways and means used to promote education-abroad opportunities, however, often have to be reexamined very thoroughly when advising these students. Advising nontraditional students also often requires additional time and resources. The remainder of this chapter suggests a variety of pragmatic and proactive strategies that you can use in the advising process itself to increase the numbers and diversity of students on your campus who will not only consider but also participate in education-abroad programming.

Pragmatic and Proactive Strategies

Secure Top Administrative Support. The rhetoric of increasing diversity is the easy part. Doing it is the hard part. Without the president's and the board's genuine commitment to increasing participation in education abroad, the chances of success are minimal. This does not mean doing the impossible, but rather making the fullest and deepest compact with nontraditional students to do everything that is institutionally possible to assist them. Equally important is that this compact be communicated clearly and frequently to other members of the administration, faculty, and student body. Finally, because new resources will probably be necessary, there must be an institutional willingness, at the highest levels, to secure and utilize them.

If you hear talk about doing more but see no positive steps, you must then take matters to the highest levels possible. Students are only frustrated and angered, and staff demoralized, if promises are made and then broken. The key is to remember your own expertise in education abroad and to use this to persuade those who have the authority to make a difference to do so. At some level, your argument has to emphasize principles to which your institution is publicly committed: namely, providing all students with equal access to all the fruits of higher education, preparing all students for the international, interdependent world of the next century, and providing a competitive edge vis-à-vis other students in the job market.

Build Faculty Support. The advising process cannot succeed without strong faculty involvement and support. With regard to encouraging nontraditional students into education abroad, this support is even more crucial. The case for studying or working abroad, when made by a faculty member from a similar background or with like disabilities, will always be doubly persuasive. When they themselves have had international experience and can talk about how this has helped them in their work and life, students are going to be even more persuaded. If such mentors exist on your faculty, their assistance will prove invaluable.

If, as often is the case, your own institutional programs have grown out of language-department interests, then faculty in other departments will have to be contacted to identify other geographic areas and appropriate programs that have a stronger likelihood of appealing to these students. Again, shorter programs, those with work components or in nontraditional study destinations may have an appeal.

Some minority students will indeed be interested in exploring their cultural roots—in Latin America, Africa, Asia, and so on. But it is unwise to assume that this is true for all, or even most, students. The degree to which such students feel the importance of including their background heritage in education-abroad planning is something you and the faculty need to explore during the advising process.

Utilize All Current Financial Aid and Seek Special Funding. Increasing the participation of nontraditional students is, more than anything else, limited by current economic realities. Without adequate family or personal resources, students are dependent on institutional financial aid from both private and public sources. Otherwise, most of these students simply cannot consider most education-abroad opportunities, no matter what other inducements and arguments are used. In this regard, the new federal financial aid legislation and the National Security Education Program (see chapter 4) will make a major difference because one of the purposes of this legislation is to enfranchise more students.

Every student has a unique financial picture, but it is important to work with the director of financial aid to establish fundamental policies. The bottom line should be to make sure that what aid now exists for an individual student on campus can "travel" abroad. Institutional policy must be set up in

117

a way to ensure openness and flexibility. Spelman and Scripps, for example, let every dollar of aid money go with students, with the exception of work-study funds. However, federal loans and grants can be used to replace college work-study.

Special minority scholarships from foundations can sometimes be used for education abroad. You may have to bring these to the attention of your financial aid office and assist in the extra effort to track them down. The number of programs that offer either special grants for minority students or are willing to make fee waivers abroad is growing slowly. Spelman and Scripps colleges have also encouraged students to solicit assistance from their churches and from service organizations, or from extended families. When groups are approached correctly, funds have been forthcoming. Often even rather small amounts of seed money may have surprising multiplier effects.

Other options include (1) getting your institution to guarantee fees to programs so that parents will not have to pay everything in July or December; (2) expediting loan and grant check endorsements in advance; (3) using revenue earned by sale of Eurail and Britrail passes, ID cards, and so on, to create special funds; (4) working with a limited number of specific programs to arrange special scholarship aid; and (5) working with the development office to raise special funds to support nontraditional students.

Work Closely with Student Services. Most likely your campus has designated at least one person to provide advice and counsel especially for nontraditional students. Large campuses are likely to have formal, specialized offices that provide on- and off-campus assistance for specific groups of students and to promote cultural diversity. One prominent author has observed that the move for greater internationalism and the emphasis on cultural diversity are intimately related but not always correlated effectively with each other because of the persistent social, economic, and political tensions in the United States:

> Many in minority communities speculate as to whether internationalism is a more comfortable concept for American society to deal with than cultural diversity. Not until recently, and only in limited circles, has the following notion been entertained as plausible: that understanding "international" cultures is linked to the understanding and respect for the "international" cultures represented by the many racial and ethnic groups in the United States. Ironically, rather than embodying this concept, the movement to internationalize American campuses is occurring on many of the same campuses where racial tension and violence are becoming increasingly more common.[2]

As this perception suggests, the relationship between the education-abroad office and the offices and professionals charged with providing special services and promoting cultural diversity can easily become enmeshed in struggles for recognition and resources on campus, as well as in broader, unresolved social tensions. Moreover, students can receive conflicting messages. It is therefore imperative for you to take proactive steps to work *with* these colleagues with the overall benefit of the student in mind. A broadened and deepened appreciation of cultural diversity is almost always the result of a good education-abroad experience, and this benefit ought to be applicable both on campus and in life.

Furnish Role Models. Most education-abroad professionals themselves have experienced a formative international sojourn. But given the limited substratum of American society that has traditionally furnished students for education abroad, very few professionals in the field of international educational exchange currently come from any of the nontraditional group backgrounds. This vacuum represents a very real perceptual and communications problem and makes it even harder to overcome the perception that education abroad is not for everyone.

In the short run, you should exploit every opportunity you have to hire full- or part-time staff with nontraditional backgrounds. Student peer counselors can also serve this function, as can faculty advisers willing to work within the structures of the education-abroad office.

Begin the Process of Encouragement Early. The literature of the college must give the unequivocal message to those considering admission that education abroad is not an incidental activity but an integral part of the degree and most majors. In addition, the literature must tell minority students and those with special needs that others like them have participated successfully in such activities. Sometimes this can be done simply by making sure that such students are visually represented in institutional promotional brochures, catalogs, fliers, and view-books that mention education-abroad activities—and especially in brochures for your own programs. If such materials quote students, make sure that some quotations come from minority and special students who have studied or worked abroad. Including nontraditional students in publicity materials is an effective way to promote study abroad as an accessible program.

By taking part in general campus orientation and promoting education abroad as early in the school year as possible, you are planting seeds and nurturing interest. This is also a good time to assure students that your services extend to all of them. You should also be present at orientation sessions for minority students or students with disabilities. One especially effective tack is to stress that studying overseas will give them a competitive edge. How many minority students applying to graduate or medical school will have spent a year overseas?

119

Work with Parents. For many nontraditional students, just being away at college is hard enough, so thinking about living outside of the United States is almost unimaginable. For their parents, it is, if anything, even harder to conceive, and indeed may be truly frightening. Early and ongoing interaction with the parents is therefore essential. You and your office should take the initiative and contact the parents as soon as their daughter or son shows serious interest in going abroad. Anticipate their concerns, especially feelings that their family unity appears threatened by this separation.

Whether in person, by letter, or phone, you should discuss (1) how study abroad could be valuable to their child in specific academic, career, and personal terms; (2) how the college chooses particular programs; (3) the support services that will be available (orientation, overseas support services, and services on return to address the possibility of readjustment problems). You should also be available on parents' weekend to talk the whole process over with them. Also talk about money. Sometimes parents call with very basic questions. They need support too.

Students should be encouraged to discuss their plans as early as possible with their parents. After all, this must be a three-way conversation. You also might be able to put doubting parents in touch with parents whose daughters or sons have studied overseas. At Scripps and Spelman this peer counseling tactic has proved very effective in calming fears. It is also helpful to communicate with the parents while students are overseas. Send the parents copies of all the orientation materials, and continue to send updates to them during the course of the program.

Select the Right Programs and Work with Them. A great deal of attention needs to be paid to the process of helping individual students select the right program. It makes some sense to do a measure of preselection of your own, even before you begin advising students. Choose groups of programs that you think have worked well in the past—and perhaps a list of countries best avoided. Racism and discrimination exist in just about every country, though the targets are different. Determinations must be made about which programs are able to protect students from the worst of such offenses and which are not. While it is true that qualified students can handle almost any overseas program, you should give special preference to programs that exhibit a good track record with minority students. Reputable programs will usually be honest in facing their built-in limitations of what they offer and will make adjustments when they can.

A common and well-founded perception among students is that education abroad is a largely Eurocentric undertaking. This can be disappointing for students from more diverse backgrounds who are either seeking something closer to their own cultural heritage or simply are not drawn to Europe. For these students, it is especially important for advisers to go out of their way to promote education-abroad programs in Africa, the Caribbean,

Latin America, Asia, and other nontraditional destinations. Of course, not all minority students will want to study in such locations, but it is critical to let them know that such opportunities exist in abundance.

Shorter programs need also to be pointed out, as well as programs which might have internships, practical training, volunteer work, or service learning as components. Indeed, anything that challenges or enlarges the general perception is worth doing.

It is also useful to work closely with programs before the process of application, informing them of your students' particular needs, seeking assurances that they can be met, and ascertaining potential problems abroad, in, for instance, housing or social life. Such conversations might also explore ways to offset borderline GPA, class rank, or low SAT scores—perhaps by writing cover letters or suggesting getting particularly good faculty recommendations. Acting as an advocate for minority students, you might be able to suggest that they strengthen the group.

It is much easier to be admitted to one of the numerous excellent education-abroad programs than to get accepted by very selective undergraduate institutions. Nevertheless, these programs need to be convinced that applicants are serious, informed, and qualified. You might also find that it is profitable to act as a mentor for your students when they are communicating with programs and especially to help them to prepare their applications. Mentoring is never an easy process, and students may need practical advice, assurances, and some prodding.

With regard to assisting students with disabilities, as noted above, many organizations exist to provide information about assistance and resources abroad. Such information can be found in two MIUSA publications: *A World of Options* and *A Manual for Integrating People with Disabilities into International Educational Programs* (see list of health information resources, pp.139–140). Together, these two publications provide not only an introduction to the educational background for administrators and advisers but also a list of resources, both in the United States and abroad, to make international education a reality for disabled students.

Disabled participants mainly want to know what their options are and what trade-offs they must make in order to study overseas.

Use Returned Students. At almost any college the most active and vocal support for education abroad comes from returning students. Using returning minority students to help you recruit others can provide affirmation and assurance that you yourself cannot provide alone. If they had good experiences, they will likely do much of the job for you. There is no substitute for this sort of student-to-student contact. Many programs will also be willing and able to put nervous students and their parents in touch with past participants from nearby colleges.

In addition, you might consider developing special written materials on minority and disabled student experiences abroad. With the help of a NAFSA grant, Brown University recently published a booklet quoting students' candid reflections on their choice of country, living situation, expectations, and actual treatment, and the influence of the experience on their outlook and further studies. While most of these reflections gave notes of caution and not all experiences were equally positive, the overall impression is highly affirmative.

Face Racism and Discrimination Squarely. During both individual counseling sessions and especially during orientation programs you should be open and realistic about the possibility of outright racism abroad. You should also discuss the likelihood that disabled students may have to contend with insensitive attitudes and inadequate facilities. These realities do exist and may even be present where an adviser might not anticipate them. If students know about these attitudes and customs up front they will be better prepared for the worst they might find overseas, and being prepared makes life easier. Again, the seasoned insights of returned students, direct or indirect, provide points of reference and truth that your students will respect and appreciate—not the least of which is that, whatever negatives existed for them abroad, the experience was nevertheless vital and important.

Information and advice is most useful when it is culture specific—and usually country or even region and place specific. While some generalizations are possible, what is true of Paris will not describe the reality of rural France, much less of Germany or Spain; what is true in cities will not hold for villages; what is true on campus may not be true in the neighborhoods; what is true for parents may not be true for their children. Students may also find that their "Americanness" is a more important factor in determining their treatment abroad than their racial or ethnic heritage or physical abilities. They may also find that the United States is not the only country with a complex of minority cultures.

Summary

As an education-abroad professional, you will need to work extra hard to extend the benefits of the international education experience to all students. With only 2 percent of undergraduates now studying or working abroad as part of their degree studies, and with these students representing a very narrow slice of the social, racial, ethnic, academic, and preprofessional pie that is American higher education, "getting on with the task" represents a long-overdue and immense challenge that we can ignore only at our professional and national peril. Put differently, because nontraditional students represent the majority of students, not to give more priority to their interests and needs is a formula for irrelevance and defeat.

Notes

1. *ADA Compliance Manual for Higher Education: A Guide to Title 1.* Edited by Forest C. Benedict, Kirk D. Beyer, Kathleen E. Donofrio, and John M. Toller. 1992. (Washington, D.C.: College and University Personnel Association, 1992)
2. Holly Carter, "Black Students and Overseas Programs: Broadening the Base of Participation," Council on International Educational Exchange, 1991.

11

Health and Safety Issues

Contributor: Joan Elias Gore

Most students who study, work, or travel abroad—indeed most people who go abroad for any reason—are less prepared than they should be for sudden injuries, illness, depression, or other health contingencies. The American folk wisdom of travel may have warned travelers to avoid the local water and be prepared for upset stomachs. But there are many health concerns that are less common, yet considerably more dangerous and unexpected. Some are of such recent development that travelers may not know how to take the proper precautions or how to locate overseas medical help. The recent worldwide spread of AIDS, for example, has focused attention on the need for current health knowledge in preparation for overseas living. However, even routine ailments (the flu, toothache, dizziness) or minor accidents (a broken limb) when endured far away from home, can take on a threatening and disorientating aspect, and can ruin any sojourn.

In addition to health issues, students often bring with them quite unrealistic assumptions, for example, that serious crime and criminal behavior exist only on American streets, or that foreigners will rob them blind at every opportunity and cannot be trusted. Moreover, while students may be model citizens on campus and feel that they will know how to behave abroad, the experience of being in a foreign land can be unsettling, with its tricky combination of new social demands and freedoms. Thus, aberrant or unexpected student behavior patterns, by U.S. or foreign standards, are not unknown in education abroad.

Finally, students may have to deal with social and political change abroad, which can sometimes come quite suddenly and on occasion become dangerous and even violent. They can, in their naiveté or the enthusiasm of the moment, easily get caught in the crossfire—perhaps literally. Recent years have given us numerous examples of American students and programs coming under both imagined and very real threats of international terrorism and war. Making decisions about which location is safe and which is not must be part of overall program planning, part of which must be consultation with university counsel on the question of institutional liabilities. The matter of appropriate student conduct during times of stress abroad is something which can and should be addressed during advising and orientation. Sound health, medical, and safety preparations on the part of students can contribute significantly to their opportunities to enjoy their time abroad fully and not be sidetracked by illness, injury, or other road-blocks. Put another way, ignorance can be disastrous, so advisers have a key role to play in imparting sound and helpful information.

Health Issues

You are not likely to be a health-care expert or to have training or experience in medicine or psychological counseling, so there are limits to the immediate knowledge you can offer. At the same time, the health-service personnel on your campus may not always be available to help your students, or may not understand health issues in other parts of the world. Also, devoting time, energy, and even budgets to addressing such issues is costly. Lastly, you may find yourself in the position of spending a lot of effort to impart what you think is vital information to an audience that is reluctant to listen—simply because of the tendency of young people to believe in their personal invulnerability.

How you go about providing the health and medical counsel and practical information your students need is up to you. Each campus will have to develop approaches and materials unique to its own set of programs and students. The immediate resources available to you on campus or through national networks are likely to be plentiful, but not perhaps exhaustive. You should begin at the student health service on your own campus. NAFSA stresses close cooperation between the student-health center and the education-abroad office in orienting U.S. students going abroad. Public agencies in the college or university area can be invaluable additional resources. Professional agencies for student health workers, such as the American College Health Association (ACHA), headquartered in Baltimore, are also good resources.

World Health Problems. Western Europe, the destination of about three-fourths of current U.S. students engaged in some form of education abroad, has largely rid itself of the ravages of many age-old plagues, epidemics, and life-threatening diseases. This may be less true of other parts of the world. According to CIEE's *Whole World Handbook*, the two most common health problems for world travelers are diarrhea and malaria.

Almost everyone encounters diarrhea, particularly when traveling in the Third World. Mild forms of diarrhea are readily treated, but severe dysentery can have long-term effects. In parts of the world with hot, wet climates, malaria continues despite an increase in community preventive measures. If your students are to be living and learning in Africa, Asia, Oceania, Central

America, or South America they should be made aware of these problems and should be given information on how the problems are prevented through appropriate means and treated if contracted.

Sexually transmitted diseases such as gonorrhea, syphilis, and herpes continue to pose health risks for travelers in virtually any country on the globe. The HIV virus, which is responsible for AIDS, is also transmitted sexually and through contaminated blood supplies and presents a health risk abroad. The HIV virus is especially threatening since it can be transmitted through medical misuse of hypodermic needles for vaccinations, allergy treatments, medications, blood transfusions, and emergency health procedures by trained personnel. Contracting hepatitis or cholera is also a possibility in countries with untreated drinking water.

Given the severe physical consequences that can stem from contracting such diseases, it is of course crucial that students pay attention to their causes and treatment. Conversely, students should not be encouraged to think that their risks are always or inevitably going to be dramatically greater abroad, even in Third World surroundings, than they are in the United States. Also, they should not be encouraged to regard foreign health care as inferior to that available at home because the opposite is often the case. As with other advice you give, a balanced approach is the best.

Preexisting Physical Problems. Students with known and ongoing medical problems, such as allergies or diabetes, need to be informed that they must take special precautions and make special preparations in order to manage their situation overseas. They may be unaware that the availability of specialized medications is not always certain in other countries. Understanding the different names for foreign medicines and their application and dosage can be uncomfortable at best and life-threatening at worst. At the same time, students with common and foreseeable medical problems need to know that they are likely to be among many fellow-sufferers and that adequate treatment is probably widely available.

The situation for students with physical handicaps is likely to have been resolved at the earliest stages of the advising process—well before orientation. Students with disabilities must be sure at the outset, even before the application process, that adequate facilities and personnel exist overseas and that they will be welcomed and well cared for.

As noted in chapter 10, Mobility International is very active in (1) encouraging programs and campuses to prepare themselves to serve students with physical handicaps; and (2) helping students to identify programs that have the will and ability to assist them with their specialized needs. Such students know well what these needs are, and only seek assurances that they will be met so that they can participate fully in the program. With the passage of the 1991 Americans with Disabilities Act, which codifies the obligations of institutions to the disabled, program administrators would do well to check with university counsel to ensure that the program is in full compliance with the Act and its implementing regulations.

Substance-Abuse Problems. Whatever their behavior on American campuses, students free from U.S. laws and mores regarding the use of alcohol sometimes slip into—or maintain—patterns of alcohol abuse while abroad. Such abuse occurs for a variety of reasons: a mistaken impression of how alcohol is used in their new surroundings, cheaper costs in some countries, a lower drinking age, more lenient laws against drunkenness, or just a desire to experiment or fit in. Your orientation should emphasize that the abuse of alcohol can result in disruptive and offensive behavior and exacerbate psychological and physical problems.

Whereas just about all countries, with the exception of those with religious prohibitions, tolerate social drinking, the use of inebriating or hallucinogenic drugs is seldom allowed under any circumstances. Drug abuse by foreign-study students is less common but more severe than alcohol abuse. It carries with it not only immeasurable health risks but also very serious cultural and legal consequences. Risks are immensely complicated by the presence of substances unknown to the student, by shady and often criminal contacts, and by rigid legal systems that impose penalties of such severity that they can ruin a student's life. In the area of drug abuse too, the possibility of institutional liability justifies a careful consultation with university counsel to ensure that your program complies with the 1988 Anti-Drug Abuse Act (specifically the provision relating to drug-free workplaces) and other federal legislation.

Nutrition. Living in another culture necessarily entails a change in diet and altered eating routines and assumptions. These changes are usually beyond student control; they must do as the natives do, which is part of the whole experience. Sometimes, students find that their diet abroad is considerably healthier than the one they followed at home. In many countries, the natives eat less processed food than Americans, drink less coffee and sweetened soda, eat more grains, fresh fish, dairy products, vegetables, and fruits, or generally eat less and have a more active life-style.

At the other extreme, people in poorer countries may eat what they can get, prepare foods in unsanitary ways, and suffer from various kinds of vitamin deficiencies. If this is the case, students will, and should, have some reasonable concerns about how either to adjust to such a diet or to supplement it. Whatever the situation, you can be sure that what students eat, do not eat, dream about eating, or hate eating will be a very important part of their thoughts and conversations while they are abroad and for years to come.

It is not feasible, or even advisable, to try to impose American eating habits and foodstuffs on a foreign culture. It is possible to learn in advance what the foreign diet consists of, and then to make some decisions about what nutritional counsel to give students. For your programs, such information should be readily available; otherwise, get it from program representatives or people who have lived there. Because you are not a nutritionist and your students may well be going to many different countries, perhaps the most you can do is discuss the situation in each country in the information sheets you keep in the education-abroad library, and try to provide some general guidance on sound nutrition during predeparture orientation.

Emotional and Mental Problems. The possibility of known, or new, emotional and mental problems emerging overseas is seen by many experienced observers as a health and safety concern second only to alcohol abuse in its potential negative impact on an education-abroad experience. Like substance abuse, its primary impact may be on the well-being of one person, but its side-effects can carry over to others—even to an entire group. What is clear is that preexisting emotional difficulties are often intensified by living in a foreign culture. Contrary to the belief of many students and their parents that an overseas experience might be "just the thing" to cheer someone up, a stressful experience in foreign surroundings can have just the opposite effect. In addition, there may be even fewer resources in foreign settings to help a student deal with such problems.

As will be discussed in the next chapter, culture shock by itself can often have a temporarily shattering and disorienting effect on even the most secure students. It is a real and very normal adjustment phenomenon, with predictable psychological and social dimensions. It is also in almost all cases something for which students can be prepared through proper predeparture and on-site orientation. But students who carry with them serious, unresolved emotional problems can put themselves and their program in a dangerous situation. The challenge to the education-abroad adviser and program administrator is to know, first, how to prevent this situation from happening, and, second, what to do, if and when it occurs.

As discussed in chapter 9, what you say in general about the range of challenges facing *any* student who chooses to study or work abroad should stress the importance of having a clear and positive motive. Let your students know that going abroad just to get away from something does not make sense. Additionally, one-on-one counseling should give you an opportunity to judge the emotional stability and maturity of most students. If you have reservations, this is the time to share them openly and directly.

If you see no obvious problems, or if students are determined to hide problems from you or do not recognize or acknowledge them, you can only proceed as if none exists. To search or probe further (e.g., by asking your counseling center if a given student is in therapy) may constitute a breach of the confidentiality of student records. However, you may wish to circulate to the counseling center the list of students applying to study abroad—

in the same way you inform the registrar or housing office. Good counselors, recognizing the names of their clients on your list, will take the matter up in their sessions. You may want to assure yourself that the counseling center personnel are aware of the risk factors in study abroad (e.g., culture shock) so that your list will be noticed and acted upon when it circulates.

Students who will not admit problems face-to-face are also likely to disguise them on their applications, too. Most letters of recommendation ask for comments on a student's emotional, as well as intellectual, maturity. But only the especially astute faculty member may be able to discern such characteristics and then be willing to state them for the record. Thus, it is very hard to know in advance which students may have emotional or mental difficulties overseas. However, if your instincts tell you that a particular student's participation would be a really bad idea for all concerned, you should act accordingly, using whatever discretion and authority you possess. In such cases, you may wish to consult university counsel and mental health professionals at the university health service or counseling center about the right approach to take.

Foreign Medical Practice. The manner in which medical help is obtained, the way patients are treated, the conditions of overseas medical facilities, and how health care is afforded often present marked differences from U.S. practice. Students need to be prepared for the reality that not all U.S. health-care values, assumptions, and methods are going to be found in each country they visit or study in. Indeed, even the notions regarding the onset of illness or points at which expert attention is required are to some degree cultural phenomena.

In some countries, especially in northern Europe, medical standards, judged by U.S. criteria, will turn out to be superior in effectiveness and cost. In other countries, standards are low enough that some medical needs cannot be met. The key is to know in advance, and be prepared for all contingencies. The availability of emergency medical help is a particularly important area of concern. Students need to face the possibility that they may need emergency help. Their orientation materials should offer general principles for finding such help while overseas.

Medical and Accident Insurance. No reputable college or education-abroad program will allow a student to travel abroad without sufficient medical insurance coverage for all possible medical needs. (Accident and life insurance policies are also fundamental.) Many institutions can make arrangements to extend the policy that covers students on campus, sometimes for an extra fee. Sometimes this arrangement applies only to home-campus programs, sometimes to all programs. In addition, a number of national agencies now sell medical and accident insurance policies designed especially for education-abroad program participation.

It is your job to work with others at your institution to decide what sort of insurance coverage you want for your students, how to acquire it, whether or not to make its costs a part of your own fees, then how to make certain that all students sign up for it and understand how it works. In addition, students must be informed about mandatory vaccinations and other inoculations. Some programs and some visa applications require a physical examination, which you may or may not be able to arrange for students through your campus health services. All such requirements and procedures need to be communicated to students as early in the advising process as possible, perhaps as part of your handbook, then reviewed carefully during predeparture orientation.

Personal Conduct and Safety Issues

Personal Conduct. Students returning from an education-abroad experience invariably observe that they think they have matured in confidence, direction, and ambition. They talk about learning to think and act for themselves and to make significant decisions for the first time in their lives. These reflections suggest that for most students the experience of living and learning abroad carries with it a new openness and independence. One of their freedoms is to make mistakes, and one of the initial mistakes they often make is to assume that local customs, mores, and even laws are not quite real and do not quite apply to foreigners. In due course, they realize that this is not the case, and sometimes they pay for their transgressions.

It is impossible to explain to a group of students about to go abroad exactly how they should and should not behave. Much of this will presumably be covered in the on-site orientation. But it is possible, and worthwhile, to remind them, in no uncertain terms, that (1) they are indeed guests in their new country and should always behave with this in mind; (2) each program has its own rules of conduct, always for good reasons; and (3) being "foreign" does not excuse them either from knowing or from obeying the civil and criminal laws of the country.

Crime. As on American campuses (as opposed to American streets), education-abroad programs often take place in relatively protected and safe environments. These may be foreign university campuses or isolated facilities with good security. But just as some crime—theft, drunkenness, vandalism, even rape—occurs on American campuses, some of your students may fall victim to petty or serious crime while abroad.

Again, on-site orientation programs bear the burden of providing detailed information on safeguards against possible crime in the area. As part of your advising and orientation, you can impart to students a general sense of the situation in each country where you run programs and direct their questions to outside program sponsors for information on other destinations. You might also work up a list of general do's and don'ts while abroad.

Threats of Political Violence. In recent years an enormous amount of attention has been given to the threats of political terrorism and violence said to be specifically directed against Americans abroad. In point of fact, few instances have occurred. This does not mean that these threats were hollow or that in the future no Americans abroad will become targets or actual victims. Respecting the possibilities of such occurrences and taking every precaution is important. It is equally important not to be intimidated and not to add to the misinformation and panic that popular journalism has tended to promote.

Decisions about where to find programs and whether or not to send students to programs judged to be in troubled areas are made at the institutional and program level. Your role vis-à-vis your institution is to provide whatever solid and current information you can. This can be done by

 • Using E-mail to receive regularly the U.S. State Department Travel Advisories

 • Using e-mail, as well as the telephone, fax, and other means to maintain contact with the SECUSSA Emergency Information Network, so as to remain in contact with your colleagues on other campuses and programs abroad, and thereby be able to quell rumors and verify known problems

 • Working with your institution to devise a contingency plan for genuine emergencies (e.g., deciding when and how to cancel programs, bring students home, etc.).

With regard to students (and their parents), the most you can do is to assure them that your institution is responsible and informed and will act to protect their safety at all times. During orientation, lay out some ways for students to minimize risks and avoid obvious dangers. These might include advice on making travel arrangements, keeping a low profile, dressing conservatively, avoiding large groups of other Americans, and generally keeping out of harm's way and political entanglements.

The question of institutional liability for students' injuries suffered abroad is a murky one. Here, too, a consultation with your university's legal counsel may be warranted.

Predeparture Orientation

Predeparture orientation (see chapter 12) is a kind of culmination of the ongoing advising process. Students who have paid attention to the preparations that must be made before going abroad should find few surprises. The information you review and the materials you distribute on health and safety issues (as outlined above) are not intended to alarm students or parents. Rather, the materials should guide them, once more, toward intelligent, rational preparations. In view of the seriousness of health and safety issues to the success of their overseas experience, predeparture orientation should make up a commensurate portion of your program.

The following is a list of health and safety information that should be included in the materials the adviser might wish to provide to students.

Predeparture Medical Examinations. Students need to complete all appointments well in advance of departure date, including immunizations and assessment of special health problems; also, they need to take care of any gynecological and dental check-ups that would fall within the time overseas. It is very important that they obtain copies of important health records, including

- Blood type
- Eyeglass and contact lens prescriptions
- Prescriptions for medications being taken (written in generic terms to obviate the difficulty of obtaining brand-name medications overseas)
- EKGs and X-rays (when these are relevant to a student's medical situation)
- Doctor's statement about any special health problems
- Dental records, particularly if special procedures or medications are indicated.

All of these records should be taken by the student during travel.

What to Pack. Students should take extra prescription drugs (except where their importation is specifically prohibited), packing them in different places, and should avoid putting prescriptions in luggage that might be lost or stolen; instruments necessary for self-administration of medications (it is strongly recommended that diabetics take a supply of disposable hypodermic syringes and needles—except where prohibited—to protect against the possibility of HIV infection in countries where needles and syringes used by medical personnel are not the disposable type); extra eyeglasses or contact lenses and dentures; a small first-aid kit containing band-aids, antiseptic cream, sunburn ointment, aspirin or other painkiller, antidiarrhea medicine; and, depending on the region visited, water purification tablets, antihistamines for allergy relief, salt tablets, and skin moisturizer.

Printed Information about Health and Safety. Students should be strongly encouraged to take with them all relevant information sheets prepared by the education-abroad office, as well as other materials from campus and local health agencies covering some or all of these topics.

Printed materials should include

- Cautions about alcohol and drug abuse, emphasizing that customs regarding alcohol and drug use are often different in other cultures, that laws controlling drugs and alcohol are likely to be different from those in the

United States, and that penalties for abuse may be severe.

• Descriptions of persistent and epidemic diseases such as dysentery, hepatitis, malaria, and AIDS, with information on their transmission, prevention, and treatment.

• Information about the physiological and psychological consequences of jet lag, culture shock, homesickness, loneliness, changes in diet, and so on.

• General instructions for emergency medical situations—using an emergency telephone system (like the 911 system in the United States), calling an ambulance, a hospital or doctor, an embassy or consular office, or a large hotel and asking for the name of the physician who is called when a guest needs emergency attention. The International Association for Medical Assistance to Travelers (IAMAT) provides a list of English-speaking doctors worldwide.

• General advice on nutrition, including ways to supplement diet deficiencies.

• Special advice for handicapped individuals and those with temporary physical disabilities.

• Full health and accident insurance policy coverage information and identification, including notice of special limitations or instructions on applicability and instructions for filing claims while overseas.

• Region-specific health information.

• A list of prudent advice on how to minimize the possibility of being victimized by crime.

• Tips on how to keep a low profile during political emergencies.

Region-Specific Information

For programs sponsored by your institution, you have a responsibility to provide ample information on health and safety issues in each country. This information will be furnished by the program staff, faculty, and past participants, but must be put into final form through your efforts. The question is how to determine what information should be imparted during the predeparture period, and what is more effectively given during the on-site orientation and through the normal counsel of the resident director.

If you do not operate your own programs, or if sizable numbers of your students participate in programs sponsored by other U.S. or foreign institutions or agencies, you may not be specifically responsible for intensive predeparture information for every specific region. Nevertheless, one way to ensure that students are properly informed is to provide the following information:

• Special medical requirements for admission and for obtaining visas or other documents from the foreign government, including immunizations, physical examinations, and tests.

• Information on the nature, prevention, and treatment of region-specific diseases. This should include, where appropriate, information on how to handle injections, emergencies, and/or blood transfusions in areas affected by AIDS.

• Information on the local diet and eating patterns, including the need for and availability of nutritional supplements.

• Information on laws regulating the import and/or possession of medications, hypodermic needles, condoms, and other contraceptives.

• Information on obtaining medications.

• Information about the health-delivery system of the region, especially if it differs significantly from that of the United States, how patients are likely to be treated, what kind of facilities they will find, how payment for services is handled, and students' legal rights to obtain services.

• Information about how to locate routine or emergency professional medical help, including names and telephone numbers of hospitals, clinics, and doctors, information on emergency-system telephone numbers, and information on self-help programs like Alcoholics Anonymous.

• Medical and accident insurance information for policies connected with the program.

• What to include in a medical kit for travelers.

• Information on local crime and the political situation.

All reputable programs will cooperate to furnish this information.

SELECTED HEALTH INFORMATION RESOURCES FOR STUDY-ABROAD ADVISERS

The following resource list was compiled by Joan Elias Gore and Margaret Brown Paviour

"Health Concerns in International Travel," Travel Health Information Service, 5827 West Washington Boulevard, Milwaukee, Wisconsin 53208; tel. 800.433.5256 (in Wisconsin, 414.774.4600).

Health Information for International Travel. U.S. Department of Health and Human Services, Public Health Service Centers for Disease Control, Center for Prevention Services, Division of Quarantine, Atlanta, Georgia 30333; tel. 202.783.3238 for information.

IAMAT: International Association for Medical Assistance to Travelers, a nonprofit, worldwide organization with excellent information on malaria prevention and other region-specific knowledge. 736 Center Street, Lewiston, New York 14092. There is no fee for joining, but a donation is welcome. IAMAT may be joined by students or study abroad advisers.

Immunization Alert, P.O. Box 406, Storrs, Connecticut 06268; tel. 203.487.0422.

Information Center for Individuals with Disabilities, 20 Park Plaza, Suite

330, Boston, Massachusetts 02116.

Intermedic, 777 Third Avenue, New York, New York 10017; tel. 212.486.8900. Provides members with names of English-speaking physicians abroad, information on immunizations and medicines.

A Manual for Integrating Persons with Disabilities into International Educational Exchange Programs. Edited by Susan Sygall. Mobility International USA, P.O. Box 3551, Eugene, Oregon 97403.

Passport's Health Guide for International Travelers. Thomas P. Sakmar, M.D.; Pierce Gardner, M.D., FACP; Gene N. Peterson, M.D., Ph.D. 1986. Passport Books. National Textbook Company, Lincolnwood, Illinois.

Society for the Advancement of Travel for the Handicapped, 26 Court Street, Brooklyn, New York 11242; tel. 718.858.5483.

State Department Overseas Citizens Emergency Center. Information on current epidemics, health conditions worldwide. Tel. 202.647.5225, 8:15 A.M. to 10:00 P.M. (EST), weekdays.

Travel Health Information Services, 5827 West Washington Boulevard, Milwaukee, Wisconsin 53208; tel. 800.433.5256 (in Wisconsin, 414.774.4600).

A World of Options: A Guide to International Educational Exchange, Community Service and Travel for Persons with Disabilities. Edited by Susan Sygall. Mobility International USA, P.O. Box 3551, Eugene, Oregon 97403.

Summary

Students have a right to expect a safe and healthy experience during their time abroad, but they sometimes bring poor health habits with them and may act more foolishly overseas than at home. Moreover, the world beyond U.S. borders is sometimes filled with health and crime problems and political instability unlike any found at home. There is no way that all dangers and risks can be eliminated, nor will students always act in their own best interests. Your responsibility to your students is to ensure that they receive all the information and assistance they need and that they understand their own responsibility for maintaining their health and well-being. Your responsibility to your institution is to see that your program complies with relevant statutes and regulations and that institutional liability is minimized through careful planning.

12

Predeparture Orientation and Reentry Programming

Contributor: Ellen Summerfield

Predeparture orientation, participation in a program abroad, and reentry constitute a unified whole. The profound learning that leads, at its best, to multiculturalism or ethnorelativism actually begins well before departure and continues long after return.[1] Thus, the philosophy of education-abroad programming cannot be limited to the actual time spent in another country, but underlies a three-part, inclusive learning process.

This chapter focuses on basic, practical guidelines for designing and running predeparture and reentry programs. Although it touches on the advising process in general, as well as on health and safety issues, these concerns are covered more fully in adjoining chapters. Philosophical and ethical questions cannot be treated at length, but will be mentioned as appropriate.

Predeparture Orientation Programs

Setting Goals. Predeparture orientation is intended to help prepare students for a meaningful and successful experience abroad. It needs to be very wide ranging, including everything from practical microconcerns with passports and ID cards to profound macroquestions concerning one's personal responsibilities in an interdependent, multicultural world. The major goals can be summarized as follows:

- To provide essential "nuts and bolts" information
- To motivate students to learn more about the host culture as well as about themselves as Americans, prior to departure
- To help students develop cross-cultural sensitivity and become familiar with the process of cross-cultural adaptation
- To help students gain a better comprehension of world issues and examine their roles as global citizens.

Orientation is a difficult and delicate affair, and the potential for mistakes

137

and damage is ever present. You must show utmost respect for students, who are generally impressionable and may easily accept misconceptions or oversimplifications. Ethical issues and pedagogical quandaries emerge early: How do you motivate students and create excitement without raising false hopes or expectations? How do you warn them against the dangers they might meet without causing unnecessary apprehension? How do you prepare them without depriving them of the joys of discovery? How do you discuss differences among cultures without introducing or reinforcing stereotypes?

Because these questions have no easy answers, a predeparture orientation can be a stimulating process for the adviser and the students. When done well, the orientation will generate enthusiasm for learning and set a tone of openness and receptivity to new experiences. It should increase student confidence in their ability to meet people and communicate across cultures but also make them see that they are to be involved in a very complex process of two-way communication. It helps them learn to appreciate and enjoy differences and to understand their responsibilities as guests in another country. Finally, it helps to create a network of peer support, as students get to know each other and develop an *esprit de corps.*

Designing the Program. In designing the orientation program, you must decide on:

• Format—one session, weekly sessions, weekend retreat, or academic course

• Content—balances between practical and philosophical, and culture-general and culture-specific issues

• Process—intellectual or experiential; reading, telling, and showing or experiencing.

These decisions will depend on your budget, staff, and time limitations, as well as on your educational philosophy and the assessed needs of your students. Most advisers believe it is both reasonable and necessary to require attendance at a predeparture orientation program and that students who do not attend demonstrate a lack of seriousness about their impending time abroad. Some schools that run their own programs automatically suspend such students from study-abroad participation. This approach is not possible, however, in large schools and those where students enroll in many different programs. Whatever your policy, students should be informed of it when they first apply to study abroad on any program.

Designing an orientation is a creative process.[2] Clearly, no orientation, no matter how well planned, can answer everyone's needs and achieve every goal. But if you recognize that in an orientation you are striving to move toward your goals rather than to achieve them fully, you and your students can find the process gratifying, despite what may be severe time constraints.

If only a few hours are available, the adviser must concentrate on the essentials and provide students with the incentive and information to explore many things further on their own. If you can schedule a series of weekly meetings or a weekend retreat, an even more effective orientation can be designed with time for nuts and bolts as well as cross-cultural training. The advantage of weekly meetings spread out over an academic quarter or semester is that students have time to absorb new ideas. A weekend retreat, on the other hand, has the advantage of capturing the students for an intensive period. If the retreat can be held off campus, students tend to be more involved and receptive.

A one-day orientation might be structured as follows:

8:45 A.M	COFFEE AND DONUTS
9:00	WELCOME AND INTRODUCTIONS—DISCUSS PURPOSE OF ORIENTATION
9:30	PRESENTATION ON CULTURE (E.G., THE VIDEO, "GOING INTERNATIONAL PART I: BRIDGING THE CULTURE GAP") AND LARGE GROUP DISCUSSION
10:30–NOON	SMALL GROUP MEETINGS TO REVIEW NUTS AND BOLTS
NOON	LUNCH (INTERNATIONAL FOODS OR DESSERTS IF POSSIBLE)
1:00–2:00	SMALL GROUP MEETINGS WITH RETURNEES
2:00–3:30	PRESENTATION ON CROSS-CULTURAL COMMUNICATION AND ADAPTATION WITH FILM (E.G., *CHAIRY TALE*) AND/OR ROLE PLAY[3]
3:30–3:45	BREAK—REFRESHMENTS
3:45–4:45	SMALL GROUP MEETINGS—"HOW TO LEARN" ABOUT TARGET COUNTRY AND THE UNITED STATES
4:45–5:30	WRAP-UP (QUESTIONS, HANDOUTS, EVALUATION)
5:30–6:30	DINNER—DISCUSSIONS WITH FACILITATORS
6:30–8:30	SIMULATION "BAFA BAFA"[4]
8:30	ENTERTAINMENT (INTERNATIONAL MUSIC, DANCING, ETC.)

For further ideas on structuring an orientation, advisers should read Sue Clarke, "The Orientation Retreat: Preparing 200 Students for Study in 20 Countries." (In *Culture, Learning, and the Disciplines*, edited by Josef Mestenhauser, et al, 82–89. Washington, D.C.: NAFSA, 1988.)

Undoubtedly an excellent form of orientation is an academic course that allows the students to investigate cross-cultural issues in depth. Such courses are becoming increasingly popular at colleges and universities across the country. There are also an increasing number of professional-development opportunities available for advisers interested in learning to teach such a course.[5]

Whatever the format, advisers must take care to recruit the most competent resource people available. In a university setting, these might include faculty members, community experts, international scholars and students, returnees, and—if the budget permits—overseas personnel. All resource people should be briefed prior to the orientation to clarify responsibilities and strategies. For example, ask returnees to prepare an hour or two of orientation for their peers by developing an outline for the session and preparing a handout. You might also warn them about pitfalls such as assuming that one's experiences will apply to everyone or getting sidetracked into travelogues.

Since education abroad is academic and experiential, one can argue that experiential techniques are particularly appropriate as a form of preparation. The cognitive methods should not be replaced, although you should consider blending and combining the two. The experiential method can include a broad range of activities: simulations, role playing, films, games, and field exercises. The Peace Corps and the Experiment in International Living have developed useful manuals describing experiential techniques and exercises (see appendix 1). You and your facilitators should be thoroughly familiar with such activities before attempting them with a group. You should also be prepared for some learner resistance and for the fact that experiential learning is often more time consuming and risky than presentations and lectures.

If you decide to incorporate experiential techniques, you should nevertheless begin the session with traditional approaches. This will help to build trust within the group and make it easier for students to make the transition to the emotionally more risky experiential methods. Careful sequencing is also important with regard to content. It is usually better to begin with the culture general and move on to the culture specific so as to provide a framework and then to hold the students' interest. (They are naturally inclined to want to hear about their own target countries.) Whatever your decisions, you should realize that attention to sequencing, pacing, and differences in learning styles are extremely important to the success of the orientation.

It is a good idea to begin any announcement about the orientation program, and the session itself, with a brief explanation of why it is necessary. Although many students genuinely welcome the opportunity to prepare for study abroad, they naturally resist planning for far-off events, especially if the orientation is held in May and the program participants are not leaving until late August. Thus, it is important to explain what the orientation is all about and what it can and cannot do. Students should be disabused of the idea that an orientation can prepare them for all eventualities and cover all topics. Rather, they should learn that this brief time together is intended to provide a foundation on which they can build.

What you cover in your orientation depends on the profile of your students' programs. Also, your students might be receiving other orientations. All high-quality programs are likely to offer some sort of on-site postarrival orientation program; the only exceptions might be for students enrolling directly in foreign universities, though many such institutions do offer new-student orientations. While it never hurts to go over the essential matters more than once, you should know what is awaiting your students, and then design your program to complement this. This may or may not be possible.

If you are working only with your own programs, then you should easily be able to find out what is done on-site by consulting with appropriate faculty or staff. Also, most reputable programs that recruit students nationally will send you literature on their on-site orientation programs. They should in any event welcome your inquiries. Nevertheless, you may still have to design your own orientation program based on the information at hand and some guesses about what is being done elsewhere.

Nuts and Bolts. The nuts-and-bolts portion of orientation is best designed to provide all straightforward, factual, and absolutely essential practical and academic information. A good handbook that lays out basic information is indispensable and will save much valuable time in the orientation sessions. It will also allow students who feel inundated with information during the formal sessions to review the material at their leisure.

Your checklist will probably contain most if not all the following:
- Logistics:
    a. Passports, visas, other essential documents
    b. International travel arrangements (if any)
    c. Housing, host families, meals, etc. (if part of own program)
    d. Packing, luggage, and shipping regulations
    e. Phoning, mail, and other communications
    f. Foreign currency, transferring money abroad, credit cards, etc.
    g. Postarrival travel information (Eurail passes, international ID cards, youth hostel cards, guidebooks, etc.)
- Academic information
    a. Preapproval forms for course work (if required)
    b. Credit-approval policies upon return
    c. Preregistration for the next term
- Legal considerations and responsibilities, waiver forms, etc.[6]

Health and safety issues (which are covered in greater detail in chapter 11) also need to be reviewed in any orientation program: medical and dental check-ups, including required inoculations; prescription medicine, as well as over-the-counter and prescription medication in sufficient supplies; and emergency medical needs (diabetes, epilepsy, allergy to penicillin). Students should bring extra eyeglasses, contact lenses, and a copy of their prescriptions, as well as ample proof of worldwide medical insurance coverage. They also need an informed awareness of potential health hazards and precautions and complete information on how and where to get medical help abroad.

Remind your students to be alert to threatening political situations that might lead to violence or terrorism against outsiders. They should also be aware of general crime patterns and the country's basic criminal and civil laws, including disorderliness, alcohol, drugs, driving, and so forth. With regard to both health and safety, a list of emergency contacts and telephone numbers is very important to have handy. Various pamphlets available from the U.S. Department of State—such as "Your Trip Abroad" and "Tips for Americans Residing Abroad"—can serve as valuable references for advisers on nuts-and-bolts issues, including passports, visas, customs regulations, and travel advisories.

In summary, the adviser must help students gain a command of the nuts and bolts—this gives them a sense of security—but at the same time make clear to them that not everything can be covered. Educators can be driven batty by the "How many towels will I need?" syndrome. The nuts and bolts must be handled thoroughly and professionally, but must not be allowed to dominate the orientation.

Introducing Cross-cultural Issues. Even though the nuts-and-bolts portion of your orientation programs is intended to concern itself with straightforward facts and information, cross-cultural issues may emerge almost immediately. If you are prepared to weave in cross-cultural information as appropriate, the presentations will be more useful and interesting. For example, if students are to live with host families, they will probably want to know where and with whom they will live, whether there is a commute to classes, whether meals will be provided, and how they can be reached by mail or phone. But this "information"—if you are in a position to supply it— is not devoid of a cultural context.

Even the simplest matter, such as providing the names of the family members, raises cross-cultural questions. How should the family members be addressed? Are first names appropriate? Should formal or informal forms of address (for example, *tu* or *vous* in French, *tu* or *usted* in Spanish) be used? Thus, in order to prepare for everyday life with a family—the basics of how to dress, eat, bathe, greet people, show affection—students need to gain insight into how and why family life and relationships in the host culture may differ from the United States. Do families value privacy? togetherness? Are there clearly defined gender roles? Are restrictions placed on women? Does the extended family play a large role? What is the role of children? What role does religion play? If students understand that family life in France tends to be more formal than in the United States, they will not be as inclined to interpret reserve as unfriendliness. If they know how expensive hot water and electricity are in Costa Rica, they will be less likely to offend with what are perceived as "wasteful" North American habits.

Although you cannot even begin to cover all such culture-specific questions that may arise during an orientation program, by being ready to focus in detail on some, you give the message that such apparently minor matters will shortly loom very large in their lives while abroad. The more thoroughly students understand underlying cultural values—such as determining why families behave as they do—the better they will be able to define their own roles and interact comfortably.

Just as the details of housing must be placed within a cultural context, so can the discussion you introduce on academics. For example, if students are to be partially or fully integrated into foreign universities, they need to know basics of how and why the foreign system is different from our own. Because they will probably be expected to function more independently than at home, they need to know something about the underlying philosophy of education so as not to conclude that the foreign university is unorganized or inefficient simply because there may be less supervision and regulation.

If you feel you need some expert advice on these and related matters, *Cross-Cultural Orientation: New Conceptualizations and Applications* and *Theories and Methods in Cross-Cultural Orientation*, as well as other books mentioned in appendix 1, should be consulted.

Culture-Specific Issues. International educators and specialists generally agree that the "how to learn" orientation is more effective than attempting to impart extensive information on host cultures in the limited time available. Moreover, if you have students going to a range of countries, there is no way that all culture-specific questions can be effectively answered, even in a preliminary way. The orientation time is therefore best spent emphasizing why students will have to take considerable initiative in order to gain the culture-specific knowledge they will need once they leave campus and arrive on distant shores.

One late-twentieth-century reality that you might want to address in your orientation is that there are few pure cultures left, especially in countries and capital cities that have seen a lot of immigration in recent decades. Thus, to prepare students going to London to expect to meet only the English and only to hear pure British English is to add to the shock they will feel when they have a roommate from Pakistan or Hong Kong and find they cannot understand the accent of the chap next door from Derbyshire. Nor will they find only the French in Paris or the Danes in Copenhagen. Indeed, contemporary European society is often as multicultural in composition, especially in the urban areas (and especially on university campuses) as anything American students might think they are leaving behind.

For traditional students from white, middle-class backgrounds, this awareness may bring some initial disappointment. For minority students, this news may be a relief in that they may believe such heterogeneity provides more social choices and options. For students trying to immerse themselves in German or Italian, being caught in a milieu where English is the common language may also cause some problems. Indeed, this situa-

143

tion may mean that students will have a far less national (albeit more *inter-national*) experience than they had planned. This is not, in and of itself, a bad thing, but it is probably not what most U.S. students are seeking.

If these realities are neglected in your orientation, your students may feel misled. You should therefore seek to discuss the realities of multiculturalism abroad. As culture-specific knowledge becomes less applicable, culture-general truths become more important than ever, as does the necessity of learning to live with people of widely different backgrounds.

When preparing students for study abroad in non-Western or Third World countries, advisers need to give more advanced attention to culture-specific information. Readings, films and slides, experiential techniques, and presentations by experts and returnees can be very effective. Students going to Japan, for example, should have a basic familiarity with everything from how to take a Japanese bath and use chopsticks to the philosophy of gift-giving to the nature of a collective society. Orientation for students going to Latin America should range from using public transportation and reacting to expressions of anti-Americanism to sensitizing oneself to the issues facing developing nations. Students going to any non-Western or Third World country should also have some concept of gender roles in that country and should reflect on how they will feel if they will be a minority.

As these issues suggest, a thorough orientation for non-Western and Third World countries is particularly demanding and may well require more time than for countries more similar to the United States—or than can be given in a general orientation program. The complexities of world multiculturalism cannot be adequately addressed in a limited time frame. But you would be remiss not to address these matters in some way.

Culture-General Issues. Helping students begin to understand broad cross-cultural perspectives and develop cross-cultural sensitivity may be the most crucial aim of any orientation program. Unless they have lived abroad before for an extended period of time, they will probably not be conscious of the profound ways in which any culture affects our lives—our sense of time, our beliefs, our relationships with nature, work, and other people. In particular, they will not understand how "American" they are. Not knowing this, they will be shocked to find that their assumptions, values, behaviors, and perspectives—which seem perfectly normal and natural to them at home—do not necessarily apply abroad. Although there is no way to forestall the fish-out-of-water sensation experienced by almost all students, especially at first, students can be made aware that at least mild culture shock is normal and to be expected. This will bolster their chances of making the necessary adjustments.

Students who have taken courses in cultural anthropology will have at least an intellectual understanding of these ideas. For others, the concept of culture—what it is, how it affects us, and how to cope—is succinctly and effectively described in Robert Kohls' *Survival Kit for Overseas Living*. You may also wish to assign other interesting readings such as "Body Ritual Among the Nacirema," which can be found in *Toward Internationalism,* or selected chapters in *Intercultural Communication: A Reader.* The films entitled *Going International* can also be used effectively in predeparture orientation.[7] Yet reading about culture and culture shock is not the same as experiencing it. Therefore, no orientation program should assure students that to know about another culture is the same thing as being completely comfortable living in it.

Still, it is worth trying to help students build some cross-cultural skills and attitudes prior to departure. Your goals might include exercises and discussions aimed at improving self-reflection, coping with transitions, communicating verbally and nonverbally, and developing sensitivity to and tolerance for differences. In his list of sixteen skills and traits "that make a difference," Robert Kohls emphasizes maintaining a sense of humor and living with some failures (*Survival Kit,* 71–73). However one might categorize and define essential coping strategies, you need to emphasize that the process of adjusting to a new culture and learning new intercultural skills is at times difficult and painful. Students must be prepared for the fact that while living abroad is often exhilarating, there are also periods of disappointment, homesickness, and frustration.

Many advisers find it useful to introduce the pertinent concept of culture shock and even to discuss the conjectural U- and W-shaped curves of cultural adjustment charted on a graph.[8] The argument is that if students understand that some form of psychological and social disorientation is a natural part of virtually every sojourner's experience, they will probably not feel as dismayed or worried as they might otherwise be when the symptoms emerge. It is possible, however, to overdo this discussion and to send unintended negative messages, even perhaps to create self-fulfilling prophecies. Stressing survival skills or coping mechanisms alone may suggest to students that the most they can expect is to merely survive or cope in a hostile environment, whereas the key is to prepare them to surmount these possible early frustrations so as to integrate themselves more fully into their new surroundings.[9]

Role-playing, culture-learning games, and simulations, such as "Bafa-Bafa" and Don Bachelder's "Martian Ambassador," when properly conducted, give students courage and help them assess values. If students can watch themselves as participant-observers in an unfamiliar group at home, they will learn how to deal constructively with their feelings abroad.

Americanness—Know Thyself. Although students readily accept the importance of learning about the host culture of the country in which they will be living, they may not at first see the importance of refreshing and expanding their knowledge about the United States. The orientation can help them understand that, as representatives of their country, they will be expected to be knowledgeable about many aspects of American history and current affairs. Also, they should understand that their observations of the host culture will be more meaningful if they have a basis for comparison.

An important aspect of the "how to learn" approach is stressing the need to develop curiosity and ask questions of oneself—and of others when appropriate. The *Trans-Cultural Study Guide* provides an excellent basis for independent learning through questioning. With regard to answering questions about one's own country, the "info-gram" entitled "Questions Asked About America" and the books *Citizen Ambassadors* and *American Ways* provide examples of the types of questions frequently asked of Americans, along with guidelines for responding.[10]

As we begin to help students develop the skills they will need to interact effectively with host nationals, we cannot neglect to give some attention to skills needed for interaction with other Americans. After all, many of our students travel and live abroad as part of a group of other Americans. Their psychological well-being and the success of their experience often seem to depend as much on their relationships with their American peers as with the host nationals. Thus, some time spent talking about group dynamics, peer pressure, and cooperation within groups will be well invested. If possible, the orientation should include some social activities and free time to help create a positive group identity prior to departure.

Global Citizenship. As students leave the United States and step into another culture, they are stepping into new responsibilities. During orientation, it is important for them to explore questions concerning their responsibilities in an interdependent world. The difficulties associated with this type of preparation are immediately apparent because you will be confronting political, social, moral, and even spiritual questions.

But if we avoid the issue of responsibility altogether or regard it as tangential, are we not in danger of doing what Munir Fasheh calls "talking about what to cook for dinner when our house is on fire"? In Fasheh's view, "international education should be mainly concerned with the development of a sense of responsibility toward ourselves, toward others, and toward future generations, all of which are threatened by psychological, social, and material structures which education has been, at least partially, responsible for building."[11] His views concur with the ideas of other educators such as Joan Bodner, Elise Boulding, and Betty Reardon, whose books provide valuable reading for advisers searching to define their own positions.

Reentry Programming

Though campus-based reentry programs have long been neglected—and do not exist in any form at many institutions—their importance is now widely recognized by education-abroad professionals. The most commonly expressed goals of such programs include helping students to:

- Readjust to America and American campus life after an intense period of living on the educational and social terms of a foreign culture
- Articulate their experiences to themselves and others
- Assimilate and incorporate what they learned abroad into their on-going degree studies
- Consider how they might build on what they have learned for post-graduate studies or career opportunities

Reentry programs have been neglected primarily because of the false assumption that students returning to a familiar environment do not encounter any serious problems. After all, the time spent abroad represents only a small portion of a student's life. Returning "home" should be easy. The startling truth may be quite the opposite: some researchers now suggest that reentry shock—also referred to as "reverse culture shock"—can be even more severe and debilitating than culture shock, perhaps for the very reason that the problems are so unexpected.[12] It can also be traumatic for a different reason: life responsibilities (such as getting serious about a career) may have been shunted aside while abroad, and all of a sudden become pressing.

Reverse culture shock can include such symptoms as disorientation, alienation from family and friends, rejection of one's own culture, boredom, and lack of direction. More specifically, students may find that they have little in common with their old friends; that beyond polite inquiries no one seems very interested in listening to them talk about their experiences abroad; that attitudes of family and friends seem parochial; and that there is seemingly no place to go with the knowledge and skills learned abroad.[13] Moreover, being back at school seems restrictive and unexciting.

Although many institutions have become increasingly aware of the need for formalized reentry programs—or at least informal counseling—to address the above issues, they are struggling to develop techniques and models. In designing your approaches, it might be helpful to consider three phases: what might be done while students are still abroad, what might be done immediately after they return, and long-term support and advising.

What to Do Before Students Return. By keeping in contact with students while they are abroad, you can facilitate a smooth transition home. If they are kept informed and sent necessary information for their return—on-campus housing forms, academic registration materials, financial aid applications—most snags will be avoided and students will be less likely to feel they have been forgotten. Recent catalogs, issues of the student newspaper, and other relevant information can help the students stay abreast of changes on campus and thus be better prepared for their return. Especially since one of the sources of ongoing student anxiety concerns getting credit, you should reassure them that if they take their studies seriously, the prearrangements you have made together should assure the anticipated amount of credit.

As is the case with predeparture orientation, however, what you can do from this side depends to a great degree on the range of programs your students enter abroad. If you run only your own programs and work closely with your staff overseas, obviously you can do more than if your students are enrolled in a lot of different programs and scattered all over the world.

If your students are scattered and are in lots of different programs, you may at this stage only be able to send a newsletter containing some advice and counsel. The effectiveness of such correspondence will depend to some degree on whether it is part of a series of letters your office has written to students during their time abroad, or one of the few times they have heard from you. It may also depend on the rapport you established with students during your advising sessions and your predeparture orientation.

In such a letter, you should let students know that: (1) you look forward to seeing them again, hope the experience has lived up to expectations, and similar positive sentiments; (2) you know they might have changed and grown, and that many things may now look different; and (3) you are ready to assist them in any readjustments they feel are necessary.

If your students are on your own institution's programs, the reentry program should begin in the host country a month or two before departure—depending on the length of the stay overseas. Overseas personnel should meet with students to discuss and prepare for the reentry process. The simple act of alerting students to the potential for stress or dissatisfaction may help to minimize difficulties later on. It is important here, as during orientation, not to predispose students to react negatively upon return.

On-Campus Reentry Programs. Marking the occasion of your students' return to campus by some type of formal welcome home reception, dinner, or party is almost always worth the effort. This gives students the opportunity to come together, talk about their experiences, and celebrate with faculty and other invited guests. But such occasions may be more possible on small campuses than large ones.

Whether or not you host a social event, some sort of formal general meetings or sessions should be attempted. As with the social event, it will be hard to gather in all returned students—much harder than it might have been with predeparture programs. Still, such meetings will be welcomed by many returnees. They need the opportunity to talk about their experiences and will recognize that others who have had a roughly comparable experience will be more likely to empathize with them than the other students on campus. There will be many issues of interest or concern, from worries about credit to more personal anxieties. Moreover, students who may be going through the same type of reentry malaise can often help each other by voicing the difficulties and discussing possible solutions. This is also a good opportunity for you to be able to identify students who are experiencing severe reentry problems so that you can later recommend personal counseling, as appropriate.

The first key to having a successful group session is to make sure that everyone has a chance to participate equally. This might mean holding several sessions so that groups are small enough for informal talking. The second key is for you to discover what the students are feeling. They will likely relate that their experience abroad was "special" and "unique" and not easily explained to those who have not had it. But most important of all, the session must balance *their* understandable desires to celebrate and remember what they have accomplished with *your* objective of helping them build on this experience during the coming year and thereafter.

At the California State University, an effective one-day reentry workshop has been designed to address reentry adjustment problems by connecting them with career concerns.[14] The workshop is structured as follows:

8:00 A.M.
- ARRIVAL, COFFEE

8:30 A.M.–NOON
- INTRODUCTIONS
- SMALL AND FULL GROUP DISCUSSION OF REENTRY CONCERNS
- "RETURN FROM INTERNATIONAL PROGRAMS"—A TRAGICOMEDY IN TWO ACTS
- CONTINUING YOUR INTERNATIONAL EXPERIENCE—FULL GROUP DISCUSSION WITH HANDOUT
- WHAT DO YOU KNOW ABOUT THE WORLD?—A SHORT QUIZ WITH CHALLENGING QUESTIONS
- MEMORY LANE—A SHARING OF SOUVENIRS

NOON–1:00 P.M.
- LUNCH

1:00 P.M.–5:00 P.M.
- "THE WORLD SAYS HELLO"—A VIDEO FROM THE MONTEREY INSTITUTE OF FOREIGN STUDIES REGARDING JOBS AROUND THE WORLD
- WORKING OVERSEAS—PRESENTATIONS BY REPRESENTATIVES FROM BUSINESS, THE PEACE CORPS, AND OTHERS
- WORKING IN THE U.S./ JOBS WITH AN INTERNATIONAL DIMENSION—PRESENTATION BY REPRESENTATIVES FROM EDUCATION, TRAVEL, BUSINESS, AND SO FORTH
- WHERE TO FIND THE JOBS?—DISCUSSION OF SOURCES AND BIBLIOGRAPHIES
- EVALUATION AND CLOSING STATEMENTS

The academic course is a more ambitious and comprehensive reentry model, and it is being used successfully at a limited number of colleges and universities.[15] This course is designed and taught by one or more members of the faculty, often in conjunction with the education-abroad adviser. Sometimes the course is directly linked with a predeparture course or course component, and it usually combines cross-cultural theory with culture-specific content. Students draw on their recent experience of entering a foreign culture, living in it, then leaving and returning to their home culture. They are also given opportunities to develop and extend the culture-specific knowledge they gained from living in a particular country or region. In some cases, such a course also enrolls foreign students, as part of their orientation to living and learning in the United States. Although this is not a course for every student, for some it is extremely useful and gratifying.

Program Evaluation. An important part of reentry is the evaluation process. Students should have the opportunity to evaluate the program they experienced and to reflect on their own progress and achievements. The instruments for capturing their insights must be sophisticated and ample time needs to be devoted to the task. The results are invaluable both in making adjustments to your own programs and in advising students about your own and other programs. In addition, it is highly recommended that you hold individual interviews or group sessions to discuss your conclusions (see chapter 16).

Postreturn Counseling. Once the students have been welcomed home, completed their evaluations, and resumed their normal studies, there is a strong temptation to view the cycle as complete. But very important work still lies ahead. You can play an important role in helping students identify with appropriate professors, courses, and departments. Many advisers routinely inform faculty of which students in their classes have been abroad and may have special expertise or perspectives to share in class. You are in a position to encourage all students who studied foreign languages overseas to continue to do so through course work, independent study, and other opportunities such as language houses and conversation circles.

Should students find that their experiences abroad have caused them to rethink or modify their majors, you can help them identify new areas of study and refer them to appropriate departments. They may even wish to explore new majors or minors in international studies, international business, or international relations. Even if students make no changes in their major or minor fields of study, you can help them to identify courses with international content. Advisers can also assist students who wish to pursue graduate study in an international field.

In addition to providing academic counseling, you can also facilitate returnees' involvement in cocurricular activities. Among the many ways for returnees to act as resource people and at the same time continue their own learning are:
- Becoming involved with international students (Big Brother/Sister, host family, ESL tutor, International Club)

- Acting as peer counselors to help with recruiting and orientation
- Joining international organizations (Amnesty International, peace groups, etc.)
- Participating in other international activities on campus and in the community (speakers' bureau, international symposia)

Career Counseling. There is no question but that a large number of students, having returned from a meaningful time overseas—from whatever program, from whatever destination—will have decided to (1) go abroad again as soon as is practicable and/or (2) pursue a career that involves travel and work abroad. You should therefore make sure that these returned students visit the school's career counselor as soon as possible. On the other hand, some career-counseling offices, even those with international career resources, have little experience with students who wish to exploit what they learned on an education-abroad program toward a definite career goal. Thus, it makes sense to work with this office to develop joint programs to assist students in designing strategies to market themselves.

Summary

The increasing emphasis on developing effective predeparture and reentry programs reflects an understanding that the time abroad must be embedded in an educational continuum. Education-abroad advisers and administrators have meaningful pedagogical roles to play in working with faculty to prepare students to make the most of their new learning and living environment, maintain a line of contact during the experience, and finally assist them in the complicated process of reintegration into degree studies, campus life, and career preparation.

Notes

1. The term *ethnorelativism* is used by Milton Bennett to describe the final stage in the development of intercultural sensitivity ("A Developmental Approach to Training for Intercultural Sensitivity," in *Theories and Methods in Cross-Cultural Orientation,* 179–186).
2. For a stimulating discussion of the multidimensional approach, see Janet Marie Bennett's article, "Modes of Cross-Cultural Training," in *Theories and Methods in Cross-Cultural Orientation,* 117–134.
3. The *Chairy Tale* is an intriguing ten-minute silent film available from the Syracuse University film rental service. For suggestions on using the film, see Pusch's *Multicultural Education,* 201–203. Further information on cross-cultural films can be found in Pusch's book (pp. 270–275) and in Howard Shapiro's article "Suggestions for Improving Film Discus-

sions" in Batchelder's *Beyond Experience,* 75–77, and in Ellen Summerfield's *Crossing Cultures Through Film* (Intercultural Press, forthcoming).

4. This and other cross-cultural simulations written by Garry Shirts can be ordered from Simile II (P.O. Box 910, Del Mar, CA 92014) or the Intercultural Press. A discussion of Bafa Bafa can be found in Pusch's *Multicultural Education,* 175–177. A popular and stimulating exercise, it is, however, rather complicated and requires practice before attempting it with students.

5. The Intercultural Communication Institute (8835 SW Canyon, Suite 238, Portland, OR 97225) offers excellent summer workshops. Similar opportunities are available through NAFSA and SIETAR (The International Society for Intercultural Training and Research, 733 15th St., N.W., Washington, D.C. 20005).

6. The waiver form—or student-agreement form—should outline overall program policy and regulations, such as rules of conduct, grounds for dismissal from the program, financial and/or academic penalties for early withdrawal from the program, and a disclaimer for responsibility from accidents or injuries incurred during periods of travel or resulting from circumstances beyond the university's control.

7. Cross-cultural films and videos entitled "Going International" and "Valuing Diversity" are available from the Intercultural Press. Before showing these films, advisers should explain that they were made for the business world, but the ideas can be applied to student travelers as well.

8. The term *culture shock* was first used by the anthropologist K. Oberg in *Culture Shock and the Problem of Adjustment to New Cultural Environments* (Washington, D.C.: Department of State, Foreign Service Institute, 1958); see also S. Lysgaard, "Adjustment in a Foreign Society: Norwegian Fulbright Grantees Visiting the United States," *International Social Science Bulletin* 7 (1955): 45–51; and J. T. Gullahorn and J. E. Gullahorn, "An Extension of the U-curve Hypothesis," *Journal of Social Issues* 19, no. 3 (1963): 33–47.

9. For an insightful discussion of how language may create negative expectations, see James McCaffery, "Independent Effectiveness," in *Theories and Methods in Cross-Cultural Orientation,* 159–178; see also Peter S. Adler, "The Transitional Experience: An Alternative View of Culture Shock," *Humanistic Psychology* 15, no. 4 (Fall 1975): 13–23.

10. "Background Notes on the Countries of the World" are factual pamphlets available from Superintendent of Documents, U.S. Government Printing Office, Washington, DC 20402. "Culturgrams" are short briefings on ninety-six different countries available from Brigham Young University, David M. Kennedy Center for International Studies, Publications Services, 280 HRCB, Provo, UT 84602.

11. Fasheh, Munir, "Talking about What to Cook for Dinner When Our House Is on Fire: The Poverty of Existing Forms of International Education." *Harvard Educational Review Journal* 55 (February 1985): 123–126.

12. Nan E. Sussman discusses the hypothesis that "reentry stress and shock is more severe than initial entry shock" in her article, "Reentry Research and Training," in *Theories and Methods in Cross-Cultural Orientation,* 241.

13. A two-page "Inventory of Reentry Problems" is found in "Reentry/Transition Seminars. Report of the Wingspread Colloquium" (1976): 4–5.

14. My Yarabinec, formerly campus relations coordinator for international programs, California State University at Long Beach, has contributed this reentry workshop model. It is given here in somewhat abbreviated form.

15. For more information on such courses send requests with stamped, self-addressed envelope to Dr. Judith Martin (Department of Communication, Arizona State University, Tempe, AZ 85287-1205), or Dr. Bruce La Brack (Department of Sociology, University of the Pacific, Stockton, CA 94211).

PART THREE

Program Development and Evaluation

PROGRAM PLANNING, BUDGETING, AND IMPLEMENTATION
*Contributors: Jack Henderson, Tom Roberts,
Paula Spier, and Henry Weaver*

PROGRAM DESIGN AND STRATEGIES
Contributors: Joseph Navari and Heidi Soneson

WORK ABROAD AND INTERNATIONAL CAREERS
Contributor: William Nolting

PROGRAM EVALUATION
Contributors: Michael Laubscher and Ronald Pirog

13

Program Planning, Budgeting, and Implementation

Contributors: Jack Henderson, Tom Roberts,
Paula Spier, and Henry Weaver,

New study-abroad programs appear each academic year, often in astonishing numbers. Frequently, these programs disappear within a short period of time. What distinguishes programs that survive from those that do not is largely a matter of proper planning and implementation. The purpose of this chapter, therefore, is to demonstrate how much thought and effort it takes both to set up an academic program abroad and to sustain it over the years.

With so many established programs in place, the first question is, does your institution need another? Many colleges believe it makes economic sense to have one's own programs. This may or may not be true. As demonstrated below, starting up a new program means a major investment of human and financial resources. Depending on how it is budgeted and supported, however, it might lose money, break even, or create a small surplus.

Even if the new program makes ultimate academic and economic sense for your institution, it also represents a commitment that has to be sustained, perhaps over a long period of time, often in changing circumstances. The willingness to make this commitment is therefore essential. If there is little commitment or scanty start-up resources, it might be more prudent to consider working jointly with another institution, a consortium, or an agency—or simply utilizing extant programs.

For colleges currently offering no programs, setting up the first program overseas is likely to be a major administrative undertaking—more so than at institutions with a number of other programs already in place. On the other hand, even if you have gone through the domestic process before on your own campus, campus politics and economics have probably changed. Certainly circumstances overseas will differ from one country to the next. What worked in France may not work in Germany or China; what was possible in 1973 may now be impossible.

Given the welter of institutional contexts, below are provided three case studies on the creation of three successful programs. The first, Dickinson College's French-language junior-year program in Toulouse, focuses on how a small, liberal arts college established a department-based program for its own students. The second gives an overview of how a public state university system, the University of California, through its Education-Abroad Program, set up a multifaceted exchange program in a developing country, Indonesia. The third concentrates on how the Institute for European Studies, acting on behalf of its constituent member colleges and universities, began a semester program in the social sciences in London.

Three Case Histories

The Dickinson College Program in Toulouse
By Jack Henderson

In September 1984 the first group of junior-year students, most of them French majors, began the academic year at the Dickinson College Study Center in Toulouse. Their arrival at our new language-based junior year abroad (JYA) program marked the end of a long, complex planning process.

During the previous two decades, French majors and other students with strong French-language preparation had spent one or both semesters of their junior year in France, participating in several high-ranking academic programs sponsored by individual U.S. colleges and universities or by two consortia of institutions with which we had formal links. Those eighteen to twenty-five students per year seemed to have the best possible options—programs providing a variety of academic offerings, different locations in France among which to choose, and preferential admissions in some cases.

However, as the number of students studying abroad in the early 1980s swelled nationally, there were increased pressures on available slots in established JYA programs. At the same time, the number of our own French majors continued to grow, creating keener competition for admission into the highest-quality programs. The very best continued to be accepted, but a small but disturbing number of qualified students found that their options were severely limited.

Even more troubling, perhaps, was the unevenness of our majors' academic experiences overseas. They returned to campus for their senior year equipped with diverse levels of language ability, analytical skills, and exposure to course content. Without direct input into, or control over, their junior year academics, we had difficulty designing a senior-year curriculum that was coherent and appropriate for all. We became convinced that the integrity of our major was at stake and that we needed to create our own program in France.

The necessary expertise to design and implement a new program existed in our own department. We had both French and U.S. faculty members of different ages and at various points in their careers. All had lived and traveled widely in France; all were knowledgeable about study abroad.

In addition, our department benefited from Dickinson's strong support for international education in general and study abroad in particular. The department's needs and aspirations were recognized by both the college administration and faculty from other disciplines. So, working with colleagues from all the language departments and across the curriculum, we designed a multifaceted institutional grant proposal in international education. The result was two grants from the National Endowment for the Humanities, which provided, among other things, the start-up funds for our own program in France. (Support for our proposed JYA program was so strong that the administration had pledged start-up monies from college funds had the grant not been received.)

In designing our program, members of the department fashioned clear goals for academic content and design.

1. A first-rate overseas study component was seen as essential to provide continuity with our on-campus academic program.

2. Experience had clearly demonstrated the superior linguistic and cultural attainments of students who had spent a full academic year in France rather than only one semester. A full-year program was thus deemed mandatory.

3. Partial academic integration of our students in the French educational system was seen as highly desirable. We therefore arranged for our students to take a portion of their course work at a French university.

4. In our desire to maximize the students' linguistic and cultural integration into French life, we arranged private housing with French families.

5. Because institutional financial aid monies had not previously been applicable to study in France, we built into our program budget an annual contribution to the on-campus financial aid budget, thereby ensuring that all academically qualified students could participate in our program, regardless of financial need.

The task of choosing a location in France was extremely important if we were to realize the goals just enumerated. In addition, discussion surrounded the following issues: first, we agreed that an urban environment would offer the greatest exposure to French culture, the most opportunities for student internships, and the widest range of family contexts in which to house our students. Second, it seemed to us imperative to identify a site not already saturated with American JYA programs.

We recognized important benefits to be gained by establishing strong interinstitutional links between our institution and a French university. Such a linkage would

• Provide local university courses in various academic disciplines, including French, in which to place our students

• Encourage interaction between our students and their French peers through opportunities to join university associations, sports teams, and other kinds of extracurricular activities

• Provide access to university faculty who could teach our core courses for us and with whom we might arrange faculty exchanges with the Carlisle campus

• Attract highly qualified French university students, who could visit Carlisle, live in our French House on campus, and assist the department in its language laboratory and cocurricular activities.

We sought advice from officials at the French Cultural Affairs Office in New York. They suggested possible universities and gave us the names of key contacts. We also made use of professional contacts that our department members had at other French universities. We identified several possible sites before narrowing them down to two. In the process, we learned that officials at the University of Toulouse had been making corresponding inquiries in the United States.

Upon learning that a four-person delegation from Toulouse was planning to visit the United States, we invited them to Dickinson to discuss possible joint ventures. After a short, productive visit, the delegation invited us to visit their campus in Toulouse to meet faculty and administrators. These exchanges laid the groundwork for what was to become a long-range partnership.

Up to this point, we had spent about eight months in the discussion and planning stages. We now began the task of implementation by drawing up a chart of tasks to be accomplished on both sides of the Atlantic, many of them of a nitty-gritty nature, along with month-by-month deadlines and a designation of person(s) responsible for each task.

Among the tasks were the following:

1. Members of our department made three more visits to Toulouse to negotiate details of our formal agreements with two branches of the University of Toulouse. They also collected syllabi (where available) and visited classes in order to identify courses appropriate for American students.

2. Meetings with local faculty and administrators identified professors to teach in our program and helped to arrange for a visiting guest professor from Toulouse in Carlisle the coming academic year.

3. We established our program's legal status (as an association) in France, took photographs for the future program brochure, and established necessary banking arrangements.

4. We were careful to cultivate contacts with key representatives of the city government, as well as cultural and civic organizations (such as Association France–Etats Unis, the local chamber of commerce, and the *syndicat d'initiative*).

5. We met with representatives of French and international corporations with links to the United States and thus likely to be interested in an American educational presence in Toulouse.

6. We began to recruit families for our students through classified ads in the local newspaper plus using personal contacts established in our visits.

7. In locating a "home" for our program in Toulouse, we researched various options, including renting classroom and office space from the university (which was in short supply), renting necessary space on the open market, or purchasing property for a permanent center. We preferred the third option because it provided both permanency and an identifiable location. We were, of course, guided in our decision by our college treasurer's knowledge of the international financial market, as well as by advice given by members of the board of trustees.

The college purchased and began renovations on a villa in a parklike residential setting on the Canal du Midi. These transactions required considerable paperwork and time to hire an attorney, to secure legal documents including powers of attorney, to hire an architect and a contractor, and to supervise the conversion of a former private home into an academic center. We had to purchase furniture, office equipment, supplies, and an automobile for the director's use, as well as to arrange for telephones and other utilities. Although our students would have access to university libraries as well as to the municipal library, we sought to assure easy availability of basic materials by setting up our own modest library including multiple copies of key reference works.

Fortunately, the building was large enough to provide an apartment for our director on the top floor in addition to classrooms, a library, student study facilities, a small computer-equipped writing center, lounge, reception area, and office space on the lower two floors. At the time, the U.S. dollar was unusually strong; the result was an important investment that has since increased sharply in value.

8. Staffing concerns also occupied our attention. As noted above, we believed strongly that continuity between the home campus and the year abroad could best be assured by rotating all members of our department into the Toulouse directorship in two-year cycles. The director's responsibilities were designated as one-half teaching and one-half administrative, a model that had worked well for the college in other overseas settings. To assure permanency and continuity on-site, we hired a native administrative assistant on a nearly full-time basis. Her duties include occasional secretarial work, but more importantly, she performs many ongoing, routine, time-consuming (and often bureaucratic) tasks.

We also contracted the services of an accountant to oversee bookkeeping and to pay salaries, social security taxes, and other financial obligations. Finally, as noted earlier, to teach our core courses, we recruited and hired local faculty whom we pay on an hourly basis, according to the French university pay scale for their position. We arranged orientation meetings with them to explain the art of syllabus writing, American course expectations, grade conversion, and the like.

While all of this was happening over a period of seven or eight months in Toulouse, we were no less busy in the United States.

We designed our JYA core curriculum, to be taught for our students only, as a logical extension of the on-campus academic program by providing (1) a coherent integration of the study of language, literature, and civilization; (2) a logical progression from sophomore to junior to senior years; and (3) coordinated use of course materials both in Carlisle and in France.

Responsibilities for recruitment, selection, and orientation of students were shared by department members. One person was designated as the on-campus coordinator and served as contact person for potential applicants. We held information meetings and published a brochure describing the program in detail and noting the prerequisites we had established: good academic standing, junior-class status, good physical and emotional health, completion of a French literary analysis course, and appropriate mastery of the French language (such as an intermediate-high rating on the ACTFL/ETS Oral Proficiency test).

Completed applications included recommendation forms from faculty in French and other departments; applicants were also interviewed by the coordinator. Admission decisions were made at department meetings. After acceptance, each student was paired with a student returned from France to facilitate the orientation process. Group orientation meetings in the spring semester were supplemented by a Toulouse Program *Orientation Handbook* sent to participants and their families.

By the time the first group of students arrived in Toulouse, nearly everything was in place. The first year was not without a few hitches. But overall, our careful planning had resulted in a highly successful program.

The University of California System Program in Indonesia
By Henry Weaver

The primary reason for a university (or, in our case, a university system) to begin a program overseas should be to expand and diversify its academic program. Faculty at the University of California (UC) encouraged the Education-Abroad Program (EAP) to open a program in Indonesia to allow increased opportunities for UC students to learn the Indonesian language, for area studies, and for study of the arts in Indonesia. We were also aware that Indonesia, the fifth most populous country in the world, had almost no study-abroad programs.

Fortuitously, the California legislature had just acted to make development into the Pacific Rim a state priority. It made funds available to provide incentive scholarships for students and to facilitate faculty exchanges. At the request of the university president, EAP developed a five-year proposal for increasing programs in the Pacific Rim. With resources available, a program in Indonesia became part of the larger Pacific Rim planning.

Most academic interest in Indonesia came from three campuses of the

University of California where Indonesian was being taught (Berkeley, Santa Cruz, and Los Angeles). Berkeley taught several years of Indonesian; Santa Cruz taught two quarters; and a student at UCLA could study the language on a special basis. At the request of EAP, the South and Southeast Asia Center at Berkeley helped to set up consultations with many UC faculty throughout the system. Its own interest was primarily in the social sciences and the language. At Santa Cruz and UCLA a network of involvement with Indonesia also existed, though primarily in the arts. Students were already involved in field work in music, dance, and theater. Faculty on different UC campuses therefore had different but complementary interests, contacts, and innovative ideas for an Indonesia program abroad.

We researched the relative standings of the major universities in Indonesia, including their ability to teach the language to foreigners. What we learned reinforced the conclusion that visits to the University of Indonesia might be necessary, as well as to the principal teacher-education university in Jakarta, and to several institutions in Bandung, Bogor, Yogyakarta and Denpasar. Malang was not investigated because other U.S. universities were already active there.

Ford Foundation representatives and an Indonesian who formerly taught at UC confirmed most of the information that we had gathered. In Indonesia, higher education is controlled by the ministry of education and national concerns are taken into consideration in designing exchanges. Contacts with the director of higher education were made on the first visit.

In addition to looking at course availability, quality of instruction, and library resources, each university visit also examined practical living needs: What were the options for students' living and eating quarters? What would they cost? How could they be arranged? What were the health conditions and what medical resources were available?

As a public system, UC is committed to exchange relationships, so the cost consideration began with a discussion of how the university could meet the needs of the host university. Would it be best for students from the host country to go to the United States as undergraduates or as graduate students? Would they seek degrees, or be able to earn credit that would transfer back? Would faculty exchange or training be desired? Were there currency controls that limited the way in which exchange-related payments could be made? What steps would be necessary for approval of tentative programs within the host university and beyond?

At the time of the first field investigation, the broad strokes of the academic program we wished to establish were clear, but there were a lot of specific concerns:

• High-quality language instruction was essential. Since some UC campuses offered no Indonesian language, course work would need to be available at the beginning level as well as at more advanced levels.

• We needed courses in the social sciences, including area studies.

• Some students needed courses in music, dance, art, and theater, ideally in various locations, since the *gamelan,* for example, is played quite differently in West Java, Central Java, and Bali.

• What support systems did UC students in Indonesia need to function at a satisfactory academic level and with due concern for their physical needs?

• How could we ensure that evaluation of students' work would be forthcoming in adequate time and in a usable form to get credit recorded on their transcripts?

• How would we gather the information that the academic senate uses to examine each course in which students enroll?

• Would enough students participate in the program to make it cost-effective to place a UC professor in the field to take care of these details, or would a local liaison be available to do the job?

After extensive investigation, a rather complex UC program emerged. Gadja Mada University, in Yogyakarta, was chosen as the primary contact and a summer language program was arranged. Here seemed to be an institution with a progressive attitude. It was well administered and had an openness to new ideas. Institutions specializing in the arts were available in Yogyakarta, Bandung, and Denpasar. Padjadjaran University in Bandung could also be entered for some fields of study.

• Students could come from any UC campus and study at three different levels.

• Students with no Indonesian would be encouraged to begin one summer, find a method of language maintenance during the next year, and then return for a full year the following summer.

• For students staying the full year, the summer study would be an intensive language program (ILP). The rest of the year could be taken in regular courses taught in Indonesian by continuation at Gadja Mada or by transferring to one of four other institutions.

The plan for the Indonesian program was presented to an all-university committee of the faculty senate, which oversees the Education-Abroad Program. The plan was then submitted to the Board of Regents for approval before drawing up contracts. When these were executed by the university counsel, they were submitted to the Indonesian universities involved. After these institutions had ironed out some differences from the original planning, they presented the contracts to the Indonesian ministry of education for approval. When these steps were completed, the contracts were signed and the program was ready to begin.

Meanwhile, the EAP office on each campus needed to get enough detail to be able to recruit and counsel prospective students. This called for information fliers and, later, printed brochures. Scanty information about a fledgling program is always a source of frustration to the counselors in campus offices, who need to respond to detailed questions from students.

Once applications were received, each campus office arranged for faculty to interview prospective participants as a part of final selection. The systemwide EAP office then arranged transportation, visa information, health insurance forms, and all the usual details involved in getting students to the foreign site.

Procedures for submitting actual courses to the faculty senate for approval, getting students registered into the courses, and recording their grades onto the transcripts were well established at UC, so these procedures were followed routinely. The UC Study Center in Indonesia was responsible for translating the Indonesian grading system into UC grades.

Finally, after the program was under way, steps were undertaken to correct our first-year problems. This involved considerable rearrangement of the ILP because some of the agreed-on methods did not materialize. The process of evaluation and change will continue as long as the program operates.

The Institute for European Studies Program in London
By Tom Roberts

The Institute for European Studies (IES), based in Chicago, administers programs on behalf of a nationwide consortium of colleges and universities, both private and public. Issues of program development are complex and require the consensus of a variety of constituencies at many points in the process. The following account illustrates the processes undertaken to establish a new program. Since the London program was established, IES has expanded to include programs in Asia and is now known formally as the Institute for European and Asian Studies.

Several members of the consortium had, over a two- to three-year period, expressed an interest to IES in developing a new program in Great Britain. At the time, very few British universities were interested in accommodating U.S. undergraduates. The issue of whether to establish a British program was brought to the curriculum committee, which consists of representatives of several consortium members. They decided to undertake a broad survey of all IES member institutions to determine "new program interest"—not limited to Britain.

Although quite reasonable and conservative, this procedure is not without drawbacks. Where immediate investment of institutional resources is not in question, institutional interest in off campus-programs ranges widely. So, although the survey results indeed indicated agreement that Great Britain would be a good place for a new program, the survey also produced a long list of other desirable program sites. The survey did help, however, to narrow the issue a bit. The committee's next step was therefore to examine the actual range of available administrative capability—taking geography, academic experience, and budget into account.

Most of the staff were, by academic background, specialists in either the humanities or social sciences. This meant that attempts to set up a program with a science or engineering bias would have proven difficult. The geographical and academic issues impinged on the budgetary—it was clearly most economical for IES to establish an arts-based program somewhere in Europe. Other factors included political stability and what other high-quality programs currently existed.

It was agreed that IES should not develop programs in areas where good study-abroad options were already available. Too many programs inevitably result in lowered academic standards in all programs offered in that country. The committee concluded, however, that few good programs (of the sort it was envisioning) were operating in Great Britain at the time. It was further decided to locate the program in London because of its many resources. The committee recommended to the full consortium at its annual meeting the establishment of a London program. The issue was formally proposed and ratified by the full body. The committee and staff were then authorized to proceed with the development of the program.

The program's precise curricular nature was worked out over a period of several months. The IES consortium consisted of close to forty colleges and universities nationwide, mostly small, liberal arts schools, but with a few larger, more broad-based institutions as well. Academic resources were available for a program with almost any curricular bias. Ultimately, the program's shape was dictated by (1) IES staff resources (i.e., academic expertise); (2) student interest, as determined by a survey (results were somewhat inconclusive but showed a slight preference for a program in the social sciences); (3) a historical bias of IES toward social science–based programs; (4) contacts overseas, who were largely faculty at the London School of Economics and Political Science.

Working with a subcommittee made up of faculty from the disciplines to be represented on the program, the curriculum committee studied the issue of ideal program length, whether semester or full year. At this time students were leaning toward semester-long programs, as opposed to a full year. The committee found that there were numerous opportunities for a full academic year of study at several British universities; fewer options existed for the many students who could not afford to be abroad for this amount of time.

The IES staff includes a stateside director of program development (who also serves as staff representative to the curriculum committee) and a talented group of program directors of existing IES European programs. These European-based directors possessed not only expertise in administering programs but also academic contacts in London. This was particularly true of the director of IES Vienna, who was born and educated in Britain and well connected with academic circles in London. These contacts proved invaluable in establishing and shaping the program, especially in recruiting faculty.

IES custom is to use only indigenous faculty to teach in its programs. Initial interviews were carried out in London by the director of program development and the Vienna IES director. All appointments were screened and ratified by the curriculum committee, which also reviewed and approved all course syllabi, descriptions, and reading lists. During this process of faculty selection and course approval, a fair amount of interchange took place between the U.S. academics (mainly the members of the subcommittee) and their British counterparts concerning course content. Under discussion were the level of the course (in this case upper-division work because all IES programs were geared to junior-year students), contact hours, length of course, credit weightings, and grading.

During this period the IES director of program development and the director of the Vienna program worked out many of the program's logistical details, such as (1) arranging for student housing; (2) finding office space for the program administrator; (3) resolving tax and legal issues; and (4) locating classroom space and library resources, which are critical to a freestanding program. It was decided to provide students membership in the Senate House library of the University of London and the library of the London School of Economics. In addition, a small textbook and reference library would be established on the program premises; classes would also be held at this site.

The committee then turned its attention to the selection of a program director. IES believes strongly in directors who are able to commit to a longterm tenure. Another criterion was solid academic qualifications because the director would need to deal effectively with the local British faculty. The director also should be sensitive to the needs of American students and the requirements of the U.S. system. Most important, however, was IES's conviction (born out of long experience) that the tasks of running an overseas program are demanding and specialized; they take time to master. Longrange continuity in this post was therefore seen as essential.

It is almost impossible to find a U.S. academic who not only has appropriate qualifications but would also be willing to leave an American college or university position for an extended period. Given these facts and criteria, an indigenous academic seemed the only appropriate course—though, as with any appointment, finding the right person was most difficult. Once selected, the director was put through a training program that included a visit to the campuses of several IES consortium members in the United States and some time at the administrative headquarters of IES in Chicago. The newly chosen director also spent an extended period at an IES center in Europe watching an experienced program director in action.

As the program was taking shape, the process of publicizing this new IES offering began. Within a consortium, the very process of program development is an element in the publicity of the program. But this notice is never enough on its own. IES staff prepared brochures and posters for nationwide distribution, as well as arranged for specific on-campus promotion by representatives of the consortium. Such promotional efforts were judged to be especially important because IES has no direct access to students on campus or the recruiting advantages of the campus-based programs. Yet, to ensure selectivity while providing sufficient numbers of students to make the program financially viable, it must attract a large number of applicants. Few programs, however administered (excluding those specially funded from nontuition sources), will long be tolerated at a deficit.

As may be evident from this discussion, the program-development process within a consortium is long and fairly expensive. The planning stages of the programs took from four to six months, preparation of the programs another similar period; publicity did not start until the planning phase was finished and required a lead time of eighteen months. The total elapsed time from the initial idea being broached to the curriculum committee until the first students began studies overseas was more than two-and-a-half years.

Critical Issues and Questions

Each of the above case histories presents an idiosyncratic situation and a sequence of specialized responses coming out of the needs and interests of particular institutions, both here and overseas. Nevertheless, as is evident, several issues are common to all three. Further, the planning and implementation stages were similar in all three cases. Perhaps the most critical stages occur at the outset, in the planning and exploration phases. These stages are listed below with brief commentary. They emphasize the critical questions that must be addressed by anyone undertaking the difficult task of starting a new program.

Determining the Need. Many faculty and administrators assume that few programs are truly appropriate to the needs of the institution. This may or may not, in fact, be true. In any event, before embarking on what—as the case histories illustrate—is a complex and expensive task, the following questions should be weighed carefully:
- Have you defined carefully your specific program needs?
- Have you surveyed all available options to satisfy the specific program need?
- Have you utilized effective measures to survey existing options?
- Is your need immediate or long range? Are you responding to immediate pressure by an individual or department, or is the new program a carefully researched institutional priority?
- Have you carefully examined the motivation behind those individuals

or groups who support new program development?

    • Are there any individuals or groups on campus that might be hostile or uncooperative to a new program? Would this severely hamper the development of a program?

    • Does the need grow naturally out of your existing on-campus academic program?

Gauging Your Resources. Even if you have established that a definite need exists, you should face squarely the issue of resources:

    • Do you have the necessary expertise—academic and logistical—on campus to develop a new study-abroad program?

    • Do you have faculty and departmental support from the discipline(s) to be represented in the program?

    • Are you sure that you have a constituency on campus that will provide long-term support for a program?

    • Is the institution fully committed to the program at the highest level?

    • Do you have the financial resources available for program start-up? For continuing the program if sufficient numbers are not reached? For how long would your institution support a deficit venture?

    • If you must seek outside support—academic, logistical, or financial—to begin the program, are you convinced that this support will be adequate to carry the program through to implementation?

Exploring the Territory. If you have the need and sufficient resources on campus, the next phase is determining the resources available at the program site. These resources will determine the location and often the shape of your program—whether a free-standing branch campus, something partially or fully integrated into an existing institution, or some sort of reciprocal and direct exchange. Consider the following:

    • Does the area possess what appears to be long-term political and/or financial stability?

    • Does a strong, ongoing institutional base exist within the program area?

    • What contacts do you have in the area? Have faculty from your institution studied or lived in the program area?

    • What sort of support will your institution have to provide? Academic? Logistical? Financial? Cultural?

    • What steps do you need to take to ensure local support for your program?

These issues regarding the opening phases in program development are hardly exhaustive, but they are critical. They must be squarely faced in the process of determining if a program should be established at all. Once the programmatic need has been firmly established, attention can be turned to the many, many hard specifics involved in setting up the program.

Ironing Out the Details. As all three examples amply show, there are a myriad of tasks to be performed to set up the program. These include but are not limited to

• Establishing curricular, credit, and grading correspondences between disparate systems.

• Entering into contractual arrangements with foreign universities, other institutions, and governments; following the correct protocol (Who signs the contract?).

• Setting admissions standards and defining the process.

• Securing housing, office space, classroom space, study space, library resources, and so forth.

• Dealing with visa, health, safety, and student social issues.

• Setting budgets, handling finances, and so forth.

• Hiring faculty and staff.

Publicity and Promotion. All programs require publicity—even those with a captive group for recruitment. For programs without a built-in base, this phase is critical because almost all programs that are tuition driven will have to

• Publish brochures, fliers, and posters, and then distribute them on campus

• Mail materials to other colleges (if you are seeking students from elsewhere); plan and execute off-campus recruitment plans

• Promote the program by meeting with faculty and students (see chapter 7).

Evaluation. Programs must be periodically evaluated, and the system for such evaluation should be built into the program-planning process (see chapter 16).

Money Matters

As suggested earlier, the economic realities of programming need to be carefully considered first, last, and always. Most education- abroad administrators have little experience with budgets and other money matters. Yet programs do not live and die on their pedagogy or overseas glories alone. Deans, presidents, and those who oversee the budget must be convinced that any new—or for that matter ongoing—program makes economic sense for the institution. Moreover, because even the *idea* of overseas programming may already seem to many on your campus economically and academically risky, the burden of proof may be put squarely on your desk.

What can you do and say to overcome the misperception that education-abroad programming invariably means a loss of money to the institution (or, as it is usually termed, "tuition export")? If students are "over there," so goes the perception, they are not paying salaries or filling beds at home. Further, if this is the case, it follows that education abroad must be frivolous—something the institution can afford to become involved with only peripherally (e.g., summer programs, programs that cannot be applied toward a major, or even perhaps general-education credit, programs to which financial aid does not apply). Your institution may think programs should be limited to honors students, or it may impose other severe limits on enrollment. The results of this kind of short-term thinking are that horrendous bureaucratic obstacles are often erected in front of students. The result is that only the most determined can surmount the obstacles. In such cases, overseas education—along with your own professional status—is marginalized.

Enlightened Self-Interest. "International" (like its fellow, "multicultural") is the buzzword for the 1990s. Every university and college in the country is giving lip service to it by rewriting mission statements, producing flashy catalogs, revising the curriculum, recruiting foreign students, and the like. Your job is to turn cheap talk into concrete action by convincing your colleagues that over the next ten years there are going to be several hundred truly enlightened schools that provide access to international experience. If yours is not among them, it will not be truly competitive, and admissions and retention will be a problem.

You need not play Cassandra, but it is important to use your informed awareness of what is going on at other institutions (to which your own compares itself) to warn of the consequences of being left out of this true national and international development. Calling education abroad "a growth stock in a stagnant industry," Craufurd Goodwin and Michael Nacht in their recent book, *Abroad and Beyond: Patterns in American Overseas Education,* conclude with the following observation:

> Above all, leaders of American academe should recognize that this is a fast-moving field they ignore at their peril. If they do not act to their own advantage in a timely fashion, not only will they miss opportunities but their competitors will surpass them. The continued dynamism of the field is so great that a laggard institution cannot simply say, "Let's wait till the dust clears and then pick the best." The dust shows no sign of settling any time soon, and if an institution is not in there with the others who are stirring it up, it will have little opportunity to gain the understanding needed for sensible action later on. (p. 118)

Seen in the context of long-range institutional planning, the investment of economic resources in sound education-abroad programming can be seen as wise.

Faculty Development. The financial investment in education-abroad programming can also be sold, with your urging, as having multiple benefits for students and faculty members. As shown above, new programs inevitably require faculty input and guidance. While some faculty participate in planning and administration out of a sense of duty, for the most part they see such programming as a way to enrich the education of their students. But they also see it as an opportunity to make meaningful lasting contacts with colleagues and cultures elsewhere in the world. Not only do short-term program leadership positions become available, but also new opportunities for research and exchange.

It is a truism that faculty who are active, say, as members of your advisory committee, come out of international backgrounds and use this experience to seek grants and travel abroad again. Additionally, they are more willing to introduce new international dimensions into the courses they teach, and to encourage students who have studied abroad to utilize what they have learned into their campus studies. Thus, the investment in education-abroad programming is also an indirect investment in the intellectual development of faculty. While this may or may not be shown in the program budget, its other effects will be easily discernible. It is your job to make sure that your administration sees this cross-fertilization.

Exploring Diverse Economic Models. There is great diversity in the way U.S. colleges and universities enroll and charge students for education abroad. In some cases, education abroad is always considered an "extra," something beyond normal degree costs and credits—an attitude that contributes to the perception that overseas study is an elitist activity. In other instances—such as the University of California example above—students pay normal tuition for any educational experience and receive normal credit and full financial aid. Between these extremes, there are many variations.

Education-abroad programming at some colleges is seen as a money-maker for the university—especially if overseas fixed costs can be kept lower than home-campus costs and student numbers remain high. In these cases, the education-abroad budget may be incorporated into the overall institutional budget in the same way as are those of an academic department or the library. Fairly often an office can cover such things as its own salaries from program revenues, with space and utilities coming out of the institution's general budget. A more general model is for nearly all program budgets to face the need to break even, with actual program costs being balanced by tuition revenues. Financial aid monies may or may not be a factor in this equation.

We all know that it costs more to educate a student majoring in chemistry or engineering than one majoring in literature. It is also true that business professors earn more than art historians. In addition, colleges offer many courses that are underenrolled in relation to the real costs necessary

172

to teach them. Yet undergraduates, whatever courses they choose, almost always pay the same tuition, and these variations in costs are seen as something any self-respecting institution must, within limits, do in order to offer a full and diverse curriculum.

If we follow this institutional logic to its fair conclusion, it follows that education-abroad programming should be viewed much as chemistry or business are, not as an "extra" that must pay for itself down to the final penny. Not every dean will buy this argument, and its effectiveness relies to some degree on the conviction you and others (including students) can muster. It should certainly be tried.

In addition, you should be able to fight for enough internal budget flexibility to be able to balance an inexpensive program—in, for instance, Mexico or the Caribbean—against more expensive programs—in, for instance, Japan or Africa. Summer or short-term programs (even those that are not as academic and may appeal to a wider constituency) may need to make up for the losses on academic year programs. In short, even if the realities are that your institution sees any financial support it gives as a type of subsidy, there remain ways to return revenues and balance different kinds of programs against each other to achieve fiscal balance.

No one else's fiscal model is likely to be entirely appropriate for your institution, but exploring other models can be very useful. Any one of them may have a line item for a kind of revenue or expense that you have not thought to include in your own financial planning. What matters in the end, however, is that you remain proactive in the budget process, and that you take the initiative to present to your institutional colleagues alternative ways to implement desired policies and essential, appealing programs. Not to do this is to lose some control over your professional role and to miss opportunities to translate what you know into programs that benefit your entire institution.

14

Program Designs
and Strategies

Contributors: Joseph Navari and Heidi Soneson

As chapter 13 suggests, there are many ways to set up and structure education-abroad programs. The purpose of this chapter is to summarize the major types of program designs now in use. The academic, intercultural, and economic features, and the corresponding drawbacks of each design, will also be presented. If you are familiar with the range of designs, you should be able to (1) set up your own new programs, (2) make adjustments in existing ones, and (3) advise your students in their choices of internal and external programs, all in accordance with individual and institutional educational philosophy, needs, and resources. In Part 2 of this book, it was asserted that no "perfect" program exists for all students and that almost any program might offer the right match for certain students. The same thing may be said about institutions: the "perfect" program cannot be defined in the abstract, but rather is one that matches institutional resources, needs, and educational philosophy with the interests and welfare of a significant number of students. The corollary of this education-abroad truism is that choices and judgments need to be made by all concerned, and that this is best done with a full awareness of all relevant facts and possibilities.

Programs Sponsored by Your Own Campus

Branch-Campus Models. Branch-campus models—sometimes called "nonintegrated" or "island" programs—provide instruction via courses specifically designed for program participants by their home college or university.

Basic Characteristics

• Students are drawn solely from your institution (a variation is to offer some places to students from other American colleges and universities). Students from the host culture do not normally participate in the classroom, because the courses are not part of their own university curriculum.

• Classes are taught by faculty who are hired by your institution for the specific purpose of providing instruction to its group of students. Some may be your regular faculty, sent to the foreign site to teach specific courses. Others might be hired locally to teach specific courses; these instructors may be resident Americans or foreign nationals. The faculty will vary according to the qualifications of students, the duration of the program, and home-institution policies. The language of instruction is often English.

• Instruction takes place in rented space, perhaps in a hotel or youth hostel, but occasionally can occur in classrooms rented from an established educational institution.

• Housing is normally leased in a hotel or nonuniversity dormitory facility (e.g., youth hostel), or arranged with local families. Alternatively, an investment is made by purchasing one's own facilities. Meals and excursions are often included in the program fee.

• The academic calendar of your institution (quarter, semester, or academic year) is usually used. However, modifications may be made to simplify planning or to accommodate the holidays of the host culture.

• Such programs may also be operated as study tours with instruction carried on at several sites over a relatively short period of time (e.g., three or four weeks or during an interim or summer term). Summer branch-campus programs are very common.

• Requirements for admission are obviously set by your institution. You may have few, or many, formal admission requirements and selection procedures. These may include specific language requirements, a certain GPA, or completion of specific course work. Some programs have few formal academic requirements but rather rigorous selection procedures, requiring student applicants to write essays and undergo selection interviews.

Some Pros and Cons. One of the advantages of the branch-campus model is that it ensures a high degree of control by your institution. This means exclusive authority over academic content; methods of instruction, testing, and credit transfer; class schedules and the calendar; and housing, meals, and excursions. Control of academic content and the calendar makes it possible to coordinate more easily with home-campus curricula and timetables. It also makes it possible, for example, to articulate courses abroad with on-campus programs (e.g., general education, graduation, or major requirements), which serves the immediate needs of students.

However, branch-campus models can rarely offer a large curriculum, or, rather, can do so only by adding to their costs. Some offer no choice at all, providing students with a fixed number of mandatory courses that often consist of general-culture and language courses. On the one hand, such basic courses can serve large numbers of students. On the other, a fixed curriculum articulated to a specific major will attract only those students interested in that major. By offering a limited number of courses and by employing staff locally, the branch-campus model can often be operated on a relatively low per-student cost, both to the student and to the institution. In many cases, the cost to the student may be at or below the average cost of attending classes at home, sometimes with international transportation included. Depending also on where the program takes place—western Europe is currently very expensive by American standards—the cost to your institution can often be less than home-campus costs. Depending on how budgets are arranged and fees are charged, this model can be designed to be self-supporting or even to generate a modest surplus.

The education-abroad office itself might be able to coordinate and administer one or more branch-campus programs, but only if you have the following:

• Dependable faculty participation and reliable on-campus support services

• Opportunities to travel abroad regularly to secure arrangements for the program and to ensure that all aspects of the program are secure.

• A reliable, hard-working contact person—or resident director—at the site to make housing arrangements, hire teachers, and generally to serve as a liaison.

• Firm and lasting faculty and institutional support in cases where your faculty member accompanies the students to the branch-campus site and conducts the academic program for participating students. Unless the program is departmentally sponsored, it is important to secure such support from faculty members from across the curriculum. Also, the program should not be seen as being "owned" by a particular faculty member.

Branch-campus programs can sometimes accommodate larger numbers of students than can other types of programs, especially if the curriculum is broad and varied. They also attract students because of the many services they normally provide. These usually include transportation, transfers between airports and train stations, housing, orientation, meals, courses and credits, registration, insurance, excursions, and cultural activities as part of their program fee. As a result, the students' responsibility for securing these services is minimal or nonexistent. The study tour, for example, is an all-inclusive package that takes care of almost everything for the participants. This convenience makes such programs particularly appealing to less independent students and to parents who want these services delivered to their children (not to mention the more cautious type of university administrator).

At the same time, the branch-campus model may allow numbers of faculty from your institution to live and teach abroad for a period of time. This involvement clearly has potential long-range advantages. Not only can they engage in scholarly research in their fields but they will also become more invested in education abroad. If they are asked, however, to carry a heavy teaching load or to supervise many students outside the classroom, they need to be prepared.

One major disadvantage of branch-campus programs is that they tend to isolate American students from meaningful contact with the host country and the host culture. This is particularly true when participants are housed together, have their meals together, and are taught only, or primarily, by American faculty. More important, contact with the host country will be neither regular nor frequent, thus limiting cross-cultural learning opportunities. Students can easily become isolated in an American ghetto. Furthermore, variables that promote intercultural learning may be completely absent from branch campuses. Indeed, when there is minimal contact between the American student group and the local community, a program might actually foster prejudice and hostility.[1]

For some proponents of branch-campus programs, a degree of isolation from the host culture is purposeful. Program participants are not required to interact with (and consequently adjust to) the host country—at least initially. So such programs may be well suited for the less venturesome student who might not otherwise go abroad. The branch-campus model, for example, might attract students without sufficient confidence in their language abilities. In this sense, the Americanized environment provides a variety of foreign-study experience that might not otherwise be pursued.

Such programs may be critical at institutions that wish to add international dimensions to their curricular programs but have few students studying language in second- and third-year classes, or which have not yet developed a sophisticated rationale for study abroad as a cultural-immersion experience. Such programs may also serve the purpose of encouraging more narrowly based students in such majors as business, engineering, and the sciences to consider education abroad. Yet, if the program serves this purpose, it is likely that many of its participants will decide to return to the country where they have lived and learned, perhaps to live on more indigenous cultural terms, to build on the contacts they have made, or to pursue more ambitious interests.

Finally, whether facilities are leased or owned, your institution may find itself heavily involved in facilities management—from lights and heaters to washing machines, kitchen utensils, pillows and blankets, beer machines, and cooking crews. Also, American undergraduates, living a long way from home, will invariably be socially and academically demanding and need varieties of support and counsel. If you are not careful about the services to be provided, you may find yourself overwhelmed by logistical and personal demands. In all international programming there is pressure to overextend both the reach of the institution and the expertise of its staff. This is especially true for branch campuses. With little training and on-site experience, you are expected to operate effectively in a foreign setting, where assistance from host-country institutions is typically weak or even nonexistent.

When on-site program administrators have to spend so much time on housing facilities or on arranging meals, there may be little time and energy left for the unique learning activities that make education abroad attractive.

Direct Enrollment Models. Direct-enrollment programs stand in stark contrast to the branch-campus models. Often referred to (with some loss of accuracy) as "integrated" or "full-immersion" programs, this form of education abroad makes American students less distinguishable from students of the host country.

Basic Characteristics

• American students become temporary, matriculated (though not degree-seeking) members of the student body of a foreign institution (for example, a university, polytechnic, or higher education institute).

• Taught by regular faculty, American students in some cases take courses from the regular curriculum alongside native students; in other cases, courses are designed specifically for foreign students (though not necessarily for Americans).

• The host-country language is the language of instruction, though a limited number of classes may be taught in English, along with a full range of language classes.

• In some cases, students apply directly to the host institution as foreign students. In many cases, however, this direct enrollment model is part of a mutual exchange between the United States and the foreign institutions, whereby an equal number of students from the home institution attend the host institution annually (see below for a more detailed discussion of reciprocally organized programs).

• Your institution controls neither the content of courses nor the range of offerings, and has little say in prerequisites, standards, or testing. The academic calendar of the host institution operates, and the program will frequently run for the full academic year of that institution.

• In order to facilitate the transfer of courses taken abroad, American students generally must undertake some form of preregistration before they leave the home campus or get pre-approval for courses.

• Most foreign institutions require U.S. students to have junior standing and competency in their language, defined minimally as two years of university preparation; in addition, intensive language work may be offered in the host country before regular courses begin.

• Many American colleges and universities provide on-site administrative staff to assist their students. This staff, usually a resident director and perhaps a secretary, provides some services not usually available to host-country students.

• Students are often housed in university dormitories, though some live with families, in boarding houses, or private apartments. Most foreign universities have housing offices. If a mutual exchange agreement exists between the foreign and the U.S. institution, housing is frequently arranged prior to the students' arrival. Foreign universities with no university-owned housing facilities generally house students with families or in private apartments. If there is no interinstitutional agreement, the students will normally have to arrange for their own accommodations and pay for them directly.

• Students are generally responsible for their own meals, which they either prepare themselves or have in university cafeterias or student restaurants. When students live with families, they usually arrange to take certain meals with their hosts.

Some Pros and Cons. The direct enrollment model is, of course, more an opportunity than a program. It enables students to experience a foreign culture on its own terms. Students become integral, social members of a new country. This integration gives them special opportunities to understand the educational system, history, customs, and mores and to meet fellow students and participate in their daily life. Students learn daily to interact with host-country bus drivers and bureaucrats, policemen and merchants, landlords and librarians, and many others. They also learn to live with families, roommates, or housemates. While American students may also have American friends, social life in a direct enrollment program is far more an individual than group experience, and whether pleasant or not at the time, most such experiences are enlarging and enlightening.

The cultural and linguistic interaction necessitated by this model promotes a deeper awareness and more sophisticated understanding of the host culture. It appears to influence students more favorably toward the host culture, in spite of the initial frustrations.[2] For language majors, or anyone serious about becoming fluent, this degree of linguistic immersion both speeds up and solidifies competency. Because direct enrollment requires participating students to integrate into the host culture with minimal supervision, students best suited for this kind of experience need to be self-motivated, independent, and flexible.

In addition, students also have the chance to experience firsthand a non-American system of higher education and its intellectual, social, and cultural life. American campus life will never look the same. More importantly, students are forced to become more responsible for their own education, learning what is expected in the classroom and on examinations and papers. Understanding how students of the host country go about educating themselves is always a revelation. Finally, the full curriculum of the foreign university is open to them, depending on their language proficiencies and prerequisites. This broad range of possible courses represents an important advantage over the limited curricula of branch-campus programs, especially for students who want to explore a variety of fields, as well as for those who must satisfy specific requirements while abroad. It is also important to students who may want to do comparative work in specific fields.

Direct enrollment programs can also be less expensive than branch-campus models because American faculty expenses are eliminated, special support services are minimal, and tuition and fees in other countries are often lower. Where there is an interinstitutional agreement, the total cost to students, including overseas and on-site transportation, can be about the same as home-campus charges.

For an American institution with only a small education-abroad staff, the direct enrollment model provides opportunities for a wide range of students. At little or no cost to your institution, student services can be provided through the foreign student office, including housing arrangements, orientation, and ongoing support. Many foreign institutions have a staff person who is responsible for initiating and maintaining bilateral exchanges. Interinstitutional agreements also create opportunities for developing other agreements at the faculty level, from teaching exchanges to joint research projects to the establishment of joint baccalaureate programs.

On the negative side, not all foreign institutions are equally ready for American students. Foreign faculty and students may not understand the very American phenomenon of "dropping in" for just a term or a year of what, for them, is a three- or four-year degree program. Nor are they likely to comprehend the notion of transferring credits toward a U.S. degree. Further, the idea of students taking a variety of courses rather than specializing in one academic area will likely be puzzling to foreign institutions. Until the recent introduction of the ERASMUS exchanges, such ideas were rare in Europe.

Thus, American students, especially if their language skills are not perfect, are often seen as brave albeit not very serious. The Americans' relatively short stays also mean that natives may not take the time to establish social relationships. All of these negatives are more likely in the major capitals and larger countries of western Europe, where there are traditionally a number of American students so that, as a consequence, befriending them is no novelty. American students, in turn, can easily feel unwanted and unwelcome.

Not all American students, alas, are equal to the challenges of direct enrollment, even though they might think they are before they depart. If this is the case, they will find no haven from "foreignness," no immediate support group of other students, and probably no American resident director to provide assurances. If neither faculty nor support-service personnel of the foreign university are accustomed to the needs of such students, problems can multiply. Direct enrollment is therefore best suited for self-confident, flexible, and resilient students; it is unlikely to appeal to a certain portion of the student population who imagine the worst.

The high language-proficiency requirements of direct enrollment in non-English-speaking countries also diminishes the number of students who can qualify—in some cases limiting it ipso facto to language majors. In addition, mismatched U.S./foreign academic calendars, a lack of clear information in advance of course availability and prerequisites, and the uncertainty of grading standards are also very real obstacles for some students and institutions. If the courses offered at the foreign institution do not match those offered at the home institution, credit transfer becomes more complicated. Students who need to fulfill specific requirements at home may therefore refrain from applying.

In short, the many clear benefits of direct immersion can be overshadowed by numerous potential problems. Interfacing two different educational systems, each with its own precedents, structures, and values, is fraught with potential pitfalls. Although the oldest and deepest ideals in the field of international educational exchange are often best fulfilled by the direct enrollment model, neither institutions nor students should enter into such an arrangement without ample forethought and planning.

Mixed Models. As we have seen, branch-campus and direct–enrollment programming represent diametrically opposed approaches to education abroad. In the one, American academic and institutional control remains largely uncompromised, in spite of the foreign setting; in the other, the educational and cultural values and rhythms of a foreign land dominate the studies and living conditions of American students. Branch campuses at their worst can represent a chauvinistic and insecure cloning of the American educational system, which just happens to take place abroad; at their best, they serve to introduce a wide range of undergraduates to studies and experiences they could never have on the home campus. Direct enrollment, at its worst, immerses American students in an education system not designed for them in a culture that remains foreign; at its best, it allows them to combine the finest qualities of two educational systems and cultures.

But between these extremes is a wide range of hybrid models, each of which attempts to maximize the advantages and minimize the disadvantages of the latter two. These mixed models seem to acknowledge implicitly that ghettoizing American students seldom fulfills the ideals of education abroad. At the same time, pretending that American undergraduates have exactly the same backgrounds, language abilities, and academic needs of their foreign counterparts can be counterproductive. Therefore, various realistic compromises and accommodations are needed to achieve the greatest success for the largest number of students. The results are program models that accommodate a wider range of students and institutions.

Basic Characteristics

Mixed programs are often housed on a foreign university campus or draw on foreign university resources. Multiple program tracks and options are available for students with different qualifications, interests, and needs. Typically, one track is made up of courses designed specifically for the American group; they are often taught in English by the program's resident director or by faculty hired by the sponsoring institution—either directly or

182

through the host institution. Course offerings focus on language instruction and on the history and culture of the host country; where sufficient numbers of students need a particular course or courses, specialized course work (such as international business) may also be offered. A second track is for students with language proficiency, who are allowed to enroll in the regular courses of the host institution.

These two tracks are usually offered concurrently. Students may be enrolled exclusively in one or in both at the same time. Housing and meals may be with families, in university dorms, or in rented buildings, but in mixed programs, attempts are made to provide some social, recreational, and language mixing of American and foreign students. Support services are provided either by the American resident director or by personnel at the foreign university. Official transcripts for course credit are prepared by the resident director or the foreign university.

Some Pros and Cons. Multiple-track, university-based programs were originally designed to help students without sufficient language preparation to keep up with the regular course offerings of the host institution. In many cases, host institutions took the lead in developing special language training for these students. Specialized courses were then offered to serve specific academic interests and/or requirements. The former were normally "culture" classes taught in the language of the host country. The latter courses, negotiated by the sponsoring institution, fulfilled home-campus academic requirements. Frequently a single course could satisfy both. The new twist is that the American institutions operating these programs took the initiative in planning these multiple tracks, and in some cases having the courses taught in English.

Some direct enrollment programs developed special courses for their students because of political unrest at host institutions. Where frequent strikes forced the cancellation of regular university courses, the development of courses outside the regular program of the host institution filled the vacuum. In many cases they became permanent offerings in these programs, even though students had access to the regular course offerings of a host institution after the turmoil passed. Economic factors have also moved American institutions in this direction. Many programs abroad devoted to single disciplines (e.g., language, film studies, or social history) have not been able to sustain sufficient numbers of students to make them financially viable. With the same infrastructure, multiple-track programs offer an enlarged curriculum.

Programs with multiple tracks acknowledge the need to provide appropriate programming for a wide range of student interests and backgrounds. They do not penalize students who have prepared themselves well in languages and areas studies. These students can take at least some regular university courses, which challenge them appropriately; but such students also have access to other general courses, taught perhaps from an Ameri-

183

can perspective. Other students, with little or no background in the language and culture of the country, can take introductory language courses, general courses, and perhaps courses in specific areas or disciplines especially prominent in this country.

At their best, multiple-track programs give less adventuresome students sufficient support to consider studying abroad. Once there, many of these students develop confidence and maturity at their own pace. Simultaneously, they do not frustrate students who disdain the prospect of living and learning exclusively with other American students from their own campus. A high amount of interaction with the host culture is encouraged for both groups, but it is not mandated. This approach lets the students choose when and how to get acquainted with the host culture.

Foreign universities are not always willing, however, to provide different tracks of courses for American students. Nor is there any reason for them to feel compelled to do so. This disinclination is more common in some countries. For a variety of political, social, or economic reasons, some universities cannot easily create new courses, even for their own students. Where these problems exist, American universities may have to provide their own instructors for the special courses they need abroad, or go elsewhere. Sometimes foreign institutions will find the incentive to work with your institution if a mutually beneficial exchange agreement can be worked out. (See the discussion below—Reciprocally Organized Programs/Direct Exchanges.)

Extensive domestic planning is required to implement a mixed program abroad; preparations will often need to be exceedingly elaborate when course options for the U.S. students abroad are expanded. The education-abroad adviser must not only oversee the general operations of the program and conduct regular site visits, he or she must also maintain a consistent base of participating faculty—whether resident abroad or from the United States. In addition, participating students require a great deal of help in choosing appropriate classes in the foreign curriculum. A well-established network of support services at the host institution is therefore essential if your institution wants to ensure that adequate arrangements are in place for housing, meals, ongoing support services and academic advising. Without this, many goals cannot be accomplished.

Independent-Study Models. The fourth education-abroad program model is institutionally sponsored, approved, and directed independent study. In short, your institution makes no effort to set up classroom instruction of its own or to arrange for matriculation in a foreign institution.

Basic Characteristics. Under faculty supervision, students conduct independent research, carry out a plan of study, or undertake some type of internship or work experience that is related to their formal studies, but they do this while living abroad; the faculty supervisor can be someone at your campus and/or at the overseas study destination.

If the student is undertaking academic research, the study destination will usually be a foreign university library, laboratory, or other facility. Students are expected to gather information and perspectives, synthesize them, do further reading and analysis, and at some later point present, in some predetermined format, what they have learned for credit assessment. Projects can vary greatly in duration; but student resources, not time spent on research and writing, will almost always determine the amount of time spent abroad. The student is in charge of making logistical preparations, including identifying a particular study destination and corresponding with prospective hosts. Housing and meal arrangements are also the participant's responsibility. Other types of support services (e.g., transportation, visas, police registration, insurance, etc.) are not normally offered. Some colleges, however, organize programs in which participants depart for the host country as a group, with a group leader, and then split up after an on-site orientation and research-methods seminar. The group leader thereafter meets with the participants on an individual basis.

Some Pros and Cons. Only the very best students are capable of undertaking truly independent research abroad. Maturity, discipline, superior background in the research area, language proficiency, organization, cross-cultural skills, patience, and stamina are only some of the essential qualities they will need to possess. Such students do exist, however, and with (1) the proper preparation and support beforehand (2) cooperation, facilities, and contacts abroad and (3) time and energy to gather together what they have learned at the end, they can produce truly impressive work. Significant cross-cultural learning can take place via independent study, particularly where cooperative activity, either research or work, occurs with host-country nationals. If, on the other hand, an independent-study project requires no such regular and daily contact, as for example in library research, opportunities for cross-cultural learning can be reduced.

Relative to other types of education abroad, few students will be attracted to this type of opportunity, though strong institutional support can make a big difference. For most undergraduates, independent projects are difficult to develop, and faculty who are called on to support these efforts are often skeptical of their outcomes. But it is better to be prepared for these rare students than to be forced to improvise when they appear on your doorstep. In some cases, only minimal assistance from the education-abroad office is needed. Because students work in cooperation with faculty members to establish project goals, a time frame, required written work, and the grading procedure, your job may be only to help them learn how to prepare to go abroad. Once the student returns to campus, he or she again works primarily with the faculty member to complete the necessary requirements. Credit is usually awarded under the rubric of "individual study" in the faculty adviser's department.

It is very difficult, however, to obtain the information necessary to plan such a project. Unless contacts at the host site are knowledgeable, the body of data that a student wishes to study may not even exist, or may not exist in an accessible form. Supervision of a research project abroad is difficult in the extreme for someone from the home campus, and faculty are often very reluctant to supervise projects abroad unless they know the student well. The problem of supervision is often cited as the principal weakness of independent study abroad.

In recent years full-time work opportunities or internship programs abroad have become increasingly popular (see chapter 15). Work experiences—paid and unpaid, short term or long term—are undertaken in a wide variety of settings: commercial offices, schools, churches, health-care facilities, social service organizations, and governmental agencies, to name just a few. Most students seeking to work abroad do so simply for the experience, or to enhance their resumes; they are not interested in reflecting analytically on what they have done or in receiving academic credit. At the same time, they want work that is very relevant to their studies or career plans.

For such students, the work experience can be treated as a species of research. Credit for the activity can therefore be based, as with academic research or study projects, on a written report, combined with evaluations from a work supervisor. You can assist such students by establishing contact with potential host companies or organizations abroad and identifying contact persons to assist with on-site supervision, housing, or orientation. Some institutions will not give credit for any nonacademic project, but this is not always the case. Faculty members from individual departments are vital resources, as they are likely to know companies or organizations abroad that would offer and oversee projects of interest to their students.

Programs Sponsored in Cooperation with Others

The four education-abroad program models described above are organized to respond to single-campus needs for the exclusive benefit of their own students. Cooperative programs can offer some significant advantages, along with some disadvantages. Formal reciprocal agreements with foreign institutions also provide a number of benefits. In each case, consortial or reciprocal, this more complex organization may alter, in small or large ways, the program model.

Consortially Organized Programs. Two types of consortially organized programs are currently being used by many American colleges and universities. The first, a so-called partnership consortium, is created when two or more American institutions join forces to operate one or more programs abroad for the students of all member institutions. The second program, often called an agency consortium, is run by an independent organization that acts on behalf of member colleges and universities to set up and help administer one or more programs abroad. The relative advantages and disadvantages of these two types of consortia will be considered individually.

Partnership Consortia. When two or more institutions share in the operation and governance of a study-abroad program, in theory each member shares equally in the obligations and benefits of the program. The terms of the partnership are usually determined by a formula that regulates the numbers of students participating from the cooperating institutions and the financial obligations of each. By sharing resources and operational responsibilities, more viable and effective study abroad programs should be possible. There are a variety of advantages and disadvantages associated with consortially organized study-abroad programs of this type. Each institution must weigh these in the light of its own needs and resources.

The pooling of students is an obvious advantage because a single institution might not have sufficient numbers of students to mount a program on its own. This may be particularly important when an institution wishes to operate a program in a country that may be relatively unknown and unpopular with students, but nonetheless is important. The same can be said for the sharing of faculty resources. Where faculty go abroad as resident directors or instructors, it is always better to have a larger pool from which to select a staff. Pooling resources in consortially operated programs may be applied to expertise. One campus may have strong faculty expertise in the history of a particular geographic area, but be lacking in political science or anthropology. By coordinating varied patterns of expertise from among a number of institutions, stronger study abroad programs are possible. There is also a slight advantage in having a group of students abroad from a variety of American institutions. The mix may help prevent the American group from becoming too ghettoized. Insofar as learning takes place between peers, diverse rather than homogeneous groups are preferred. Working together also provides some leverage when negotiating with foreign institutions over costs, facilities, courses, and support services.

The reduction of fixed program costs (as they are spread out over a larger number of student participants) tends to be the greatest strength of consortially operated programs. But fixed and variable program costs must be identified, and the percentage of fixed costs isolated relative to the total cost in any particular program. Fixed costs are those that a program must pay regardless of the number of students who participate (e.g., the costs of teachers, administration, and facilities overseas). Variable costs are those tied directly to each student participant (e.g., tuition, transportation, books and supplies, insurance, meals, excursions, cultural events, and lodging). In general, where fixed costs are high relative to total cost, a consortial program will usually save money for the sponsoring institutions, but probably not for students. Where fixed costs are low relative to total costs (or nonexistent as is the case in some direct enrollment programs based upon reciprocity), it makes no difference financially whether a program is consortially organized so long as institutions can find students to go.

But with the added offices and individuals involved in the operation of such programs, information often does not get where it needs to be. Information also moves more slowly. In addition, because institutions play a governance role in the operation of these programs, more time is required to generate the information necessary for program operations. The problem of good communication is compounded if the cooperating institutions are geographically distant. Holding joint predeparture orientation programs, for instance, becomes difficult if not impossible.

Consortially organized programs often involve the loss of some autonomy on the part of each participating college, and governance can be cumbersome. Institutions may not, for example, be able to send all the students they would like because the numbers of participating students are often governed by an agreement among all the members. Representatives of the participating institutions must meet periodically to set policies and in some cases to select students and/or resident faculty or staff. A number of principles have therefore emerged for governing consortially organized programs. The most common is to have the program administered out of a fixed office or location. This location could rotate or remain at one of the cooperating institutions. In either event, all program-abroad matters are addressed to this central administrative office. If resident directors are sent abroad from the participating institutions, the directorship often rotates among the member institutions. Frequent changes in personnel or administrative operations at any institution, however, can also significantly compound even routine communication difficulties. Still, the greater breadth of experience means that a partnership consortium carries with it a high degree of stability.

Agency Consortia. The second type of consortium gives over to an independent agency (a nonprofit or profit-making organization) the responsibility for much of the logistical and academic details of establishing and maintaining one or more programs abroad. In this type of consortium, the agency works with the host institution to arrange housing, and provides orientation and ongoing support services. It sometimes conducts one or more predeparture orientation programs. In addition, some agencies coordinate the academic program and the transfer of credit, working with member institution representatives. The agency may be responsible for hiring resident directors (with the approval of member institutions) and monitoring the program on a regular basis. Programs run in this way can follow any number of models: independent campuses for member-institution students only, direct enrollment into a foreign institution, or hybrid curricula that include both special and regular university course work.

Regardless of the overseas program design, the agency consortium model has several domestic advantages. Participating institutions are relieved of the burden of making the logistical arrangements abroad, and, in the case of branch-campus programs, finding a faculty member each year who is willing to accompany the students abroad. Because the central organization is also responsible for establishing and maintaining the programs abroad, students at the participating institutions have ongoing access to a wide variety of possible study sites, while the education-abroad office can focus on advice, recruitment, orientation, and other campus support. The agency can also effectively ensure that on-site orientation programs, advising, and classes meet the specific agreed-upon standards of participating institutions and the personal and academic needs of students.

The costs of membership in an agency consortium vary quite a bit. Some bring together public colleges and universities with reasonably low tuition; others cater to private colleges and universities; some are established so that both public and private institutions find cost-benefits. Some consortia have set a fee for the program, which includes all costs including the airfare, orientation program, room and board, and excursions; others fix fees for only room, board, and tuition. Those with reciprocal agreements have participating students pay fees to the home institution, in addition to an administrative fee to the central organization. This feature is quite attractive to state institutions with low in-state tuition rates. Several agency consortia have special financial aid for qualified students.

But there are also some potential drawbacks. Most agency consortia require an annual membership fee, and in some cases this is significant, especially if few of your students participate. In addition, there is usually a per enrollment administrative fee that is passed on to students, increasing their costs. If fees are set on the basis of private college tuition, public college students often find the costs unaffordable.

In addition, the home institution does not have complete control over the selection and placement process. In some cases, only a few students from each participating institution are eligible for certain programs. Where the consortium places students at several sites abroad, students may not be placed at the institution of their choice or even placed at all. In sum, the admissions process can be lengthy and complex, and the results not always pleasing or easy to explain to students.

Finally, because most consortia operate by consensus, with the agency simply administering decisions, a given institution will not have its way on all matters. Your program can easily get caught between consortium policy and the preferences of your administration, and matters such as the course content, the structure of the program, or the calendar can be divisive issues. If a given institution finds itself continually at odds with other members, however, it can withdraw. But before taking precipitate action (especially if you work for a small college or a larger institution with limited commitments to education-abroad programming), remember that membership in a consortium offers program choices far beyond those that your institution is able to provide.

Reciprocally Organized Programs/Direct Exchanges. Any of the study-abroad program models described above may be organized reciprocally. *Reciprocity* means, very simply, that two educational institutions, one American and one foreign, agree to some form of student exchange, or student-faculty exchange. Usually this swap involves an equal number of individuals taking each other's places, over equal periods of time. Originally, exchange programs between universities were based on the principle of student-for-student, with each paying room, board, and tuition at his or her home institution and no monies changing hands. In practice, however, many universities have found it difficult to send an equal number of students in both directions within the same period. Consequently, a variety of exchange mechanisms have been developed that are not limited to the student-for-student exchange. Thus, reciprocity may now also involve asymmetrical numbers of students and unequal periods of time spent abroad; it may also include faculty members as well as students.

Reciprocity can occur only if each institution is able and willing to accept students without an actual payment of tuition. This is possible in many countries where higher education is free to foreign students. It is also possible in many private American institutions that, through appropriate accounting procedures, can register a student without a tuition payment. It is also possible at many American state institutions where tuition may be waived on the basis of reciprocal agreements calling for an exchange of "equal service" and not equal numbers of students. But not all American colleges or universities are set up to accommodate this necessity.

Typically, reciprocity also requires that exchanged participants pay directly for their room, board, and personal expenses. Obviously, many students from developing countries cannot participate in these types of exchanges without further funding from one nation or the other. Another condition is that special services costing extra money not be required beyond those which an institution regularly offers to its current foreign students. Thus, students needing significant language training or health care, for example, might not find either, and therefore not be able to participate. However, when each host institution is already servicing large numbers of foreign students, the cost of educating several more may be marginal.

Imaginative planning (and bookkeeping) sometimes means that the body or dollar balances called for in reciprocity agreements can be spread out over several years. This variation allows a system of credits and debits to develop, and provides time for the cooperating institutions to balance these credits or debits by sending more or fewer students in particular years, depending on the credits or debits that have accumulated. This adaptation works very well, particularly where room-and-board costs are covered directly by the participating students. Where this is the case, monies must be accumulated by an institution, presumably from its own students, before it can receive students from the cooperating institution. In a given year, sufficient room and board money may not be available to meet the demand from the cooperating institution. This is not a problem when each institution has reserve funds to cover these "bumps" in the exchange. Again, private institutions may have some advantages in these regards.

A third adaptation is based on exchanging a fixed ratio of students in staggered years. These exchanges begin in year 1 with x number of students moving in one direction. This number becomes a base figure that dictates in a subsequent period how many students the cooperating institution may send. This mechanism works particularly well where the calendars of the two cooperating institutions begin during different times of the year. For illustrative purposes let us assume a relationship between an American and a Latin American university. The American institution's calendar begins in September, the Latin American's in March. They agree to exchange three American students for one Latin American student. In September, the Latin American university sends five students to the American university. In March, the American university reciprocates and sends up to fifteen of its students to its Latin American partner. If it sends fewer or more, these gains or losses are simply transferred to the next cycle, with the exchange balanced in each succeeding year. The ratio of students sent between the institutions is determined by agreement, and will depend on the respective services provided by each. This adaptation to direct exchange is particularly useful when room and board on both sides are delivered to the participating students.

Some reciprocal agreements are based on allocations of money, rather than an exchange of students. Under these agreements one of the cooperating institutions agrees to generate x dollars for each student it sends abroad, and to reserve that amount to support students coming from the partner institution. This kind of mechanism can easily be combined with those adaptations where uneven numbers of students are being exchanged. This approach simplifies the question of equity, and provides great flexibility to the institution that has received monetary credits in a foreign country. The institution can send students, but it may wish to use the credits to support a single faculty member at the partner institution, or to buy equipment, library materials, and so forth. Obviously, these types of agreements must be specific on how financial credits can be used, because in most instances they do not represent actual funds that can be spent for salaries or library books.

Reciprocal exchanges require that additional staff time be committed to the incoming exchange students. Ideally, this will primarily be the work of the foreign student office and other offices on campus that provide services

191

for foreign students. If this is not possible, the extra responsibilities of arranging housing and meals, orientation, immigration, and academic counseling are likely to be too much for you and your office. Assuming others on your campus can assume responsibility for these matters, your office is still likely to need some time to provide some counsel and social occasions for the students—and they also may be indispensable to you in promoting the exchange opportunity to American students.

Reciprocal exchange agreements afford significant advantages. Where costs might be otherwise prohibitive, they present opportunities. In countries where currency controls restrict the numbers of students studying abroad, programs organized reciprocally can provide some relief. There are also significant nonfinancial advantages. Reciprocity gives each institution a stake in the relationship, so that each works harder to make sure it succeeds. This networking tends to create additional activities, in some cases developing into additional programs, further strengthening the links between the two institutions. Finally, reciprocity in education-abroad programming diversifies the student body on your campus and contributes to the international education of students who do not study abroad.

Notes

1. See S. Bochner, "The Social Psychology of Cross-Cultural Relations," in *Cultures and Contact,* ed. S. Bochner (New York: Pergamon, 1982), 16.
2. Otto Klineberg, *International Exchanges in Education, Science, and Culture* (Paris: Moulton, 1966), 9.

15

Work Abroad and International Careers

Contributor: William Nolting

As noted in previous chapters, education abroad includes academic and experiential programming. This chapter is about the myriad possibilities open to students and recent graduates for working abroad. Such opportunities have been available since the end of World War II; indeed, many of the postwar programs founded in the late 1940s and early 1950s to promote transatlantic understanding and cooperation included strong experiential components. Work-centered programs remain accessible to students from any college or university—as well as to nonstudents. But until recently, only certain institutions—such as the universities of Michigan, North Carolina, Minnesota, Wisconsin, and Illinois; Michigan State, Harvard, Brown, and Stanford universities; and Goshen College—have been truly proactive in setting up advising offices and support services that provide genuine encouragement and counseling for this kind of experiential education. At most institutions students often have to fend for themselves.

Over the past two or three decades, as more and more universities have offered study-abroad programs, it became commonplace to assume that few students were interested in any educational activities abroad unless they could receive academic credit for their efforts. For some students of limited means, who need to enter credit-bearing programs in order to qualify for financial aid, this may still be the case; however, the cost of most work-abroad options is a fraction of that of study-abroad, and some are even self-financing. U.S. student and institutional attention to work options has steadily grown over the past decade. There are many reasons for this interest: student preference for a nonacademic cultural-immersion experience; their desire to live abroad inexpensively and independently for an extended period of time; the ambition to return overseas, after a previous study- or travel-abroad experience; and the desire to prepare themselves for an international career.

Work abroad has been relatively neglected at most colleges and universities because it simply falls into the bureaucratic cracks. Work-abroad options may well be an utter mystery to study-abroad advisers whose responsibilities have been institutionally limited to academic programs. While it might seem logical for career-planning or employment offices to handle work-abroad advising, such offices frequently lack the international expertise needed to advise in this area.

Traditional study-abroad offices have refrained from promoting work-abroad opportunities because they do not view such programming as their responsibility. Most have their domain exclusively defined as providing access to *credit-granting academic opportunities*. Some education-abroad advisers and administrators fear they might jeopardize their hard-won faculty support if their offices become too clearly identified with experiential education. Such learning tends to be seen as irrelevant to the goals of an academic institution. The professional schools of the same universities, however, value internships highly, often making them a mandatory part of the degree, while career offices tout the value of employment abroad. Undergraduates on many campuses have, meanwhile, been left to wander in a bureaucratic limbo.

Again, this narrow view is changing. Institutions are not only responding to student interest but they are also learning to appreciate the immense value students derive from international work experiences. Additionally, the job market is beginning to tell students and institutions that such experience is good career preparation in a tight and increasingly internationalized economy. Though the best administrative location for any advising function is debatable, the larger question may be how much importance a given college or university grants to nonacademic education of any sort—whether this be learning in the workplace, service or volunteer settings, or any place outside of the proverbial classroom, the results of which may not be amenable to ready evaluation by tests and papers.

Putting these larger questions aside—whether student intellectual growth, personal maturation, and career preparation can or should be limited to American academic modes—the bulk of this chapter has a practical rather than theoretical focus and is intended to introduce the education-abroad adviser to reasonably accessible work-abroad options. The descriptions herein are based upon the reports of hundreds of University of Michigan students and alumni, but these opportunities are available to anyone. Relatively few publications address this subject, although a number of books written for a general audience have recently become available; the best of these are listed in the annotated bibliography in the appendix.

Work versus Study Abroad: Similarities and Differences

One of the best arguments for education-abroad offices to advise on work-abroad options is simply that some of the most significant benefits of a study-abroad experience (as detailed below), are also among the main benefits of a work-abroad experience. Indeed, some would argue that these goals can be even more fully realized in programs that are not specifically set up to meet American academic credit criteria.

Cultural Immersion. Most work-abroad settings are, almost by definition, "full immersion." Unlike many U.S.-sponsored study-abroad programs, the work-abroad participant is likely to be the only American, or one of just a few, working and living in a fully indigenous setting. Whereas most study-abroad students have to work hard to break out of an often comfortable American ghetto, where English is spoken and familiar customs and mores prevail, work-abroad students have no choice but to do what the locals do.

Language Learning. Classroom learning tends to be passive and is largely a solitary endeavor. In a work setting, social interaction is almost always a given. The give-and-take—the immediate feedback—of a workplace can be enormously beneficial in learning a foreign language. Most work-abroad participants demonstrate dramatic gains in their language skills. It should be emphasized, however, that this holds for those already possessing a solid foundation in the language, equivalent to two years' study at the college level. Progress will be greater in the spoken than in the written domain. And one is more likely to learn the slang or dialects associated with everyday life than the formal, or "high," language.

Cross-cultural Learning. As mentioned, the opportunity to meet host-country nationals is assured in most work settings. What is different, however, even from full-immersion study-abroad settings is that one is more likely to experience differences of social organization, such as class and cultural distinctions, than would be likely in the relatively elite, homogeneous, and loosely organized environment of university life. The pace of work, the way in which managers treat workers, and forms of gender, ethnic, or class discrimination may be very different from practices in the United States. Such experience can vastly increase one's interest in, and capacity for, later study of other societies and cultures.

Personal Development. Growth in self-confidence and independence, in tolerance and empathy, in flexibility and adaptability, and in pragmatic know-how and cultural insight is likely to be as great or greater than in most study-abroad settings. Most work settings offer less hand-holding and well-intentioned protection. Although this independence can be stressful, most students adapt readily, discover inner resources, and consider this challenge one of the primary benefits of their experience.

The possibility of academic or job failure is a given in any overseas experience. Many U.S.-sponsored study programs therefore have some provision for on-site counseling; relatively few work opportunities offer this. Some individuals who might struggle in an academic setting may prosper in the more group- and action-oriented environment of a work setting, just as many average students excel in their careers after graduation! By the same token, some academically outstanding students have difficulty dealing with the uncertainties and need for improvisation involved in "pounding the pavement" looking for work or performing a job with loosely defined tasks.

Relevance to Academic Major. For students with certain majors, internships can be much more feasible than a study-abroad program. In engineering, for example, very few study- abroad opportunities exist in the core curriculum because of problems in matching courses with overseas universities. When the University of Michigan, for instance, started a study-abroad program for engineers, the program was placed in the sophomore year because of greater ease in course matching. Engineering internships, on the other hand, are easily available in the summer for juniors, seniors, and graduate students, who can go on paid internships without delaying their graduation date. Yet relatively few work opportunities exist in the humanities, except in related applied fields. An English major can teach English as a foreign language. A history or political science major could do a parliamentary internship.

Antioch, Earlham, Kalamazoo, and Goshen colleges (and perhaps a half-dozen others) have begun to build evaluated, for-credit field experiences into nearly all of their study programs in an effort to combine the best of the academic and work models. These experiences may take the form of job placements before or after a study term, volunteer activity during the academic year, or a field-based independent study built around an internship.

Grade Point Average. If maintaining "academic rigor" abroad is seen as the only institutional goal of the overseas experience, this way of thinking has implications not only for the types of opportunities that are open to students but also for the types of students who qualify for programs. Students with high GPAs are admitted and those with lower GPAs are often not— even though some evidence suggests that a high GPA is not the primary factor in ensuring maximum educational gain abroad. Classroom and test-taking superiority, as measured by the GPA, is less important in admitting students to most, though by no means all, work-abroad programs. Attitude, work habits, and motivation are seen as considerably more important. Thus, a much wider range of students can qualify for work abroad than for study abroad.

Timing of Participation. Work abroad tends to attract slightly older and more intellectually and socially mature students. While most study-abroad participants go during their junior year, most work-abroad participants go after the junior year, after graduation, or as graduate students.

Location. The majority of work-abroad participants, like study-abroad students, end up in western Europe. Unlike study abroad, at least as many work opportunities are available in eastern Europe, Asia, and in many developing countries.

Cost. Cost is one area in which study and work abroad differ significantly. Most work-abroad options are substantially less expensive than study-abroad options for the same location and length of time, although university-sponsored internships with academic course work are an exception.

Noncredit work options may not even delay graduation, since many take place in the summer or after graduation. Still, there may be "opportunity costs"—either lost time when one could be earning credit towards an advanced degree, or lost income compared to what one might be earning in a job back home. But one can argue that the latter options carry their own "cost of a lost opportunity" compared to working abroad, particularly since the majority of work options are limited to students or the young and unattached.

Working Abroad and International Careers

There is a distinct difference between working abroad and actually being in an international career. Many of the options covered below are available to those with little previous work experience and are not especially competitive. The internships in particular can serve as a first step toward an international career. Most of the work options discussed below, however, are generally *not* positions on a career ladder.

Those in international careers may not actually work abroad except for brief business trips. Also, international careers are notoriously competitive. Even an entry-level position may require a combination of extensive background in a discipline related to the career, for example a degree (a master's is often preferred) in business administration or journalism; and career-related work experience. Not surprisingly, in view of this complexity, preparation for an international career often takes place in several stages, as the following chart shows. Those interested in an international career should start by researching it thoroughly in the guides listed in the work-abroad section of the bibliography.

Five Typical Patterns of International Career Development

Pattern 1
- Peace Corps volunteer
- Graduate school in the United States

- Private voluntary organization
- Agency for International Development or the State Department (sometimes followed by work in a public multinational)

Pattern 2
- College year abroad
- Small international educational organization
- Larger international educational organization
- A foundation or a U.S.-based university (as a director of international programs)

Pattern 3
- Business school
- Trainee in a multinational corporation
- Overseas assignment #1 (one or two years after trainee position)
- Overseas assignment #2 (two to four years after overseas assignment #1)
- U.S.-based assignment
- Possible future overseas assignments

Pattern 4
- International studies major
- Foreign service exam
- Foreign service officer in series of overseas posts (two-year cycle)
- Washington, D.C., post
- Other overseas post (may either stay in the foreign service or move into work for an educational or private voluntary organization or for another branch of the U.S. government)

Pattern 5
- Study of technical field (e.g., engineering, agriculture, health)
- Five to ten years of domestic experience
- Project team member with an international consulting firm on a series of overseas contracts
- Independent consultant to U.S. government agencies, multinational corporations, or international private voluntary or educational organizations.

SOURCE: Howard Schuman, *Making It Abroad: The International Job Hunting Guide,* © *1988* (New York: John Wiley, 1988), 135–136. Reprinted by permission of John Wiley & Sons, Inc.

Do most students who seek to go abroad, either for work or study, want an international career? Experience suggests that they do not—at least initially. The vast majority of students interested in a work-abroad experience wish to spend three to twelve months abroad; a few will consider a two-year stint such as the Peace Corps. What these students consciously seek is a serious, nonacademic cultural-immersion experience. Career considerations are secondary. However, many who return from an extended period of working abroad do go on to develop an international career, often by pursuing graduate study or an international-track professional degree in business, public health or medicine, engineering or natural resources, law, or international relations, to name just a few.

Advising for Work Abroad

Advising for work abroad is more complex than advising for study-abroad. One must use a variety of sources (see bibliography) because there is no single exhaustive directory comparable to the IIE books on study-abroad. There are more apparent choices with respect to time, location, and other program aspects. Yet despite the wealth of choices, a perfect fit for a very specific wish, such as a paying position in philosophy in Paris for someone lacking unique qualifications, may be impossible to find. In advising, one cannot neglect any of the following issues, each of which implies specific options. All answers taken together may indicate many or only a few feasible possibilities for any given student.

Visa Status and Work Permits. A work permit is required in any country in order for legal paid employment—an often unknown fact that should be discussed with students. "Off the books" work is often possible, but this limits the type of work to the lowest-paying jobs and puts the individual at risk for exploitation, for on-the-job injury without legal recompense, or for deportation. Visas permitting work are usually far more difficult to get than visas for study or tourism, because jobs of citizens are at issue. Special reciprocal work-exchange programs (usually for students or recent graduates), discussed below, are an important exception to this rule.

Unpaid work, whether in an internship or volunteer capacity, usually does not require a work permit. Some types of work compensated primarily in room, board, and spending money, such as au pair work, are often exempted from the need for a regular work permit. If one has a skill possessed by few citizens of the host country, a work permit can often be obtained, depending on the particular country's regulations. Very few recent graduates are in this position, except for positions in teaching English as a foreign language, where simply being a native speaker of English is a unique qualification. Thousands of Americans work legally in this capacity throughout Asia and, recently, eastern Europe. But some popular destinations such as Spain and Italy, despite high local demand for native speakers of American English, very rarely grant work permits to U.S. citizens.

Duration. Find out when and for how long the student wants to work abroad.

Options for Undergraduates. For undergraduates, work-abroad summer

199

programs are one option. There are internships of all kinds, CIEE and InterExchange Work Permit programs, and volunteer work camps. During the academic year, internships and some CIEE and InterExchange work programs and some "service learning" programs are also available.

Options for Recent Graduates. For recent graduates, there are CIEE work programs of up to six months; some internship programs are also available, though many require that application be made while applicants are still students. Programs of a year or longer are primarily English-teaching positions or positions with organizations such as the Peace Corps.

Options for Graduate Students. Options for graduate students include internships related to the field of study, usually in the summers between years of graduate school.

Student Standing. For CIEE and InterExchange Work Programs, students must begin their participation within six months of having last been a student. For certain internships (e.g., IAESTE, AIESEC), it is possible to go following graduation, but successful applicants must have applied while still a student. Some internships (e.g., U.S. Foreign Service, Ford Foundation) are only for those who will be returning to school.

Location. Most short-term paid positions and many internship programs are in western Europe. Likewise, most short-term volunteer possibilities (workcamps) are in Europe. Most positions in teaching English as a foreign language are in East Asia (Japan, Korea, Taiwan) or eastern Europe. Most long-term volunteer possibilities such as the Peace Corps and nonprofit or religious organizations are in developing areas such as Africa, Latin America, and South and Southeast Asia. Internships are increasingly offered outside Europe (nearly half those listed in the Michigan State directory, for example).

Foreign Language Knowledge. For countries with languages other than English, some knowledge of the language is very useful, if not always required. The CIEE Work-Abroad programs in France, Germany, Costa Rica, and Spain require applicants to have the equivalent of two years' study of the appropriate language at the college level. Many internship programs have a similar requirement. For most overseas teaching positions, knowledge of the host-country language is not required but would be extremely helpful for daily living.

Academic Major. Paid internships are available mainly for applied fields such as engineering or business. In humanities-related fields, paid internships are rare and may be only indirectly related to the major. An art history major, for example, may find an internship at an art auctioning house.

Previous Work or Leadership Experience. Any type of experience beyond the purely academic is a plus. Obviously, for technical positions (such as engineering internships) there is no substitute for academic training—but even in this case prior work experience is advantageous. For a parliamentary internship, prior experience working for a local politician or even in student government would be viewed positively. For positions in teaching English as a foreign language, previous experience as a tutor or conversation partner, even if volunteer, is most valuable. For many volunteer positions, previous volunteer work in the United States demonstrates commitment to the ideal of volunteering.

International Career Preparation. The best path of entry into any career, given the proper academic preparation, is to work in a career-related capacity. Internships are usually the most accessible way of gaining such experience, but many desirable internships related to international careers can be found in the United States. Another common path is to study or work abroad for a year or longer, perfecting one's knowledge of a foreign language and culture, then to return to the United States for graduate school training in a practical discipline.

Degree Credit. Because many summer internships and other work experiences are available, even a noncredit work experience will not necessarily delay graduation. In the case of nonpaying internships, such as those with the U.S. foreign service or the United Nations, it may be difficult to justify the expense without gaining credit in exchange. This can be viewed as an excellent long-term investment—which may indeed pay off in just a few years when it comes time to apply for the first full-time job.

Some students want to take time off, yet are eager to continue their education in a nontraditional manner. A recent University of Michigan graduate is not atypical. Feeling aimless after his sophomore year, he left to work in Britain with the CIEE program for six months, He had ordinary jobs in pubs, but this was his first acquaintanceship with a foreign culture. He was able to save enough in this time to travel in Africa for a year and a half during which he volunteered at a United Nations refugee camp in Somalia. Upon returning to the university, he designed his own major, studying the role of international agencies in developing countries.

Credit-granting internships offered by universities are one way to have one's cake and eat it, too. But the student must be careful to ascertain whether a full semester's credit will be granted—some universities will recognize only actual classwork, not internships, for credit. Credit may also be arranged in the form of an independent study, based on the work experience, with a professor from the student's home institution.

Money. Working abroad will usually be less expensive than either study or travel abroad, but there is a wide range in the cost of various work-abroad opportunities.

It is possible to break even or save money in some types of work. A surprising number of internships pay well enough to cover living expenses, though not airfare. These internships tend to be in practical fields such as business or engineering. Even some university-arranged internships come with a modest overseas stipend.

Undergraduates. For most undergraduates, the CIEE and InterExchange work abroad programs offer the best possibilities to be self-supporting. But this varies greatly, depending on the economy of the particular country, from fairly good chances of saving money, including enough to reimburse the cost of airfare (Britain, France, or Germany), to being barely able to cover on-site living expenses (Costa Rica, Jamaica, and even Ireland). An up-front investment of $1,000 or more is necessary to cover the cost of airfare as well as the cost of living until the first paycheck.

Graduating Students. For those who are graduating, English teaching is another possibility for earning money. Earning power varies, as usual, with the local economy. A good income is possible in Japan, Taiwan, or Korea. In eastern Europe, although the pay may be very good by local standards, unfavorable currency-conversion rates make this a break-even proposition at best. Finally, numerous long-term (at least two years) volunteer possibilities actually cover all expenses, including overseas transportation, and pay a stipend. In the case of the Peace Corps, there is a resettlement allowance payable at the end of duty, which amounts to more than $5,000 for the two-year stint. Nearly all other volunteer positions that pay are also long term, generally for two years.

Most internships arranged by universities have tuition charges, but offer academic courses and credit—as well as logistical support—in return. Financial aid can often be applied to credit-granting internships. Other internships, especially those with international organizations or with the federal government, are unpaid. Living expenses can be considerable, with no credit or financial aid available as compensating factors. Most short-term volunteer opportunities—for less than one year—will cost something, either a fee or the cost of airfare. Many do, however, provide room and board in exchange for the work.

Citizenship. Citizenship can be a factor for some overseas work opportunities. U.S. citizenship or permanent residency is required for the CIEE Work-Abroad Programs, for some internship exchange programs (e.g., Carl Duisberg Society, American-Scandinavian Foundation), and for government positions such as State Department internships or the Peace Corps. International students in the United States may well be interested in doing an internship in a third country. The internship organizations IAESTE and AIESEC both are ideal for this.

Types of Work Abroad

Internships. Career-related traineeships are usually arranged by universities, special internship organizations, or by businesses, governments, or nonprofit international agencies. Some paid internships are available, especially in technical or business fields (e.g., IAESTE, AIESEC, American-Scandinavian Foundation, Carl Duisberg Society, some U.S. government positions, Ford Foundation). Unpaid internships include those with the United Nations and many U.S. government positions. Tuition is charged for most university-sponsored programs, which also usually include classes for academic credit. These may cost the same as or sometimes less than study-abroad programs of similar duration and location.

Advantages. Internships are one of the best preparations for international careers. Academic classes and credit are available for many university-sponsored internships. Many are well-organized; placement, housing, and so forth are often handled by sponsoring organization. Some offer a group experience, either in classes or organized social activities.

Disadvantages. Assignments are sometimes very demanding, leaving little time for travel or other activities. Conversely, some internships involve excessive busy work at the expense of professional tasks. The intern can often take an active role in shaping the nature of assignments. The placement may occasionally not be made until after the student's arrival; specific placement requests may not be possible. A student who wants an internship in an art museum may end up working in an auction house for rare stamps. Ultimately, however, he or she may find that the art business and the stamp business have much in common. In some programs, social contacts may be limited to older professionals uninterested in socializing outside the workplace. U.S. government internships overseas will be in an all-American environment.

Application Requirements. The selection process may be extremely competitive. A good academic record is usually required. Prior language study is often essential if the internship is in a non-English-speaking country. Prior related work experience is very helpful. Internships are available mainly to undergraduate and graduate students, though some are also available to nonstudents. Watch for early-application deadlines!

Duration. Summer or semester-length internships are typical; a few are longer.

Location. Most international internships are located in Europe (and in the United States!); a great many are available in other locations worldwide.

Sample Sponsoring Organizations. Special internship organizations offering paid positions include IAESTE/AIPT, which has technical, scientific, agricultural, and hotel management placements worldwide—(410) 997-2200; AIESEC, which provides business placements worldwide—(212) 979-7400; American-Scandinavian Foundation, for technical positions in Scandinavia—(212) 879-9779; and the Carl Duisberg Society, for business and technical positions in Germany—(212) 760-1400. (See the bibliography for comprehensive directories of internships.)

Government and business: U.S. Foreign Service, paid and unpaid, worldwide—(703) 875-7207; Proctor & Gamble—(513) 983-1100, and Coca-Cola (404) 676-2121, both M.B.A. students only. U.S. Agency for International Development, three-year internship—(202) 663-1451. These particular internships are very competitive.

International organizations: United Nations, unpaid—(212) 963-1091; European Community, paid and unpaid, mostly in the United States—(212) 371-3804 or (202) 862-9500; Ford Foundation, paid, for graduate students in the social sciences only—(212) 573-4927. These particular internships are very competitive, others less so.

Universities: Hundreds of programs are available for undergraduates and graduates in most disciplines and in most regions of the world. (Many of these are academic internships in which students take classes as well as hold an internship.)

Nonprofit organizations: CARE—(212) 686-3110; CONCERN—(714) 953-8575. These particular organizations hire for graduate students only, but others welcome undergraduates as volunteer interns.

Medical students: Elective overseas positions are available for upper-level students.

Short-Term Paid Work. This section describes the main U.S.-based programs of this type. See the bibliography for resources listing other options.

The CIEE Work-Permit Program. The Council on International Educational Exchange's Work-Abroad Program can procure a short-term work permit that allows students or recent graduates to enter a country and seek work of any kind. This program is unique. Usually work permits can be obtained only after receiving a job offer, which would usually not be forthcoming without a work permit! CIEE's Work Abroad Programs are reciprocal exchanges with a limited number of countries: Great Britain, Canada, Costa Rica, France, Germany, Ireland, Jamaica, New Zealand, and size-limited pilot programs with Australia and Spain.

CIEE charges $125 (1992) for the work permit and for limited assistance from its overseas counterparts in finding a job and accommodations. How much students earn depends very much on the economy of their chosen country and can range from as much as $200–$350 per week in Britain (enough to allow savings) to $20 per week in Costa Rica or Jamaica (barely adequate to cover living expenses). CIEE provides reliable income figures with their literature. Students should be advised to take along $500–$1,000 to tide them over until the first paycheck.

CIEE permits are virtually the only way to get legal permission to look for work without already having a job offer. Permits can be used for any type of work. In Britain, approximately 25 percent of the participants find career-related, internship-like positions. The majority of participants find jobs in restaurants, pubs, or clerical or sales positions.

Nearly all jobs involve total cultural immersion because colleagues at work are nearly always local citizens. Participants see the opportunity to experience a foreign culture in a work setting as the most valuable aspect of the program. Social contacts tend to be with people from a variety of class backgrounds. Most participants also feel satisfaction at having succeeded, in a very real sense, on their own. Costs can be low. Participants in Britain, and sometimes France or Germany, are sometimes able to cover their expenses and save. This is much less likely in the other countries.

This is a do-it-yourself program. Some assistance in finding a job and an apartment is provided in Britain and France, and relatively little in the other countries (except for the Spain program, in which CIEE assists applicants in finding a job before departure). Even under the best of circumstances, the stress during the job and apartment hunt can be high. In this sense it is probably as close to the traditional immigrant experience as a student will ever come. On the other hand, few participants fail to find a job.

Applicants must have carried at least an eight-credit-hour load in the semester prior to participation. Two years' study of the appropriate language is required for France, Germany, Costa Rica, and Spain. Participants must be U.S. citizens, though some countries allow U.S. permanent residents to participate. Application is noncompetitive, with no limit on places for all countries except Australia and Spain, where places are filled on a first-come, first-served basis. For applications and further information, contact: CIEE (212) 661-1414, ext. 1126, 1129, or 1130.

Other permit programs. Other organizations can also assist individuals in getting a permit, typically for up to eighteen months, but they require that the individual have a job offer first. Those seeking positions can let potential employers know that the employer would be relieved of the burden of obtaining the work permit, which might increase the chances of getting a job offer. In practice, an employee is rarely hired sight unseen. These permits are most useful for extending a permit for more time than is possible with CIEE (necessitating a return to the United States for the new permit), or for cases in which an individual has the necessary connections—perhaps made during a study-abroad experience—to land a job offer.

These organizations—all of which also arrange for internship placements in technical, business, or hotel/culinary areas—include the Association for International Practical Training (AIPT)—(410) 997-2200, for Australia, Britain, Finland, France, Ireland, Japan, Germany, Malaysia, or Switzerland; The American-Scandinavian Foundation—(212) 879-9779, for all the Scandinavian countries; and the Carl Duisberg Society—(212) 760-1400 for Germany. IAESTE, a branch of AIPT, can obtain permits for fifty-two countries, but only for students.

For students who prefer to be placed in a paying job of a casual variety rather than finding their own, InterExchange—(212) 924-0446, arranges placements for modest fees ranging from $100 to $225 (1992). Placements are offered in Czechoslovakia and Finland (teaching English); Australia, Germany, and Switzerland (resort jobs); Norway, Finland, and France (agricultural work); and for women only, au pair placements in Austria, France, and Germany (see below).

Other Types of Paid Short-Term Work. A well-established tradition in Europe, au pair work involves living in a private home and helping with housework and childcare. Enough time should be provided each week for the au pair to attend classes part time. Room, board, and a small stipend are provided. As au pair work is considered to be for purposes of educational exchange, it is exempted from work permit regulations by most European countries, although formal contracts are necessary. Most au pair placements are for six months to one year or sometimes summer only. Au pair placements for men are rare. The Experiment in International Living's "Au Pair Homestay Program" arranges for placements for a fee of $1,200 to $1,400; call (412) 422-3202 or (202) 408-5380 for more information.

Work Without a Permit. Working for pay without a work permit is illegal. The illegal worker is without any legal protection from exploitation, or injury on the job, and may be deported if discovered by the authorities. Student travelers do occasionally find casual work without a permit, usually of a menial and low-paying variety, but it is generally not recommended.

Teaching English as a Foreign Language (without credentials). Positions teaching English as a foreign language may be arranged by a sponsoring organization or simply found by the individual in an on-site interview. Duties vary widely from assisting a teacher to having full responsibilities for several large classes a day.

Pay varies widely depending on the economy of the country. Positions in East Asia (Japan, Taiwan, Korea) can pay very well. If the position has been arranged by a sponsoring organization, airfare may be included and housing—otherwise scarce and expensive—provided. If the position is self-sought, beginning expenses can be very high, including airfare, housing (deposit of several months' nonrefundable rent), and a trip to another country to obtain a work permit.

In areas with poor economies, such as eastern Europe or China, pay can be high by local standards, but unfavorable currency-conversion rates makes these in effect volunteer positions. Living expenses can be covered, but not the cost of airfare. Many volunteer organizations, private or church-related, provide placements.

Some organizations such as WorldTeach or Georgetown University charge a fee for placement into an EFL teaching position. Training is provided and housing is arranged. Some academic credit may be available.

Advantages. Teaching English is one of the few long-term overseas positions available to graduates with little work experience. Considerable cultural-immersion is possible, especially for those who have knowledge of the host country's language before coming. Program-sponsored placements are generally well organized; teachers in these programs are treated particularly well as honored guests or cultural ambassadors.

Disadvantages. Most of the working day is spent speaking English, which makes learning the host country's language difficult. For those who arrive with little knowledge of the host country's language, friendships tend to be mainly with other English-speaking expatriates. Those who find their own positions may have difficulty negotiating for housing or details of contracts. Breaking of contracts by the employer, with work time unpaid or failure to deliver a promised return airfare, is not unknown.

Application Requirements. In most cases, a bachelor's degree is required. Applicants must be native speakers of English. For most positions outside western Europe, no other credential is required, though having English as a major and some TEFL experience is a big advantage. Volunteering as a tutor for one's own university's English program for foreign students is an easy way to get experience. No knowledge of the host country's language is usually required, though this actually represents a disadvantage in the long run.

Duration. Nearly all positions are for at least one year. A few summer- or semester-long placements are available.

Locations. Most positions are in East Asia (Japan, Taiwan, Korea, China) or eastern Europe. Some are also available in Latin America and Africa. In western Europe, TEFL positions are very competitive and formal TEFL credentials are often necessary.

Sample Sponsoring Organizations. Governments: The Japanese English Teaching (JET) program recruits teachers for Japan through Japanese consulates—(202) 939-6700; the PRC Embassy recruits EFL teachers for the People's Republic of China—(202) 328-2563.

Universities: Earlham College, Japan only—(317) 983-1324, and Princeton-in-Asia, most of Asia—(609) 258-5300, have well-organized programs that place teachers into paying positions.

Fulbright English Teaching Assistants: Available for future teachers of French or German, these positions are competitive—(212) 984-5330.

Private language schools: Two large chains recruit from the United States for their overseas branches; AEON, Japan only—(213) 550-0940, and ELS, Asia and South America—(213) 642-0982.

Short-term placements: InterExchange (for Czechoslovakia and Finland) offers placements for six months, for a fee of less than $200—(212) 924-0446. The YMCA has two summertime overseas programs, Interns Abroad—(202) 797-4470, and International Camp Counselor Program—(212) 563-3441.

Teaching-intern-for-a-fee: Georgetown University—(202) 298-0200, and others offer TEFL placements for a fee ($1,500 is typical); six credit hours are given for one year's teaching.

Volunteer-for-a-fee: WorldTeach—(617) 495-5527, and AFS Intercultural Programs—(800) AFS-INFO place teachers for a substantial fee ($1,000–$3,000), which includes training and logistical arrangements.

Peace Corps: Teachers of EFL are still placed by the Peace Corps. Recruiting requirements are strict, although formal TEFL credentials are not required for most positions. Call (800) 424-8580 for more information.

Other volunteer organizations: Education for Democracy—(205) 434-3889, places teachers throughout Eastern Europe and the former Soviet Union. Many church-related organizations, such the YMCA—(206) 382-5008, Brethren—(708) 742-5100, and others place English teachers into non-missionary teacher jobs. In most cases, volunteers are expected to pay for their airfare.

Professional Teaching Positions in Overseas K-12 Schools. A completely different realm of possibilities exists for those with certification to teach in kindergarten through high school. There are Department of Defense (DOD) schools at overseas U.S. military bases. Teaching at these schools is similar to teaching in U.S. public schools. For applications, call (202) 325-0885.

The other large groups of overseas schools are private international schools (some of these are supported by the U.S. State Department), which are English-language schools for the offspring of expatriate diplomats and businesspersons. Teaching in these schools is like teaching in an elite private school with an international student body. The easiest way to land a position in one of these schools is to attend one of the special job fairs for international schools. Major fairs are held in February, and a few smaller fairs take place in June. For more information, contact the two largest job fair organizers: University of Northern Iowa—(319) 273-2083; and International Schools Services—(609) 452-0990. International Schools Internship Program recruits "teaching interns" (certification not necessary) for overseas K-12 schools; call (508) 580-1880. Also, many universities offer tuition-charging student teaching programs abroad.

Volunteer Work Abroad. Traditionally, volunteer work abroad has been seen as service work. Though this is still true, today many volunteer organizations see their role as one of solidarity with and empowerment of indigenous peoples. Volunteers not only give, but also receive, an education in respect for the richness of traditional cultures and an understanding of the sometime deleterious effects of policies of developed countries upon the developing world.

Volunteer opportunities seem to fall into two categories: short-term (a few weeks to a few months), of which the best-known example is the so-called "workcamp"; and long-term (from six months to two years or longer). Most volunteer positions are with small nonprofit organizations or are church-affiliated.

Paid volunteer positions, in which the participant's expenses are entirely covered, are virtually all for periods of two years or longer (e.g., Peace Corps, Brethren, Mennonites). The Peace Corps alone provides additional benefits, including a "resettlement allowance" of about $200 for each month served, provisions for deferring or partial cancellation of educational loans, and some tuition support for further study. Volunteering in exchange for room and board is a possibility for surprisingly many volunteer positions, both short- and long-term. Apart from a small application fee, the partici-pant's main expense is transportation to and from the site, and pocket money (e.g., YMCA, most workcamps, many TEFL positions).

The idea that a true volunteer position should be unpaid is still alive and well, particularly with organizations based in developing countries; in such cases all expenses are absorbed by by the volunteer.

Fee-charging volunteer programs are of two main types: those which offer a structured learning experience with the possibility of earning aca-demic credit (e.g., Partnership for Service Learning, Goshen College); and those that provide placement, training, and on-site support for a fee (e.g., WorldTeach, Amigos de las Americas). Fees for the latter tend to be mod-est, generally less than those of a U.S.-sponsored study program of similar duration in the same location.

Advantages. Volunteers are needed for a huge variety of work, ranging from the unskilled to the professional, in virtually all areas of the world. Vol-unteering is frequently the only realistic possibility for working in develop-ing countries.

Volunteer positions in developing countries, especially long-term ones, are perhaps the best initial preparation for those interested in a career in de-velopment work. Nearly all volunteer positions offer a high degree of cul-tural immersion. In many cases the volunteer may be the only American, or one of a few, in a given volunteer project. "Workcamps," short-term projects organized mainly in Europe, provide a well-organized, very inexpensive group experience with young people from all over Europe, and might be worth considering as an alternative to summer study, paid work, or travel abroad. The CIEE Travel Grants (Bowman Scholarships) can be used to support service work in Third World countries. Many community service groups (e.g., Rotary) or churches are willing to assist volunteers with ex-penses.

Disadvantages. Service work is not for everyone. Idealistic young per-sons in particular may be frustrated at being able to do little about condi-tions they would like to see changed. The Berry and Chisholm publication, *How to Serve and Learn Abroad Effectively: Students Tell Students,* gives excellent guidance for those considering service work. Culture shock can be great for sojourners to developing countries. Not every volunteer organization has a strong support network in place, though many do.

Application Requirements. These vary widely depending on the organization, length and type of assignment. For example, screening for the Peace Corps is thorough and the application process can take six months to a year. For other positions such as workcamps, applications are noncompetitive and are on a first-come, first-served basis. Organizations affiliated with religious groups may insist on membership in the religion or at least a willingness to examine the particular belief.

Duration. Most workcamps last two to three weeks in the summer. Other volunteer possibilities vary in length from a few weeks to two or three years.

Locations. Short-term possibilities, such as workcamps, and a few long-term ones are available in Europe. The vast majority of long-term positions, and some short-term positions, are in developing countries—primarily in Africa, Latin America, and South and Southeast Asia, with relatively few possibilities in East Asia. Volunteer positions in eastern Europe are gradually opening up.

Sample Sponsoring Organizations. Government: The Peace Corps—(800) 424-8580.

Major International Organizations: The United Nations Development Corps—(800) 424-8580, ext. 2243; Project Hope—(703) 837-2100. Note that "volunteer" positions with these organizations are only for those with a great deal of training in specific technical or health areas.

Service-Learning, with academic credit possible: The Partnership for Service Learning—(212) 986-0989; Goshen College—(800) 348-7422. Kibbutz Aliya—(800) 444-7007; International Christian Youth Exchange—(212) 206-7307; Lisle Fellowship—(313) 847-7126; Minnesota Studies in International Development, a service internship program—(612) 626-2234.

Nonprofit volunteer-for-a-fee organizations: WorldTeach—(617) 495-5527; Amigos de las Americas—(800) 231-7796; Los Ninos—(619) 661-6912.

Regilios-affiliated organizations: Brethren Volunteer Service—(708) 742-5100; Mennonite Central Committee—(717) 859-1151; American Zionist Youth Foundation—(212) 751-6070

Short-term workcamps: CIEE—(212) 661-1414, ext. 1139; Volunteers for Peace (VFP)—(802) 259-2759.

Opportunities in eastern Europe and the former USSR: Call the Citizen's Democracy Corps, a clearinghouse for volunteer organizations in this part of the world, at (800) 394-1945.

Summary

American colleges and universities must be clear about their primary mission as academic institutions. Education-abroad programming will probably always be dominated by credit-bearing study programs, but students learn in many different ways and have many different needs, only some of which can be satisfied by educational programs that are purely academic in their structures, methods, and values. As an alternative to academic programs, many students are now seeking work opportunities abroad, in part because of their belief in the intrinsic educational value of such experiences, in part because of economic advantages they provide, and in part for career preparation. All of these motivations are valid and need to be supported by advisers and institutions.

16

Program Evaluation

Contributors: Michael Laubscher and Ronald Pirog

Program Quality

There is no more lively or important topic in the field of education abroad than program quality. Experienced advisers and program administrators know that it is hard enough to agree in principle on what defines a "good" program and what identifies a "bad" one. It is even more difficult to reach a consensus on whether a particular program is good. You will nevertheless be asked qualitative questions about programs every day. Although lists can be drawn up and some institutional consensus reached, objective, conclusive, final, and unanimous answers are nearly impossible to provide.

Some advisers have declared flatly that there is no such thing as a good or a bad program, only those that meet or do not meet the needs of particular students or specific institutions. And even these relativistic judgments may not, they add, be clear in advance; one can judge programs only in retrospect.

Further, students are likely to have a set of criteria for judging the value of their experience that is quite different from that used to determine its creditworthiness. Sometimes these criteria are quite visceral (e.g., how much "fun" they had or how many new places they visited). More often, students are eager to reflect searchingly on how they have grown, how they see the world differently, how alive they felt when they were abroad, or how they have a new sense of direction. Moreover, whatever a student's immediate conclusions, they are quite likely to alter with time. All of which is to say that if our professional and personal concerns are with the total educational value of the overseas experience, we should not rush to easy and oversimplified judgments.

This philosophical perspective does not, however, eliminate the institutional pressures you will feel to present pragmatic conclusions. Judging the quality of a program has become more and more difficult, in part because of the proliferation of overseas programs. Each academic year the typical education-abroad office is inundated with new literature about existing programs as well as material on newly developed ones. The *1992–93 Academic Year Abroad,* published by the Institute of International Education (IIE), lists 2,060 programs worldwide; *Vacation Study Abroad* lists another 1,400 summer and short-term programs. In addition, a host of noncredit programs do not appear in these volumes.

But even if your institution has restrictive policies or a limited list of "approved" programs, the need to assess program quality has not been eliminated. While quality in this academic sense is defined somewhat narrowly as creditworthiness, it is nevertheless not so simple. It is therefore crucial for you to have a systematic process for evaluating your own programs objectively and frequently. Besides, students will want to know what you think about other programs.

Given the large number of existing overseas programs, the promise of many new ones, and the difficulty in keeping current, this chapter provides some basic evaluation guidelines. The first section focuses on internal or institutional self-evaluation—assessing programs sponsored by your own institution. The second section focuses on the external evaluation—judging programs sponsored by other U.S. colleges and universities and consortia, foreign universities, and agencies. Although your institutional standards should be the same when judging the overall quality and appropriateness of all programs, the means of evaluation are likely to differ.

As stressed in previous chapters, your institution must have established pedagogical guidelines and goals for education abroad as part of its mission statement. Likewise, you must be thoroughly knowledgeable about them— they should be prominent in the review process. Without such a frame of institutional reference, determining not only the quality of your own programs but also judging which external programs best compare to these standards will be impossible.

Program evaluation is complicated precisely because many intangible elements are being judged. On the one hand, a program may get high marks because it complements or supplements work done on the home campus and thereby conforms to the institution's standards of quality. On the other hand, the whole point of studying abroad is to learn different things in a different way. Therefore, another measure of a program's quality may relate to its ability to present entirely new and different academic, cultural, and personal experiences—typically regarded as integral to the ideals of education abroad. The problem, however, is that these singular elements are not readily and systematically understood (or, if understood, not fully appreciated) by your faculty because they were introduced through a "foreign" system of learning, or (even more suspect) through initiative and personal involvement that are difficult to grade or otherwise evaluate. Nevertheless, in spite of the difficulty of assessing every single aspect of student learning or program strength abroad, the ongoing evaluation is a necessary task and provides a vital service to the home institution and to the individual student.

The Internal Evaluation

At its most complete, an internal evaluation involves on-site information-gathering visits by a team from your campus. The team should consist of independent educators drawn, at least in part, from the field of international education or even an accrediting agency. This level of evaluation can be both expensive and time-consuming. Regardless of the level on which the evaluation takes place, an institutional self-assessment should be an ongoing, systematic, and integral part of any institution's education-abroad programming.

In establishing a regular approach to self-evaluation, you must take the lead in examining the relationship between the institution's education-abroad programs and its overall mission. Specific objectives, evaluation criteria, and assessment procedures must be identified in the context of the mission statement. The following discussion of program evaluation will therefore be general, with a few concrete examples for the sake of clarity. Obviously, specific criteria and evaluation procedures will differ from one institution to the next in accordance with its particular goals and objectives.

Criteria. Evaluation criteria must be general enough to allow for flexibility but specific enough to give the assessment a concrete direction and focus. The following are general criteria included in most institutional guidelines:

• Does the program help to fulfill the institution's overall mission, general goals, and strategic plan?

• What inherent academic quality or distinction does the program provide?

• Is the program's pedagogical methodology compatible with its defined goals?

• To what extent does the program complement (rather than duplicate) course work available at the home campus?

• What rationale is given for basing the program abroad?

• What rationale is offered for the program's particular location?

• How desirable is such a program, given the institution's academic mission and the mission of cross-cultural education in general? That is, what is the level of need?

• How available and adequate are the resources and support services abroad to ensure a viable program of high academic quality?

• To what extent does the program take advantage of the features and resources unique to education abroad, such as the level of cultural immersion, the degree of integration into the host institution's academic and student life, the length of time spent abroad, and the nature and degree of exposure to the host culture and language?

• What is the level of student and faculty interest in maintaining this particular kind of program?

Each of these general criteria can be further refined. In their very useful guide to program evaluation, *Study Abroad Programs: An Evaluation Guide* (May 1979), the Task Force on Study Abroad of the American Association of Collegiate Registrars and Admissions Officers (AACRAO) and NAFSA: Association of International Educators present program evaluation criteria in the form of eighty-nine specific questions. These are divided into four general areas:

Basic information
• The adequacy and accuracy of printed materials.
• The clarity of the program's objectives and the ways that the program and its location and resources contribute to the fulfillment of those objectives.
• Admissions requirements, their relation to the program's objectives, and the ways in which they are enforced.

Academic aspects
• How does the curriculum contribute to fulfilling the program objectives? How does it benefit from the host environment? How does it compare with the home curriculum in terms of level and degree of difficulty?
• What are the qualifications and attitudes of the faculty teaching the courses abroad?
• What are the academic resources (e.g., library and laboratory facilities, language labs, etc.)? How do they support the program's curriculum?

Interaction with host culture
• Predeparture and on-site orientation—are they adequate?
• To what degree does the program promote and facilitate student interaction with the host culture?

Administrative aspects
• What is the extent and adequacy of administrative support at the home campus?
• How effective is the on-site support structure, including the resident director and administrative support staff?
• How is the program affiliated, if at all, with the host institution?
• Are housing and meal arrangements adequate?
• Are there sufficient support services (for example, personal and academic advising and health services)?
• How much does the program cost and what will this include? How accurate is the cost information available to the students?
• Are the travel arrangements adequate?

Copies of *Study Abroad Programs: An Evaluation Guide* are available from NAFSA, 1875 Connecticut Ave., N.W., Suite 1000, Washington, D.C. 20009.

Sources of Information. In order to conduct an effective and thorough evaluation, you and your colleagues will need to consider input from a wide variety of sources: returning students, on-site faculty and staff, the home campus's faculty and academic units, the study-abroad staff, and outside evaluation teams.

Returning Students. The study-abroad office should systematically obtain as much information as possible from returning students. One method would be to send out survey questionnaires to all students immediately upon their return from abroad. In spring 1986 the NAFSA Field Service, with support from USIA, funded a SECUSSA seminar at Penn State University to develop a survey instrument for collecting information from returning study-abroad participants. This instrument is generic and, so, can accommodate the needs of a wide variety of institutions. It can also be adapted for use in collecting information about other institutions' programs; administrators could also use it to collect information from students as a part of the institution's ongoing self-assessment program (appendix 3 shows how Penn State has adapted the instrument for that very purpose).

Although survey instruments can be useful, they also have their limitations. It is therefore advisable, whenever possible, to include personal interviews with a random sampling of returned students to solicit oral comments. The interviewer should be prepared with specific questions (some of which may be prompted by information already obtained from the survey responses), and students should be encouraged to volunteer whatever information they consider relevant and significant.

Reports from On-Site Staff. The study-abroad office should receive annual reports from its on-site staff. The resident director or coordinator can identify problem areas and provide an insider's perspective on the relative success of the program on an annual basis. Although individual faculty members abroad may not be able to provide as extensive an assessment of the overall program, they can certainly report on their students' academic caliber and performance. In addition, their general views on the program as a whole can be solicited indirectly through the resident director/coordinator or through personal interviews conducted during a site visit.

Site visits. Site visits are an essential component of any ongoing self-evaluation. You, or someone from your office or advisory committee, needs to make periodic visits to each program sponsored by your institution. This is done to ascertain that acceptable levels of administrative and logistical support are being maintained, and to nurture rapport with, and elicit support from, the host faculty and staff. Provisions should also be made, either through the resident faculty director or via a faculty representative visiting from the home institution, to assess course compatibility in terms of content and academic quality.

Faculty Oversight. Your advisory committee, or a special faculty review committee, should be involved in program review. Whatever form the committee takes, its perspective on the extent to which specific programs abroad are compatible with and fulfill the home institution's academic mission is fundamental.

Outside Evaluators. Every effort should also be made to obtain the services of an outside evaluation team as a way of providing an objective cross-check of the institution's internal review—if not annually, then at least every three to five years. As an example, the Commission on Higher Education of the Middle States Association of Colleges and Schools (CHE/MSA) has been providing a study-abroad evaluation service to its member institutions since 1981. A CHE/MSA evaluator reviews all the pertinent written information about the program, then visits the program site for a day or two during its actual operation.

During the site visit, the evaluator interviews as many students, faculty, and administrative staff members as possible and tries to assess a wide range of activities, including promotion and recruitment, selection and admission, orientation, any relevant financial aspects of the program, and the fit between, the curriculum and the mission and objectives of the home institution. The evaluator also talks to faculty about their perceptions of the program; students are asked about their perceptions of the faculty and their overall experiences, both academic and cross-cultural. The evaluator then prepares a written report for submission to the home institution's chief executive officer and study-abroad office. The NAFSA Consultation Service, operated for thirty years, is an excellent source of affordable expertise. A brochure describing the service is available from NAFSA at 202.462.4811. CIEE also provides an evaluation service to its members, and informal arrangements are possible with many consortia.

Follow-Up. No program review is complete without adequate follow-up, nor is any program without room for improvement. Maintaining the quality and integrity of a program is a never-ending process. One of the more frustrating experiences is to discover that a program you and others considered nearly perfect one year may be seen to be a near-disaster the next. Any number of factors can contribute to the relative success or failure of a program in a given year, as well as to perceptions about it.

By drawing on as many different sources as possible to ensure adequate cross-checks and differing perspectives, the program evaluation process must carefully interpret all available information in light of clearly defined institutional criteria. Only then can the institution make appropriate judgments or necessary changes. Given the dynamic conditions and circumstances surrounding education abroad, every program must be considered a potential subject for revision and refinement. A systematic approach to self-evaluation and follow-up will help the institution maintain effective programs that fulfill its goals.

Evaluating External Programs

Most U.S. students who participate in credit-bearing programs are enrolled in programs sponsored directly by their own institutions. This pattern ensures a good measure of home-campus control over academic and economic matters abroad. It also means that when an institution concludes, through its own internal review, that a program is not working well, it can be changed or dropped. However, the ultimate control any college or university has over education-abroad programming comes from the simple fact that it has the authority to grant or deny academic credit as it sees fit, in accordance with its own standards. Thus, whether students undertake programs sponsored by their own institution, or those sponsored by others, the criteria for creditworthiness presumably remains the same.

If an institution has set up its own programs and has confidence in them, it is much better able to judge student performance and to award credit than if students participate in programs sponsored by others. Few institutions can offer *all* the programs its students might be interested in. Even campuses with many of their own programs have to consider allowing at least some (and often many) students to look elsewhere. Many campuses, especially small ones, offer few or no programs of their own, so all students seeking an education-abroad experience must look elsewhere. It is clearly to the advantage of such students to know, well before they depart (and ideally at the very outset of the advising process), what credit they can expect to receive. This means that you will have to have some way to evaluate outside programs.

Unfortunately, given the current number and range of programs, there is no easy way to assess their quality. Even compiling a list of approved programs can be a laborious task. Most reputable U.S. institutions, consortia, and agencies do their own internal evaluations, but the results are often not made widely available. Nor is it very feasible for you to do site visits, even brief ones, to every program some of your students are interested in. If you can find the time, money, and energy to visit programs abroad, however, such an undertaking would be very worthwhile. Some organizations and agencies regularly sponsor such opportunities. Most, however, do not.

Criteria. The general criteria discussed above for evaluating your own programs ought to be equally applicable for judging other programs. In both

219

cases the questions are simply whether the program meets home-campus academic standards: Does it offer something unique and important that cannot be obtained domestically? Does it provide a truly intercultural experience? Are students properly fed, housed, and counseled? Is student performance adequately and fairly judged?

If programs are seen to duplicate any of your own programs in curriculum, location, or emphasis, additional criterion might concern *comparative* overall quality or perhaps cost. In the case of the programs that compete with your own offerings, there should probably be compelling academic reasons for giving the nod to an external program—if a choice has to be made. In programs of comparable quality, economic considerations that benefit students may occasionally conflict with economic considerations that redound to your own program or institution, This sort of dilemma pits institutional loyalties against student needs and is never easy to resolve.

Sources of Information. Invariably there will be less information about external programs. Additionally, what is available may be less objective. But you should still be able to assess external programs and get the answers you, your colleagues, and your students need.

IIE Guides. At the earliest stages of assessment, you will often need a succinct and accurate overview of each program.. The IIE guides provide this. The guides identify each program by location, operating dates, academic subjects, eligibility, and amount of credit that can be earned. The guides also spell out costs and what is covered, housing, application deadlines, the source of accreditation, plus some history and how to receive further information. Although this information is furnished by sponsors and may not be absolutely accurate in every particular detail, IIE does its best to keep it current, to define carefully what its terms mean, and to be impartial. No qualitative questions can be answered by these listings, but hard information can be obtained.

Program Materials. Perhaps understandably in the age of consumerism and hype, materials sent to your campus by other universities, consortia, and agencies trying to interest you and your students in their programs are likely to be unbalanced mixtures of hard information and soft sell. The current level of verbal and visual hyperbole is very sophisticated. Let the reader beware. At the same time, respectable programs provide good, ample, detailed information in their materials. Brochures, fliers, posters, even perhaps videos must be examined critically. In view of the sheer number of overseas programs, the task of critically evaluating each piece of literature can be a formidable one.

To reject the information (even that written between the lines) because it is often mixed in with the promotional hype is to ignore excellent resources and perspectives. Furthermore, it will usually be apparent from the litera-ture when a program is trying to obscure some deficiency or is contradict-ing itself. The revered Lily von Klemperer lived by the maxim "truth in ad-vertising." Her invaluable essay, "How to Read Study-Abroad Literature" is essential reading (see appendix 5). Some of her wisdom is paraphrased below:

- If not the quality, then at least the suitability and compatibility of a pro-gram is reflected in the way it is presented.
- Be wary if you cannot easily identify the program sponsor or be told how to receive more information.
- Be wary of vague information about the actual academic location of the program, academic calendar, size, methods of instruction and testing, and available courses.
- Be wary if eligibility requirements (class status, minimum age, cumu-lative grade point average, foreign language competency, prerequisites, etc.) seem too variable.
- Be wary if the administration/faculty/staff (credentials, on-site experi-ence) are not identified.
- Be especially wary if costs and what is covered are not carefully enu-merated and dated.

In sum, a good brochure tells you what a program costs, as well as what is, and is not, included. Features such as orientation, flight information, homestays, internships, housing type and selection policy, extracurricular activities, and trips/excursions should be spelled out in detail. The refund policy should also be clearly documented as well as the relationship of pro-gram costs to the value of the dollar.

Program Representatives. Not all programs send representatives to cam-pus to discuss their programs. If you have the opportunity to host such per-sons, a great deal of useful information and insight can be gained. To make the most out of this visit, you should make sure that you have first reviewed all relevant materials, including student evaluations, in order to be able to get at matters that are not clear or discuss current developments in the pro-gram or on your campus. If you have questions or concerns, this is the time to bring them up.

In addition to your own private conversation, it also can be very helpful to arrange for the program representative to meet with your advisory com-mittee, appropriate faculty in key departments, and perhaps the academic dean. Often representatives also wish to hold general information meetings with interested students. Unless this is impossible, you should support this initiative as a way for students to learn more about the program. Former participants and visiting foreign students from the country in which the pro-gram is located might also be invited. As with reading program materials, it is important to consider what is and is not said in these meetings.

221

Student Evaluations. As in the case of an internal evaluation of programs, reading the evaluations of, and conducting interviews with, students who have returned from participating in a program overseas can be an invaluable source. Unlike the situation with your own programs, where you have access to a large amount of collective opinion, it is unlikely that the number of student assessments of external programs will be numerous, at least for a given semester or year. A word of caution: Try not to give too much weight to any one student's evaluation, positive or negative; the more readings you have, the closer you get to being objective.

It is also accepted practice to (1) request evaluations of a program from students at other institutions, (2) check evaluations from previous years to determine patterns of change, and (3) request student assessments from the program itself. When serious discrepancies or concerns arise from these comparisons, further discussions with students or with the program are in order.

Students as Guinea Pigs. If the desired information about a particular overseas program is not forthcoming, it is sometimes necessary to use one student as a guinea pig. Obviously, you need to be frank with the student about credit prospects. When the student returns and the record is available for review, a decision will then have to be made about whether to approve the program, place it on an informal "worry list," or drop it altogether from consideration. Prudence dictates, of course, that a single student's evaluation be weighed together with the insights of colleagues, the opinions of students at other universities, or by initiating contact with the program directly.

Contact with Colleagues. Making contact with trusted colleagues at comparable institutions is another valuable resource in the evaluation process. In some regions, where numerous advisers from similar types of colleges or universities are geographically proximate, occasional meetings can be held several times a year for the purpose of comparing notes on programs. Too-public discussions about particular programs (for instance at NAFSA conferences or SECUSS-L over the electronic mail network) are prone to cause hard feelings and also in some cases can lead to legal complications. On the other hand, open and free discussions about how to improve the general quality of education-abroad programs and programming are essential.

Other sources. Other sources, which may or may not yield pertinent information, include the following:

• A survey of one's own campus to learn whether a faculty member or other person may already have knowledge about the program in question, may have visited the site in question, or may plan to be in the area on sabbatical and could visit a site or sites.

• Foreign students on campus may be familiar with programs in their country or be willing to visit a certain program upon their return home.

• Students who are overseas (studying or just traveling) might be able to visit a particular site or meet with students from other programs and share their impressions.

- Parents who plan to visit children on a particular program might be contacted as well to solicit their impressions.
- Alumni living overseas might be willing to visit a site in their area.

Direct enrollment. Most of what has been said thus far pertains to overseas programs sponsored by U.S.-based institutions or organizations. The process of evaluating overseas programs becomes more difficult and complicated when a student intends to enroll directly into a foreign institution or program without going through an intermediary sponsor. Fortunately, there are an increasing number of foreign institutions that have set up international program offices to deal with overseas students. Contact them directly or read their literature.

An organization such as AACRAO also provides information about the transferability of work done through direct enrollment at foreign institutions. Your colleagues in the admissions office and the registrar's office might also be able to provide some assistance. Finally, a number of private organizations (and consultants) specialize in evaluating transcripts from foreign institutions; while this sort of credential evaluation is usually for foreign students, it can be applicable for American students who have studied in a foreign university.

The regional and national conferences of NAFSA (with counterparts in Japan and Europe) provide excellent settings for direct contact with the representatives of foreign institutions. A safe method in evaluating quality is to use institutions abroad that are already being served by U.S.-based sponsors or have existing exchange programs with U.S. colleges and universities, especially if those institutions are comparable to your own. Another approach, though more time consuming and cumbersome, is to check with the accrediting agencies of the country in question (e.g., the ministry of education), with the U.S. embassies/consulates in that country, with the U.S. Department of Education, or with the many handbooks dealing with the subject of evaluating overseas institutions. Your main objective in all of these approaches is to use whatever method or resource is available to ensure that the program meets the two basic criteria of comparable quality and suitability.

PART FOUR
Appendixes

STUDY, WORK, AND TRAVEL ABROAD: A BIBLIOGRAPHY

"GETTING ON WITH THE TASK"
REPORT OF THE NATIONAL TASK FORCE ON UNDERGRADUATE
EDUCATION ABROAD, 1990

PENN STATE UNIVERSITY'S PROGRAM EVALUATION GUIDE

NAFSA CODE OF ETHICS, 1992

"HOW TO READ STUDY ABROAD LITERATURE BY LILY VON KLEMPERER, 1974

Appendix 1

Study, Work, and Travel Abroad
A Bibliography

Contributors: Heidi Soneson, Catherine Gamon, and
William Nolting

Resources preceded by an asterisk (*) are essential for any education-abroad library. Following the bibliography is a list of organizations and publishers that provide resources as well as publication catalogues and/or free information on education abroad.

Adviser's References

INTERNATIONAL EDUCATION

Abroad and Beyond: Patterns in American Overseas Education. Craufurd Goodwin and Michael Nacht. 1988. Cambridge University Press. $10.95 paperback; $32.95 hardcover.

Goodwin and Nacht's IIE-sponsored analysis of the fast-growing field of study abroad. Contains discussion of the issues study abroad presents to U.S. higher education—and the consequent policy decisions administrators face.

AIFS Advisors' Guides. Various authors and dates. AIFS. Free.

Published quarterly by AIFS, these guides are written for study-abroad advisers and others in the field of international education. Study-abroad topics include political advocacy, nontraditional programs, promoting ethnic diversity, and reentry.

Black Students and Overseas Programs: Broadening the Base of Participation. Holly Carter 1991. CIEE. $10 plus postage and handling.

Addresses the issue of underrepresented groups in overseas study. Contains papers written by faculty, administrators, and students.

Building the Professional Dimension of Educational Exchange. Edited by Joy Reid. 1988. Intercultural Press. $19.95 plus postage and handling.
The first book devoted exclusively to defining the theoretical and operational domains of the international educational exchange professional.

CIEE Occasional Papers. Various authors and dates. CIEE. Costs range from $3 to $6. Papers 1–19 are bound in a single volume that costs $16.
These 28 occasional papers focus on various aspects of the study-abroad field, including studies on U.S. student populations overseas, international business programs, the nature of international education, and essential considerations in developing successful programs in the developing world. The compilation of the first nineteen occasional papers documents the evolution of international educational exchange between 1965 and 1975, and provides a historical perspective that lays the foundation for the present state of international educational exchange.

Crises, Emergencies, and the Study Abroad Program. Edited by Deborah J. Hill. 1989. Renaissance Publications. $10.50 plus postage and handling.
A collection of 10 essays exploring crises and emergencies as they relate to the student studying abroad. The essays are divided into three main sections: "Safety," "Mental Health," and "Crisis Prevention."

"Educating for Global Competence: The Report of the Advisory Council for International Educational Exchange." 1988. CIEE. $5.
In this report, an advisory group of distinguished figures from U.S. education, business, and government, chaired by Thomas A. Bartlett, chancellor of the University of Alabama, reviews the current state of study abroad and makes recommendations for the future.

* *Educational Associate.* Available to designated institutional representatives and included in IIE's institutional membership fee.
This IIE membership newsletter, published five times annually, provides a chronicle of trends and resources in international education.

Film and Video Resources for International Educational Exchange. Lee Zeigler. 1992. NAFSA. $12 (nonmembers)/$8 (members) plus postage and handling.
Lists films and videos available from a multitude of sources for use with incoming foreign student and in preparing U.S. students to study overseas. Listings include a brief description as well as ordering information.

* *Increasing Participation of Ethnic Minorities in Study Abroad.* 1991. CIEE.

Free.
Advice on increasing the enrollments of nontraditional students.

* *International Educator*. NAFSA. Semiannual. $12. Included in annual membership fee.
Presents essays on major issues and trends in the field of international education. Contributors are leaders in the field of international educational exchange.

International Exchange Locator. Liaison Group for International Educational Exchange. 1991. Available from IIE. $25 plus shipping and handling.
Provides information on organizations responsible for educational exchange, committees and subcommittees of the House and Senate that deal with exchange issues, and related federal agency officials.

Missing the Boat: The Failure to Internationalize American Higher Education. Craufurd Goodwin and Michael Nacht. 1991. Cambridge University Press. $42.95 plus shipping and handling.
An in-depth look at the international experience of U.S. faculty, commissioned by the Council for the International Exchange of Scholars. An appraisal of the personal and professional benefits and risks of faculty travel abroad.

* *NAFSA Newsletter*. NAFSA. Published 8/year. $35 in the U.S.; $38, Canada and Mexico; and $50, Overseas. Included in the membership fee.
Each 32- to 40-page issue contains current information about developments in foreign student advising, the teaching of English as a second language, community programs, admissions policies, and study-abroad programming. The newsletter provides commentary on major governmental actions, carries in-depth examinations of issues and articles on practical applications of knowledge in the field, and explores the latest developments in international educational exchange.

* *NAFSA Standards and Policies*. 1991. NAFSA. First copy free; additional copies $2 each.
A vital reference collection for educators ambitious to internationalize their institutions. Includes a compilation of important policy findings from over a decade of NAFSA research and experience.

A New Manual for Integrating People with Disabilities into International Educational Exchange Programs. Cindy Lewis and Susan Sygall. 1990. Mobility International USA. $18 postpaid.
Provides information on different types of disabilities, issues and needs to be taken into consideration, and organizations to assist students with

disabilities.

A Profile of the U.S. Student Abroad—1984 and 1985. Jolene Koester. 1987. CIEE. $10 plus postage and handling.

This paper presents the findings of Jolene Koester's ongoing statistical research on U.S. students going abroad. The report, based on data from 1984 and 1985, analyzes the reasons for student travel abroad and assesses its impact.

Profiting from Education. Gail Chambers and William Cummings. 1990. IIE. $7.

A discussion of the successes and failures of establishing overseas campuses in and from Japan, including specific recommendations regarding the issues facing U.S. and Japanese higher education.

Research on U.S. Students Abroad: A Bibliography with Abstracts. Edited by Henry D. Weaver. 1989. CIEE. $12 plus postage and handling.

This bibliography provides a comprehensive listing of studies about U.S. students studying abroad. It contains approximately 250 entries abstracted by Barbara B. Burn, Jerry S. Carlson, Jürgen C. Kempff, Judith N. Martin, and John Useem.

Students Abroad: Strangers at Home. Norman L. Kauffmann, Judith N. Martin, and Henry D. Weaver. 1992. Intercultural Press. $19.95.

Examines the study-abroad experience from the student's point of view and provides a theoretical framework for understanding the effects of a study-abroad experience on students.

* *Update.* Monthly. CIEE. Free.

CIEE's monthly newsletter reports on developments in the field of international educational exchange as well as programs and events organized by the Council. Designed for advisers, administrators, and educators.

U.S. Students Abroad: Statistics on Study Abroad. Edited by Marianthi Zikopoulos. 1988. IIE. Out of print; available in libraries.

Provides essential statistics on students abroad.

CREDIT TRANSFER & EVALUATION OF PROGRAMS ABROAD

Recording the Performance of U.S. Undergraduates at British Institutions: Guidelines Toward Standardized Reporting for Study Abroad. Edited by David Rex and Thomas Roberts. 1988. NAFSA. $6 (nonmembers)/$4 (members) plus postage and handling.

This booklet provides guidelines to officials at British educational institutions for reporting the academic performance of U.S. study-abroad students. The credit and grading practices of the U.S. higher-education system are explained, and the background and rationale for American reporting requirements are provided.

* *Study Abroad Programs: An Evaluation Guide.* Prepared by the AACRAO-NAFSA Task Force on Study Abroad. 1979. NAFSA. $7 (nonmembers)/$5 (members) plus postage and handling.

Through a series of carefully phrased questions, this guide provides a systematic analysis of the major components of study-abroad programs. An evaluation procedure will reveal the strengths and weaknesses of a given program and identify improvements to make the program more effective and viable.

Transcripts from Study Abroad Programs: A Workbook. Edited by Eleanor Krawutschke and Thomas Roberts. 1986. NAFSA. $9 (non-members)/$6 (members) plus postage and handling.

This workbook, designed for those responsible for making credit-transfer determinations and those advising students on study abroad, provides guidelines for necessary documentation in an ideal transcript, an analysis of current transcript practices by college- and agency-sponsored programs, and recommendations for on-campus procedures.

Transfer Credit Practices of Selected Educational Institutions. 1990–92. AACRAO. $20 (nonmembers)/$15 (members).

This publication lists the acceptance practices of one "reporting institution" in each state regarding transfer credit completed at other colleges and universities in that state. Indicates whether institutions are members of regional accreditation associations. Also lists selected institutions outside the United States, with an indication of their accreditation status.

GENERAL CROSS-CULTURAL

American Cultural Patterns: A Cross-Cultural Perspective. Edward C. Stewart and Milton J. Bennett. 1991. Intercultural Press. $15.95.

A classic study of the assumptions and values of mainstream American culture as contrasted with other cultures of the world. Using the value orientation framework of Kluckhohn and Strodtbeck, Stewart divides the patterns of perception, thinking, behavior, and belief which characterize American culture into four major categories: form of activity, form of social relations, perception of the world, and perception of the self. He then compares and contrasts them with other cultures and provides a model for cross-cultural analysis.

Applied Cross-Cultural Psychology. Richard Brislin. 1990. Sage Publications. $21.95.

This volume introduces the reader to the application of cross-cultural psychology in a number of basic areas. Certain common themes or issues run through the articles: ethnocentrism, culture-general vs. culture-specific approaches, cultural awareness, and cultural differences.

The Art of Crossing Cultures. Craig Storti. 1990. Intercultural Press. $14.95.

An analysis of the personal challenges inherent in the cross-cultural experience, based not only on psychological and communication theory, but on the vivid perceptions of an assortment of the world's greatest writers and the literature they have produced.

The Basic Works of Edward T. Hall. Intercultural Press. $32.80.

A collection of cross-cultural works by Edward T. Hall: *The Silent Language, The Hidden Dimension, Beyond Culture*, and *The Dance of Life*.

The Cultural Dialogue: An Introduction to Intercultural Communication. Michael Prosser. 1985. Intercultural Press. $14.95.

A review of the basic concepts of intercultural communication. Examines the components of communication and the cultural context in which communication occurs.

Culture Shock. Adrian Furnham and Stephen Bochner. 1986. Routledge, Chapman and Hall. $16.95 plus postage and handling.

The first comprehensive study of the adjustment experience of tourists, travelers, and sojourners.

Culturgrams: The Nations Around Us. 1991. Brigham Young University, Kennedy Center for International Studies. $40 postpaid.

Culturgrams provide clear and concise information on customs and courtesies, life-styles, the people, and the history and government of 102 nations, and provide a quick overview for prospective travelers.

Human Behavior in Global Perspective: An Introduction to Cross-cultural Psychology. Marshall H. Segall, Pierre R. Dasen, John W. Berry, and Ype H. Poortinga. 1990. Alan & Bacon. $24.95.

The authors begin by reviewing the history and present state of the major issues in cross-cultural psychology, including a methodological case study of one of the first avenues of research on the subject—the perception of visual illusions. The heart of the book lies in the authors' thorough examination of culture, cognition, personality, and social behavior within a cultural context. The last section of the book focuses on cultural change and cultures in contact.

InterActs. Series edited by George W. Renwick. Various dates. Intercultural Press. Various prices.

A series of books analyzing how Americans and nationals of other countries see and do things differently and how these differences affect relationships.

Intercultural Interactions: A Practical Guide. Richard Brislin, Kenneth Cushner, Craig Cherrie, and Mahealani Yong. 1986. Sage Publications. Available from Intercultural Press. $21.95.

A cross-cultural orientation and training manual based on techniques developed at the University of Illinois. The practical suggestions are accompanied by theoretical essays.

Introduction to Intercultural Communication. John C. Condon and Fathi Yousef. 1975. Macmillan. $30.00. Also available from Intercultural Press. $27.95.

This comprehensive introduction to intercultural communication examines cultural behaviors and practices, explores the process of intercultural communication, and introduces the concepts of culture, values, and value orientation. This book makes the subject accessible to the general reader as well as to students and professionals in the field.

On Being Foreign: Culture Shock in Short Fiction. Edited by Tom Lewis and Robert Jungman. 1986. Intercultural Press. $16.95 plus postage and handling.

This international anthology provides insights into culture shock and cross-cultural adjustment through the eyes of fictional characters from twenty short stories.

Toward Multiculturalism: Readings in Multicultural Education. Jaime Wurzel. 1988. Intercultural Press. $24.95 plus postage and handling.

A selection of 19 articles that examine a wide assortment of behaviors in a variety of cultures, illuminating both the dynamics of multiculturalism worldwide and the nature and challenges of multiculturalism in the United States.

Transcultural Study Guide. 1975 (reprinted 1987). Volunteers in Asia. $5.95 plus postage and handling.

A series of questions under various categories, designed to help students make the most of an educational experience abroad.

PREDEPARTURE ORIENTATION AND REENTRY RESOURCES

BAFA BAFA. R. Garry Shirts. 1977. Simile II. $69.50.

A classic simulation game of intercultural experience, in which participants assume the roles of two different cultures.

Barnga: A Simulation Game on Cultural Clashes. Sivasailam Thiagarajan and Barbara Steinwachs. 1989. SIETAR International. Also available from Intercultural Press. $15.

This game simulates the effect of cultural differences on human interaction. Participants play a simple card game in small groups and undergo a mini-culture-shock similar to the experience of actually entering a different culture.

Cold Water. Noriko Ogami. 1987. Available from Intercultural Press. $125 for purchase/$35 for rental.

This videotape, consisting of interviews with a number of foreign students, deals with issues of cross-cultural adjustment and with values. It can be used effectively in predeparture orientations for U.S. students as well as in other cross-cultural training situations, and is accompanied by a facilitator's guide.

Cross-Cultural Orientation: New Conceptualizations and Applications. Edited by R. Michael Paige. 1986. University Press of America. $27.95.

An in-depth series of articles dealing with central ideas associated with cross-cultural orientation. Eleven of the twelve chapters in this volume were originally presented at an international conference on cross-cultural orientation held in Minneapolis, Minnesota, in November 1984.

Cross-Cultural Reentry: A Book of Readings. Clyde N. Austin. 1986. ACU Press. $14.95.

This collection of 25 articles deals with reentry issues in general, issues related to specific groups, and strategies for reducing reentry stress. Includes exercises and other materials for use by individuals or in workshops and seminars.

Going International films/videotapes. Copeland Griggs Productions. $350/purchase; $75/rental; $25/preview per film/videotape plus postage and handling for nonprofit organizations.

These seven films/videotapes examine different aspects of cross-cultural experience from the perspective of individuals who have lived abroad as well as professionals in the field of cross-cultural communication. Several are particularly useful in predeparture or reentry sessions for college students. Available in film and videotape formats.

Hostage Crisis: A Simulation. Moorhead Kennedy and Martha Keyes. 1987. The Moorhead Kennedy Institute. $150.

This simulation is based on the actual experience of an American diplomat held as a hostage in Iran for 444 days during the Iran hostage crisis. The simulation encompasses three sessions of role playing and an additional debriefing session. Among other values, it heightens the participants' capacities for critical thinking, and compels them to deal with conflicting views in solving problems.

A Manual of Structured Experiences for Cross-Cultural Learning. Edited by William W. Weeks, Paul B. Pedersen, and Richard W. Brislin. Intercultural Press. $9.95.

Fifty-nine exercises designed to stimulate learning in multicultural groups. Sections include clarification of values, identification of rules, recognition of feelings and attitudes, and community interaction. These exercises have long been used by cross-cultural specialists in experiential teaching and training.

Orientation Handbook for Youth Exchange Programs. Cornelius Grove. 1989. Available from Intercultural Press. $19.95 plus postage and handling.

Although designed for youth exchange programs, this handbook contains cross-cultural training materials that may also be used with college students. These materials are drawn from the series of orientation handbooks that have been compiled and published by AFS International Intercultural Programs.

* Survival Kit for Overseas Living. 2nd ed. L. Robert Kohls. 1984. Intercultural Press. $7.95 plus postage and handling.

The Survival Kit provides a series of practical, do-it-yourself exercises for Americans planning to live and work abroad. It offers guidelines on how to set objectives for an overseas experience, how to become a foreigner with style and understanding, how to get to know your host culture, and how to combat culture shock. New edition includes a chapter on going home and dealing with reentry, and has an expanded resource list.

Theories and Methods in Cross-Cultural Orientation. Edited by Judith Martin. Special edition of *International Journal of Intercultural Relations*, vol. 10, no. 2, 1986. Out of print, but available in libraries.

A series of articles addressing theoretical issues related to cross-cultural orientation and training.

Updates. Series originated by Alison Lanier. Intercultural Press. $19.95 each.

A series of books designed specifically to meet the needs of families relocating abroad. Each book covers the basic issues important to a successful transfer and adjustment to a new country and culture. Included in the series are books on Saudi Arabia, Germany, Belgium, France, Japan, and Hong Kong.

There are numerous other cross-cultural reference materials of potential use to a study-abroad adviser and/or library. The Intercultural Press is the most comprehensive single source of such reference materials. Many materials are also available through SIETAR, at a discount to members.

Study/Work/Travel Abroad Resource Library

GENERAL MATERIALS ON OPPORTUNITIES ABROAD

Advisory List of International Educational Travel and Exchange Programs, 1992–93. Council on Standards for International Educational Travel. $8.50.

A listing of educational and exchange programs that have requested inclusion and have subsequently met certain standards for international programs set forth by CSIET. Includes a section on evaluating programs.

* *Basic Facts on Study Abroad.* 1992. Available from CIEE, IIE, or NAFSA. NAFSA: single copy free, $35/100; IIE: $35/100; CIEE: single copy free, $35/100.

This key brochure, produced jointly by NAFSA, IIE, and CIEE, lists resources, publications, and tips for those planning to study, work, or travel abroad. *Basic Facts* aids students in selecting an educational program abroad, provides information on financial aid resources, and directs students to organizations involved in study abroad. We recommend having multiple copies available for students.

Bridging the Global Gap: A Handbook to Linking Citizens of the First and Third Worlds. Medea Benjamin and Andrea Freedman. 1989. Global Exchange. $11.95 plus postage and handling.

A compendium of information on the growing movement to end hunger and poverty and build peaceful international ties through direct action. Includes a 100-page resource guide to internationalist organizations.

* *A Guide to Educational Programs in the Third World.* 1991. CIEE. Single copy free; $25/100.

This booklet provides brief descriptions of more than two hundred programs offered by CIEE member institutions for study and work in developing countries. Also included is a general statement on the benefits of studying in the Third World.

Learning Vacations. Gerson G. Eisenberg. 1989. Peterson's. Out of print; available in libraries

Lists a variety of vacation study options in the United States and abroad.

1991 Directory of Study Abroad Programs and Travel Services. Edited by Deborah J. Hill. 1991. Renaissance Publications. $14.95.
A reference guide to international program offices, study-broad directors, tour operators, travel agents, teachers, librarians, and students of all ages. Includes descriptions of domestic and international programs and tours in many areas.

Study Abroad 1992–1994. UNESCO. Available from UNIPUB. $24 plus postage and handling.
Listing of international scholarships and courses; covers study-abroad in the most general sense and is therefore useful to foreign students in the United States as well as U.S. students intending to go abroad.

The Teenager's Guide to Study, Travel, and Adventure Abroad. Marjorie A. Cohen. 1991. CIEE. $11.95 plus postage and handling.
A listing of opportunities especially appropriate for junior high and high school students, from the publishers of *Work, Study, Travel Abroad* (see below).

* *Transitions Abroad: Guide to International Study, Work, and Travel.* Transitions Abroad. $18/6 issues; $34/12 issues. Also available in bulk ($50/100 copies).
This periodical is an independent resource guide to living, learning, employment, and educational travel abroad. Published six times a year, it emphasizes practical, usable information in timely and informative articles and first-hand reports. Includes an annual Educational Travel Directory of information on employment, education, travel, and living abroad.

Travel Programs in Central America. Annual. San Diego Interfaith Task Force on Central America. $6.
Guide to over three hundred organizations. Lists study programs, delegations, environmental and work brigades, human rights organizations, and short- and long-term service opportunities in all fields. Includes a trip calendar. Updates published throughout the year.

* *Work, Study, Travel Abroad: The Whole World Handbook 1992–93.* 11th ed., 1992. CIEE. $12.95. Bulk orders are available St. Martin's Press.
This is the most important single reference book to have on study, work, and travel abroad. Refers reader to hundreds of organizations that can supply information as well as to academic and experiential programs abroad. Good country-by-country information, but far from complete with respect to work options.

A World of Options: Guide to International Exchange, Community Service, and Travel for Persons with Disabilities. Cindy Lewis and Susan Sygall. 1990. Mobility International USA. $16.

Lists a wide variety of programs for study, work, or travel abroad, with an indication of "implications for persons with disabilities" for each entry.

STUDY ABROAD/SYSTEMS OF HIGHER EDUCATION

* *Academic Year Abroad 1992/93.* Edited by Sara J. Steen and Ed Battle. Annual. IIE. $39.95 (Included in IIE's institutional membership fee).

The most comprehensive listing available of academic year, semester, and quarter programs abroad. Now includes sections on programs sponsored by accredited U.S. colleges and universities and programs sponsored by non-U.S. colleges and universities, language schools, and other U.S. and foreign organizations.

AACRAO World Education Series. AACRAO. Currently about 25 titles available. Dates vary. Prices range from $2 to $10 each.

Written primarily for admissions officers evaluating credentials of incoming foreign students, this series offers useful objective information and subjective evaluations on systems of higher education as well as individual institutions.

Australian Study Opportunities 1988/89. IIE. $18.95 plus postage.

This guide to Australian higher education provides institutional profiles, course offerings, and costs for all Australian post-secondary institutions, as well as an overview of study in Australia written especially for the overseas student.

Commonwealth Universities Yearbook. Association of Commonwealth Universities. Annual. Available in the United States from Stockton Press. $240 plus postage and handling and handling.

This four-volume set provides information on five hundred universities and institutions in thirty-one countries or regions of the Commonwealth. Chapters on universities contain lists of administrative and teaching staff, addresses and telephone numbers, and statistics.

Higher Education in the United Kingdom 1992–93: A Handbook for Students from Overseas and Their Advisers. The British Council and the Association of Commonwealth Universities. 1990. Available from Oryx Press. $32.95.

Contains an introduction to the British educational system as well as information on courses and degrees.

238

Higher Education in the European Community: Student Handbook. 6th Edition. Edited by Brigitte Mohr. 1990. Available from Oryx. $24.95.

A useful summary of information on systems of higher education in member states of the European Community. Note: additional free information is available from the embassies, consulates and information offices of the countries concerned, as well as from such organizations as the German Academic Exchange Service (DAAD).

The Insider's Guide to Foreign Study. Benedict A. Leerburger. 1988. Addison-Wesley Publishing Co. Out of print; available in libraries.

Lists over four hundred programs abroad for students and vacation travelers, as well as sources of further information.

Planning for Study Abroad. 1989. IIE. $24.95, IIE Educational Associates; $49.95, others.

IIE's advising video presents the essential facts on study abroad. Information comes from students themselves, who help their peers think about opportunities—and issues—that international study presents. Guidance in areas such as academic credit and finance is offered by study-abroad advisers.

Study Abroad: The Astute Student's Guide. David Judkins. 1989. Williamson Publishing. $13.95 plus postage and handling.

A compilation of some of the major study-abroad programs, this guide also helps students consider all aspects of studying abroad in order to make more informed decisions when choosing a program.

Study and Research Opportunities in the Middle East and North Africa. Edited by Leslie C. Schmida. 1985. AMIDEAST. $7.95.

Information on study programs, research opportunities, and funding for educational activities.

Study Holidays. Published by the Central Bureau (England). 1992. Available in the United States from IIE. $18.95 plus postage.

Lists over 600 organizations offering language and civilization courses in Europe.

"Studying in the French University: A Guide for U.S. Advisers and Students." Mary Anne Grant. 1990. NAFSA. $4 plus postage and handling.

Provides basic information on the French educational system for U.S. study abroad advisers counseling students interested in enrolling in a French university.

"Studying in the German University: A Guide for U.S. Advisers and Students." Axel Markert. 1990. NAFSA. $4 plus postage and handling.
Provides basic information on the German educational system for U.S. study-abroad advisers counseling students interested in studying in a fully integrated German program.

"Studying in the Spanish University: A Guide for U.S. Advisers and Students." Miguel A. Parmantie. 1990. NAFSA. $4 plus postage and handling.
Provides basic information on the Spanish educational system for study-abroad advisers counseling students interested in enrolling directly in a Spanish university.

The Underground Guide to University Study in Britain and Ireland. Bill Griesar. 1992. Intercultural Press. $14.95.
Provides practical considerations on studying and living in Britain and Ireland including university selection, application procedures, credit, transportation, insurance, and housing.

* *Vacation Study Abroad 1992.* Edited by Sara J. Steen and Ed Battle. Annual. IIE. $31.95 (Included in IIE's institutional membership fee).
Similar in format to *Academic Year Abroad*, this directory lists short-term and summer study programs offered by both U.S. and foreign organizations. This and its companion volume (above) are essential to a study abroad reference library.

World List of Universities. International Association of Universities. 1992. Available from Stockton Press. $130 plus postage and handling.
Brief descriptions of universities and other institutions of higher education around the world.

The World of Learning. Annual. Stockton Press. $310 plus postage and handling.
According to the publisher, *The World of Learning* is the standard and authoritative guide to educational, scientific and cultural institutions and organizations all over the world." Considered by some as the most crucial of several references providing such information.

FUNDING FOR INTERNATIONAL ACTIVITIES

Annual Register of Grant Support. Annual. National Register Publishing Co. $165.
Provides comprehensive listings of scholarships, fellowships, and grants, many of which are international in scope.

Fellowships, Scholarships, and Related Opportunities in International Education. Edited by James Gehlhar. 1989. Center for International Education, 201 Alumni Hall, University of Tennessee, Knoxville, TN 37996-0620. $10.

This publication lists granting agencies to which U.S. students may apply for financial assistance for study and/or research overseas. New edition forthcoming.

* *Financial Aid for Research and Creative Activities Abroad, 1992–1994.* Gail A. Schlachter and R. David Weber. 1992. Reference Service Press. $40 plus postage and handling.

Over eleven hundred references and cross-references to international funding opportunities.

* *Financial Aid for Study Abroad: A Manual for Advisers and Administrators.* Edited by Stephen Cooper, William W. Cressey, and Nancy K. Stubbs. 1989. NAFSA. $12 (nonmembers)/$8 (members) plus postage and handling.

This sourcebook primarily addresses application of federal sources of financial aid to the study-abroad programs of undergraduate students, as well as how to utilize this information to help shape institutional policies.

Financial Aid for Study and Training Abroad, 1992–1994. Gail A. Schlachter and R. David Weber. 1992. Reference Service Press. $30 plus postage and handling.

Over seven hundred references and cross-references to international funding opportunities, covering most fields of study throughout the world.

Financial Resources for International Study. 1989. IIE and Peterson's Guides. Out of print; available in libraries.

Compiled by IIE and published by Peterson's, *Financial Resources for International Study* collects in one book all the most relevant information on grants and fellowships available to U.S. undergraduates, graduates, postgraduates, and professionals planning study or research in other countries.

Foundation Grants to Individuals. 7th ed. 1990 (revised biennially in October). The Foundation Center. $40.

If you are looking for money for educational assistance, for travel or study abroad, for emergency help or medical aid, or for special research or projects in the arts, sciences, social sciences, or humanities, you should investigate the grant-makers described here. New edition expected mid-1993.

Free Money for Foreign Study. Laurie Blum. 1991. Facts on File, Inc. $14.95.
Lists more than one thousand grants and scholarships for study abroad.

Fulbright and Other Grants for Graduate Study Abroad. IIE. Revised annually. Single copy free.
Describes IIE-administered fellowships available to U.S. graduate students wishing to study and/or conduct research abroad.

The Grants Register, 11th ed. 1993–95 (revised biennially in December). St.
Martin's Press, Inc. $89.95
Bills itself as "the standard directory of scholarships, fellowships, prizes
and other sources of financial aid for professional and academic work beyond the undergraduate level."

The International Scholarship Book. Daniel J. Cassidy. 1990. Prentice Hall,
Inc. $22.95 paperback; $29.95 hardback.
Lists private-sector funding sources for graduate and undergraduate
study abroad.

International Student Identity Card Scholarship Fund. CIEE. Free.
Describes scholarships the Council on International Educational Exchange offers to help support U.S. high school and college students planning an educational experience in the Third World. Includes eligibility
information and application instructions.

EMPLOYMENT ABROAD—BACKGROUND INFORMATION

The Canadian Guide to Working and Living Overseas. Jean-Marc Hachey.
1992. Best Gagné, Ltd. Available from Intercultural Systems, P.O. Box 588
Station B, Ottawa, Ontario, Canada K1P 5P7; tel. 613.238.6169. $34.50 plus
shipping and handling.

The Directory of Jobs and Careers Abroad. Alex Lipinski. 1993. Peterson's.
$16.95 plus postage and handling.
Written from a British perspective, this book provides information on
finding a job overseas. Contains a listing of careers and contacts worldwide, with chapters detailing specific opportunities in over thirty countries.

* *Harvard Guide to International Experience.* William Klingelhofer. 1989. Office of Career Services, 54 Dunster Street, Harvard University, Cambridge,
MA 02138; 617.495.2595. $15.
Offers information on working and volunteering abroad with numerous
student quotations and general advice (occasionally Harvard specific).

Passport to Overseas Employment. Dale Chambers. 1991. Simon & Schuster. $15.
A guide to short-term, career, and volunteer work opportunities. Includes a section on study and internship programs, and a brief chapter on grant opportunities.

INTERNATIONAL INTERNSHIPS

* *Academic Year Abroad* and *Vacation Study Abroad.* Edited by Sara J. Steen and Ed Battle. Annual. IIE. $39.95 and $31.95 plus postage and handling. (Included in IIE's institutional membership fee.)
These references—found in every study-abroad library—have indexes for internships, practical training, and student teaching, listing mainly university-sponsored programs that charge a fee.

* *Development Opportunities Catalog: A Guide to Internships, Research, and Employment with Development Organizations.* 2nd ed. 1990. Overseas Development Network. $10 ($7/students; $15/institutions).
Describes internships, employment and research opportunities for college students and recent graduates interested in Third World development. Lists over forty development organizations with positions abroad and in the United States.

* *Directory of International Internships: A World of Opportunities.* Compiled and edited by Thomas D. Luten, Charles A. Gliozzo, and Timothy J. Aldinger. 1990. Career and Placement Services, Attn: International Placement, 113 Student Services Building, Michigan State University, East Lansing, MI 48824. $20.
This essential reference is based on a survey in which forty-five thousand questionnaires were distributed. Lists a wide variety of experiential educational opportunities abroad, for academic credit, for pay, or simply for experience.

* *Guide to Careers in World Affairs.* New edition forthcoming. Foreign Policy Association, Inc. $10.95 plus postage and handling.
Lists many internships with major organizations not found elsewhere.

International Directory of Youth Internships. Cynthia T. Morehouse. 1992. Apex Press. $7.50 plus postage and handling.
Provides information on UN agencies and nongovernmental organizations, positions available, and required qualifications.

International Health Electives for Medical Students. Edited by Galofre and Luketich. 1990. American Medical Student Association Publications, 1890

Preston White Drive, Reston, VA 22091. $13.
> Electives abroad for upper-level medical students. New edition forthcoming.

* *International Internships and Volunteer Programs.* Will Cantrell and Francine Modderno. 1992. Worldwise Books. $18.95 plus postage and handling.
> Identifies programs that can serve as "stepping stones" to international careers, for both students and professionals.

Internships 1993. Annual. Edited by Brian Rushing. Peterson's. $28.95 plus postage and handling.
> "How-to's" and listings, plus a chapter on international internships.

Internships and Careers in International Affairs. Edited by James Muldoon, Jr. 1989. Publications Department, United Nations Association of the United States of America, 485 Fifth Ave., New York, NY 10017. $7.
> Lists internships based primarily in the United States with major international organizations, including the United Nations.

Internships in Foreign and Defense Policy: A Complete Guide for Women (and Men). 1990. Women in International Security. Available from Seven Locks Press, P.O. Box 68, Arlington, VA 22210. $10.95 plus postage.

* Student Intern Program, United States Department of State. Intern Coordinator, U.S. Department of State, P.O. Box 9317, Arlington, VA 22219. Free.

TEACHING ABROAD

English in Asia: Teaching Tactics for the Classrooms of Japan, China, Korea, Taiwan. John Wharton. 1992. Global Press. 202.466.1663. $12.95 postpaid (20% discount for students).
> Practical overview of English teaching methods in these countries.

* *Jobs in Japan: The Complete Guide to Living and Working in the Land of Rising Opportunity.* John Wharton. 1991. Global Press. $14.95 plus postage and handling.
> The guide gives names and addresses of English language schools and professional organizations in Japan and discusses the details of living in Japan.

Living in China: A Guide to Teaching and Studying in China Including Taiwan. Weiner, Murphy, and Li. 1991. China Books and Periodicals, Inc., 2929

Twenty-fourth Street, San Francisco, CA 94110. $16.95.
    The most comprehensive and up-to-date guide to China (mainly the PRC). Useful for students, too.

* *Teaching Abroad 1989/91.* 4th ed. Edited by Edrice Marguerite Howard and Carol Weeg. 1988. IIE. $21.95 plus postage and handling.
    Comprehensive but dated guide to international K-12 schools and teaching exchange programs. New edition planned for 1993.

* *Teaching English Abroad.* Susan Griffith. 1991. Vacation Work. $7.95 plus postage and handling.
    The only book to cover English teaching opportunities worldwide. Lists long- and short-term teaching jobs for trained and untrained teachers. Suggests short TEFL courses, other preparation, strategies, and specific addresses.

Teaching English in Taiwan: The Underground Guide. William Combs. 1990. Combs Vanity Press. $14.95.
    A comprehensive guide to teaching English in Taiwan.

VOLUNTEER WORK ABROAD

* *Alternatives to the Peace Corps: A Directory of Third World and U.S. Volunteer Opportunities.* 1992. Edited by Becky Buell, Susan Clarke, and Susan Leone. Food First Books. $6.95 plus postage and handling.
    Contains listings of volunteer service organizations as well as organizations offering study tours and alternative travel opportunities.

Archaeological Fieldwork Opportunities Bulletin. Annual. Archaeological Institute of America. Available from Kendell Hunt Publishing Co., 2460 Karper Blvd., Dubuque, Iowa 92001; 800.338.5578. $10.50.
    Lists current and ongoing archaeological programs in over 299 sites throughout the world.

Beyond Safaris: A Guide to Building People-to-People Ties with Africa. Kevin Danaher. 1990. Global Exchange. $12.95 plus postage and handling.
    A new handbook on how to help build and strengthen links between U.S. citizens and grass-roots development efforts in Africa. Includes volunteering, studying, social responsible travel, and an annotated list of organizations.

The Directory of Work & Study in Developing Countries. David Leppard. 1991. Vacation Work. £9.95 or dollar equivalent postpaid.
    Current and comprehensive, but written exclusively for a British audi-

ence; U.S. addresses are omitted, reducing this directory's usefulness.

Environmental Vacations: Volunteer Projects to Save the Planet. Stephanie Ocko. 1990. John Muir Publications. $16.95.
>An introduction to the world of "eco-volunteerism." Provides a narrative description of some of the major organizations offering volunteer experience in environmentally related areas.

* *How to Serve & Learn Abroad Effectively: Students Tell Students.* Howard Berry and Linda Chisholm. Partnership for Service Learning, 815 Second Ave., Suite 315, New York, NY 10017. $7.
>This is not a directory to opportunities, but still an essential guide to help one decide if volunteer service is the right choice.

The International Directory of Voluntary Work. David Woodworth. 1993. Peterson's. $15.95 plus postage and handling.
>Lists many volunteer opportunities in Europe not found elsewhere, as well as worldwide listings.

* *International Workcamps.* CIEE. Free.
>CIEE's international workcamps program is designed for those interested in community service with a group of international volunteers. The brochure includes an application and describes options in twenty countries of eastern and western Europe as well as North America.

Invest Yourself: The Catalogue of Volunteer Opportunities. Edited by Susan Angus. 1991. CVSA. $8 postpaid.
>Listings for over two hundred nongovernmental volunteer service organizations.

* *1992 International Workcamp Directory.* Annual. Volunteers for Peace. $10.
>Contains over seven hundred workcamp announcements for the summer and fall of the year of publication. Lists volunteer work opportunities in western and eastern Europe. Issued each April.

* *The Overseas List: Opportunities for Living and Working in Developing Countries.* David M. Beckmann, Timothy J. Mitchell, and Linda L. Powers. 1986. Augsburg Publishing House. $14.95.
>Comprehensive guide to organizations, information, and resources on working overseas in developing countries. While oriented to those with a religious vocation for working in the Third World, it constitutes a valuable sourcebook for anyone looking for service-oriented experiences abroad.

* *The Peace Corps and More: 114 Ways to Work, Study, and Travel in the Third World.* Medea Benjamin. 1991. Global Exchange. $6.95 plus postage and handling.

Lists organizations that allow you to gain Third World experience while promoting the ideals of social justice and sustainable development.

* *Volunteer! The Comprehensive Guide to Voluntary Service in the U.S. and Abroad.* 1992–93 edition. Edited by Adrienne Dorney. 1990. CIEE. $8.95 plus postage and handling.

This essential reference is by far the most useful guide to short- and long-term volunteer opportunities.

Volunteer Vacations. Bill McMillon. 1991. Chicago Review Press. $11.95.

A directory of 125 organizations sponsoring projects in the United States and abroad.

SHORT-TERM EMPLOYMENT ABROAD

The Au Pair and Nanny's Guide to Working Abroad. Susan Griffith and Sharon Legg. 1989. Vacation Work. $5.95 plus postage and handling.

Provides advice on how to find and prepare for a child-care job in another country. It includes a director of agencies worldwide, their fees and job opportunities, visa regulations, and cultural considerations.

* CIEE Work Abroad Participant's Handbooks. Annual. Included in the program fee; not for sale. One copy of each available to study-abroad offices upon request from CIEE, Work Exchanges, 205 E. 42nd St., New York, NY 10017

All eight are helpful. Handbooks for Britain and Ireland contain very useful addresses for writing ahead to arrange interviews.

The Directory of Summer Jobs in Britain and *Emplois d'Été en France.* Annual. CIEE. $13.95 plus shipping and handling each.

Lists of employers, potentially useful to CIEE work abroad participants.

1993 Directory of Overseas Summer Jobs. Annual. Peterson's. $14.95 plus postage and handling.

Lists temporary jobs in over forty countries. It also contains facts on visa regulations, work permits, and health related issues.

* *Work Abroad.* Annual. CIEE. Free.

Contains information and application forms for the CIEE work-abroad program, which grants short-term working papers to U.S. college students for France, Germany, Britain, Ireland, New Zealand, Costa Rica, Jamaica, and Canada.

Working Abroad. Annual. InterExchange, Inc., 161 6th Ave., Room 902, New
York, NY 10013. Free
Information and applications for work-abroad programs.

Working Holidays 1991. Published by the Central Bureau (U.K.). Available
in the United States from IIE. $22.95 plus postage and handling.
Lists organizations worldwide which offer a wide variety of youth employment opportunities, paid and volunteer. Written exclusively for a
British audience, it omits relevant American addresses.

* *Work Your Way Around the World.* Susan Griffith. 1993. Peterson's. $17.95
plus postage and handling.
This up-to-date classic is the only guide to finding casual work on the
spot worldwide. Valuable especially for the countries for which CIEE
permits are available but which provide few support services, as well as
for countries for which no work exchange program exists.

INTERNATIONAL CAREERS

*After Latin American Studies: A Guide to Employment for Latin
Americanists.* Kregar Majeski & Sekelik. 1991. Center for Latin American
Studies, 4EO4 Forbes Quad, University of Pittsburgh, Pittsburgh, PA 15260.
$5 postpaid.
Essential for Latin Americanists.

The Almanac of International Jobs and Careers. Ronald Krannich and Caryl
Krannich. 1991. Impact Publications. $14.95 plus postage and handling.
This companion guide to *The Complete Guide to International Jobs and
Careers* (see below) provides contact information on organizations offer-
ing international job opportunities.

* Application for the Foreign Service Officer Program. Recruitment Division, Department of State, P.O. Box 12226, Arlington, VA 22219. Free
Registration materials for the Foreign Service exam given each fall.

Career Opportunities in International Development in Washington, D.C.
Edited by Kathleen Poer and Sally Scott. 1988. Zeta Group, Johns Hopkins
University, School of Advanced International Studies, 1740 Massachusetts
Avenue, N.W., Washington, D.C. 20036. $5.
A listing of over seventy-five Washington-based organizations offering
career work in the field of international development.

Career Preparation and Opportunities in International Law. Edited by John Williams. New edition forthcoming. American Bar Association, Order Fulfillment Dept., 750 N. Lake Shore Dr., Chicago, IL 60611. Price not available.

Essays by practitioners on preparation and careers in various settings.

* *Careers in International Affairs.* 1991. Edited by Maria Pinto Carland and Daniel Spatz. School of Foreign Service, Georgetown University, P.O. Box 344, Mt. Vernon, VA 22121. $15.

One of the best "how-to's" and listings of prospective employers.

* *The Complete Guide to International Jobs and Careers.* Ronald L. Krannich and Caryl R. Krannich. 1992. Impact Publications. $13.95 plus postage and handling.

A guide to skills and strategies necessary for finding employment abroad. Includes a large section with listings of organizations and other resources for the job-seeker.

Directory of American Firms Operating in Foreign Countries. 1991. World Trade Academy Press. $195 plus postage and handling.

Lists foreign businesses in countries that own or have substantial investments in some 2,600 firms in the United States and 3,000 American companies with subsidiaries and affiliates in 127 foreign countries. Country-specific lists also available from the same publisher.

Employment Abroad: Facts and Fallacies. Edited by Rachel Theus. 1990. International Division, U.S. Chamber of Commerce. $7.50 plus postage and handling.

Offers "realities" of international employment.

* *Guide to Careers in World Affairs.* 1992 edition forthcoming. Foreign Policy Association, Inc. $10.95 plus postage and handling.

The best single work in the field. More than 250 listings of sources of employment in international business, law, journalism, consulting, non-profit organizations, and the U.S. government. Also includes essays by practitioners of each field and a survey of major employers with specific information on qualifications and internships.

How to Get a Job in Europe: The Insider's Guide. Robert Sanborn. 1993. Surrey Books. $17.95 plus postage and handling.

Provides general strategies for finding employment as well as country-by-country information. Includes information on temporary and volunteer work in addition to career employment. This is the least expensive source for this kind of information.

How to Get a Job in the Pacific Rim. Robert Sanborn and Anderson Brandao. 1992. Surrey Books. Available from Impact Publications. $17.95 plus postage and handling.

Same format as *How to Get a Job in Europe.*

How to Find an Overseas Job with the U.S. Government. Will Cantrell and Francine Modderno. 1992. Worldwise Books. $28.95.

Comprehensive guide to finding work in this area.

The International Businesswoman of the 1990's. Marlene Rossman. 1990. Impact Publications. $19.95 plus postage and handling.

An introduction to the field of international business.

International Careers. Arthur H. Bell. 1990. Bob Adams, Inc. $12.95.

Outlines a six-step method for finding international employment and offers information on U.S. firms abroad, foreign employers, and temporary overseas employment opportunities.

* *International Careers: An Insider's Guide.* David Win. 1987. Williamson Publishing. $10.95 plus postage and handling.

Strategies for crafting an international career; stresses the need for sustaining focus on direction within the discontinuous path typical of international careers. Few specifics on individual organizations.

* *International Jobs: Where They Are, How to Get Them.* Eric Kocher. 1989. Addison-Wesley Publishing Co. $12.45.

One of several directories listing organizations involved in international activities and suggesting how to go about exploring job/career options. New edition expected in fall 1993.

The Job Hunter's Guide to Japan. Terra Brockman. 1990. Kodansha International. Impact Publications. $12.95 plus postage and handling.

Interviews with expatriates working in professional positions, demonstrates possibilities and limits on integration.

* *Making It Abroad: The International Job Hunting Guide.* Howard Schuman. 1988. John Wiley & Sons. $14.95 plus postage and handling.

Thoughtful and encouraging guide to job hunting strategies, with dozens of career histories but no specific references. Includes a section on cross-cultural adjustment.

Opportunities in Foreign Language Careers. Edwin Arnold. 1993. National Textbook Co. $10.95.

A book useful to those interested in utilizing foreign languages in career employment. Provides tips on finding work in teaching, foreign trade, government, and other vocations from airlines to travel and tourism.

A Select Guide to International Careers and Opportunities. 1989. Brigham Young University, the Kennedy International Center. $4.50 postpaid.
A useful guide for the student interested in a career in international relations. This book lists organizations and agencies where additional information can be obtained.

Teaching Opportunities in the Middle East and North Africa. 1987. AMIDEAST. $14.95.
Lists job opportunities for teachers, trainers, and administrators.

Working in France: The Ultimate Guide to Job Hunting and Career Success à la Française. Carol Pineau and Maureen Kelly. 1991. Frank/A.L. Books. Available from the CIEE. $12.95 plus postage and handling.
An exhaustive, practical guide for finding a career position in France. First-hand case histories.

The World Says "Welcome" When You Know the Language. 1987. Monterey Institute of International Studies, ("Monterey Tapes"), 425 Van Buren Street, Monterey, CA 93940; tel. 408.647.4123. $89.
This videotape provides an overview of international career opportunities using foreign languages, and can be used effectively in promoting study abroad/foreign language study.

Worldwide Jobs 1993. 1992. Peterson's. $19.95 plus postage and handling.
Profiles 250 leading multinational companies that hire for international positions. Includes information on necessary qualifications and available opportunities.

TRAVEL

Adventure Holidays 1993. Vacation Work Publications. Peterson's. $12.95.
Ideal for anyone seeking adventure in any of 100 countries overseas. Lists over 360 organizations that offer exciting alternatives to the package tour vacations.

AIDS and International Travel. 1990. CIEE. Single copies free.
Provides advice to international travelers on this important topic and growing area of concern.

AILA U.S. Consular Posts Handbook. 1991. Fourth edition. American Immigration Lawyers Association. $22 plus shipping and handling.

A worldwide guide to 240 State Department consular posts. Includes international and domestic addresses, telex and fax numbers, and names of consular officers.

Background Notes Series. U.S. Department of State. Published irregularly. Available from the U.S. Government Printing Office. $1 each; complete set of current notes is $58; annual subscription for updates is $18.
Capsule descriptions of basic features of countries worldwide.

Blue Guides Series. W.W. Norton & Co. Also available from Book Passage.

Diplomatic List. 1990. U.S. Department of State. U.S. Government Printing Office. $4.50.
Contains the addresses and telephone numbers of foreign government embassies and consular offices located in Washington, D.C., and includes names and titles of staff members.

How to Stay Healthy Abroad. Edited by Dr. Richard Dawood. 1987. Viking Penguin, Inc. Out of print; available in libraries.
A book containing a wide range of information on health issues written by numerous health professionals.

* *Let's Go* Series. Annual. Titles include Europe; Britain and Ireland; France; Italy; Greece; Israel and Egypt; Mexico; and Spain, Portugal, and Morocco. Available from most bookstores and from CIEE. Approximately $14 each.
Provides information on travel in the country, worthy sights, hotels, hostels, restaurants, and miscellaneous tips for the budget-conscious.

Living In Series. Experiment Press. $2.50–$3.00 each.
Helpful tips on the customs, language, and lifestyle of France, West Germany, Great Britain, Italy, Japan, Mexico, Spain, and the United States.

Lonely Planet Series. Available from various suppliers including Lonely Planet Publications, Book Passage, and Nomadic Books.
A wide array of "travel survival kits" and other guidebooks for "shoestring" travelers to Third World destinations.

Michelin Guide Series. Michelin Guides.

1992 International Travel Health Guide. Stuart R. Rose, M.D. Travel Medicine, Inc. $16.95 plus shipping and handling.
A comprehensive guide to the diagnosis and prevention of some of the most commonly encountered illnesses. Includes sections on trip preparation, traveling with disabilities, and a country-by-country guide listing

entry requirements and advisories.

The Pocket Doctor. Stephen Bezruchka, M.D. 1988. The Mountaineers. $4.95.
A guide to self-diagnosis and treatment of illness for travelers abroad.

Staying Healthy in Asia, Africa, and Latin America. Dirk Schroeder. 1988. Volunteers in Asia. Available from Moon Publications in early 1993. $7.95.
Provides a wealth of information for preventing and treating illness and other health problems while traveling in less-developed regions.

Through the Back Door and *22 Days* Guides. John Muir Publications. Also distributed by W.W. Norton & Co.

Tips for Travelers. Bureau of Consular Affairs. Various dates. Available from the Superintendent of Documents, U.S. Government Printing Office, Washington, D.C. 20402. $1, with 20% discount on orders of a hundred or more.
A series of guides covering visa regulations, health precautions, crime and personal security, and travel restrictions for specific countries, including the USSR, the Caribbean, Central and South America, Cuba, Eastern Europe and Yugoslavia, Mexico, the Middle East and North Africa, the People's Republic of China, South Asia, and Sub-Saharan Africa.

Travel Safety: Security Safeguards at Home and Abroad. Jack Adler and Thomas C. Tompkins. 1991. Hippocrene Books. $14.95.
This book gives thorough coverage of a range of safety issues for the traveler, from securing your home to preventing theft while abroad. Also includes a section on safety issues for women traveling alone.

* *Travel! The 1992 Student Travel Catalog.* Annual. CIEE. Free.
This guide covers rail passes, insurance, work and study opportunities abroad, tours, airfares, car rentals, hostels, and more. Included are descriptions of the services provided by CIEE and its subsidiary, Council Travel. Available in bulk.

Travel Tips International. Deborah J. Hill. 1990. Renaissance Publications. $12.50.
A practical guide for travel abroad. Offers advice on how to buy travel insurance, how to find a safe hotel, how to manage money, and where to find medical and legal assistance. Additional tips on cultural taboos, shopping abroad, flying, choosing a travel companion, discount travel, and more.

Updated U.S. Department of State travel advisories are available to subscribers on the NAFSA Net, electronic mail system. This service is free
of charge. More information on how to subscribe to NAFSA Net can be
requested from the NAFSA central office.

Organizations and Publishers

*The following is an alphabetical list of organizations and publishers that
provide the resources listed in the bibliography. The listings marked with
a double asterisk (**) are key publishers and suppliers of travel guides.*

ACU Press, ACU Station, P.O Box 8060, Abilene, TX 79699; tel.
915.674.2720.

Addison-Wesley Publishing Company, 1 Jacob Way, Reading, MA 01867.

The African-American Institute, 833 United Nations Plaza, New York, NY
10017; tel. 212.949.5666.

AFS International/Intercultural, 313 East 43rd Street, New York, NY 10017;
tel. 800.AFS.INFO; fax 212.949.9379.

American Immigration Lawyers Association, Publications Department, 1000
16th Street, N.W., Suite 604, Washington, D.C. 20036.

American Association of Collegiate Registrars and Admissions Officers
(AACRAO), One Dupont Circle, N.W., Suite 330, Washington, D.C. 20036-
1110; tel. 202.293.9161.

American Institute for Foreign Study (AIFS), 102 Greenwich Avenue,
Greenwich, CT 06830; tel. 800.727.2437.

American Scandinavian Foundation, Exchange Division, 725 Park Avenue,
New York, NY 10021; tel. 212.879.9779.

AMIDEAST, 1100 17th Street, N.W., Suite 300, Washington, D.C. 20036-
4601; tel. 202.785.0022.

Apex Press, Council on International and Public Affairs, 777 United Nations
Plaza, New York, NY 10017; tel. 212.953.6920, 914.271.2039.

Archaeological Institute of America, 675 Commonwealth Avenue, Boston,
MA 02215.

Association of Commonwealth Universities, John Foster House, 36 Gordon Square, London, England WC1H OPF, fax 1.387.2655.

Association of Universities and Colleges of Canada, 151 Slater Street, Ottawa, Ontario, K1P 5NI.
Augsburg Publishing House, 426 S. 5th Street, Box 1209, Minneapolis, MN 55440.

Austrian Institute, 11 East 52nd Street, New York, NY 10022; tel. 212.759.5165.

Bob Adams, Inc., 260 Center Street, Holbrook, MA 02342.

**Book Passage, 51 Tamal Vista Boulevard, Corte Madera, CA 94925; tel. 415.927.0960, 800.321.9785; fax 415.924.3838.

**Bookpeople, 2929 Fifth Street, Berkeley, CA 94710; tel. 800.999.4650, 415.549.3030.

**Bradt Enterprises, Inc., 95 Harvey Street, Cambridge, MA 02140; tel. 617.492.8776.

Brigham Young University, David M. Kennedy Center for International Studies, Publication Services, 280 HRCB, Provo, UT 84602; tel. 801.378.6528.

British Information Services, 845 Third Avenue, New York, NY 10022; tel. 212.752.8400.

Cambridge University Press, 40 W. 20th Street, New York, NY 10011; tel. 800.221.4512.

Canadian Bureau for International Education, 85 Albert Street, Suite 1400, Ottawa, Ontario K1P 64A, Canada; tel. 613.237.4820.

Chicago Review Press, 814 North Franklin Street, Chicago, IL 60610.

Combs Vanity Press, Suite 295, 925 Lakeville Street, Petaluma, CA 94952.

Copeland Griggs Productions, Inc., 302 23rd Avenue, San Francisco, CA 94121; tel. 415.668.4200; fax 415.668.6004.

Council on International Education Exchange (CIEE), 205 East 42nd Street, New York, NY 10017; tel. 212.661.1414.

CVSA, P.O. Box 117-G24, New York, NY 10009.

The Experiment Press, Experiment in International Living, Kipling Road, Brattleboro, VT 05301; tel. 802.257.7751.
Facts on File, Inc. 460 Park Avenue South, New York, NY 10016; tel. 212.683.2244.

Food First Books, 145 Ninth Street, San Francisco, CA 94103; tel. 415.864.8555, 800.888. 3314.

Foreign Policy Association, Inc., 729 Seventh Avenue, New York, NY 10019.

**Forsyth Travel Library, 9154 West 57th Street, PO Box 2975, Shawnee Mission, KS 66201.

The Foundation Center, 79 Fifth Avenue, New York, NY 10003; tel. 800.424.9836.

French Cultural Services, 972 Fifth Avenue, New York, NY 10021.

Gale Research Company, 835 Penobscot Bldg., Detroit, MI 48226.4094; tel. 800.877.4253.

Garrett Park Press, P.O. Box 190E, Garrett Park, MD 20896; tel. 301.946.2553.

German Academic Exchange Service, 950 Third Avenue, New York, NY 10022; tel. 212.758.3223.

Global Exchange, 2141 Mission Street #202, San Francisco, CA 94110; tel. 415.255.7296.

Global Press, 697 College Parkway, Rockville, MD 20850; tel. 202.466.1663.

Walter de Gruyter, 200 Saw Mill River Road, Hawthorne, NY 10532; tel. 914.747.0110.

Hippocrene Books, 171 Madison Avenue, New York, NY 10016.

Impact Publications International, 9104-N Manassas Drive, Manassas Park, VA 22111; tel. 703.361.7300; fax 703.335.9468.

Intercultural Press, Inc., P.O. Box 700, Yarmouth, ME 04096; tel. 207.846.5168, fax 207.846.5181.

International Publications Service, a division of Taylor and Francis, Inc., 1900 Frost Road, Suite 101, Bristol, PA 19007; tel. 800.821.8312.

The International Society for Intercultural Education, Training, and Research (SIETAR International), 733 15th Street, N.W., Suite 900, Washington, D.C. 20005; tel. 202.737.5000; fax 202.737.5553.

Institute of International Education (IIE), 809 United Nations Plaza, New York, NY 10017-3580; tel. 212.984.5412; fax 212.984.5452.

**John Muir Publications, P.O. Box 613, Santa Fe, NM 87504.

John Wiley & Sons, 1 Wiley Drive, Summerset, NJ 08875; tel. 908.469.4400.

**Lonely Planet Publications, Embarcadero West, 112 Linden Street, Oakland, CA 94607; tel. 415.893.8555; fax 415.893.8563.

Macmillan, 866 3rd Avenue, New York, NY 10022; tel. 800.257.5755, 212.702.2000.

**Michelin Guides, P.O. Box 3305, Spartanburg, SC 29304; tel. 803.599.0850.

Mobility International USA, P.O. Box 3551-C, Eugene, OR 97403; tel. 503.343.1284.

**Moon Publications, 722 Wall Street, Chico, CA 95298; tel. 916.345.5473.

**The Mountaineers, 306 2nd Avenue West, Seattle, WA 98119.

*NAFSA: Association of International Educators, 1875 Connecticut Avenue, N.W., Suite 1000, Washington, D.C. 20009-5728; tel. 202.462.4811; fax 202.667.3419.

National Register Publishing Co., 3004 Glenview Road, Wilmette, IL 60091; tel. 800.323.6772.

National Textbook Company, VGM Career Horizons, 4255 West Touhy Avenue, Lincolnwood, IL 60646-1975.

Netherlands Universities Foundation for International Cooperation (NUFFIC), Badhuisweg 251, P.O. Box 90734, 2509 LS The Hague, The Netherlands, tel. 70.351.0510.

**Nomadic Books, 401 NE 45th, Seattle, WA 98105; tel. 206.634.3453.

Organization of American States, OAS Bookshop, 1889 F Street, N.W., Washington, D.C. 20006; tel. 202.458.3533.

Oryx Press, 2214 North Central at Encanto, Phoenix, AZ 85004; tel 800.457.ORYX.

Overseas Development Network, Publications Department, 333 Valencia Street, Suite 330, San Francisco, CA 94103.

Peterson's, Department 1312, 202 Carnegie Center, P.O. Box 2123, Princeton, NJ 08543-2123; tel. 800.338.3282; fax 609.243.9150.

**Phileas Fogg's Books and Maps, #87 Stanford Shopping Center, Palo Alto, CA 94304; tel. 800.233.FOGG (California) or 800.533.FOGG (elsewhere in the U.S.).

Pilot Industries, 103 Cooper Street, Babylon, NY 11702.

Prentice Hall, Inc., West Nyack Distribution Center, Route 59 and Brook Hill Drive, P.O. Box 515, West Nyack, NY 10994.

Reference Service Press, 1100 Industrial Road, Suite 9, San Carlos, CA 94070.

Renaissance Publications, 7819 Barkwood Drive, Worthington, OH 43085.

Routledge, Chapman and Hall, 29 W. 35th Street, New York, NY 10001-2291; tel. 212.244.3336.

Sage Publications, Inc., 2111 West Hillcrest Drive, Newberry Park, CA 91320; tel. 805.499.0721.

San Diego Interfaith Task Force on Central America, P.O. Box 3843, La Mesa, CA 91944-3843.

**St. Martin's Press, 175 Fifth Avenue, New York, NY 10010; tel. 212.674.5161.

Stockton Press, 257 Park Avenue South, New York, NY 10010; tel 800.221.2123, or 212.673.4400; fax 212.673.9842.

Surrey Books, 230 East Ohio Street, Suite 120, Chicago, IL 60611.

The Swedish Institute, P.O. Box 7434, S-103 91 Stockholm, Sweden.

Transitions Abroad, Dept. TRA, Box 3000, Denville, NJ 07834.

**Travel Medicine Inc., 351 Pleasant Street, Suite 312, Northampton, MA 01060; tel. 800.872.8633.

UNIPUB, 4611-F Assembly Drive, Lanham, MD 20706; tel. 800.274.4888.

University Press of America, 4720 Boston Way, Lanham, MD 20706.

U.S. Chamber of Commerce, International Division, 1615 H Street, N.W., Washington, D.C. 20062.

U.S. Government Printing Office, Superintendent of Documents, Washington, D.C. 20402; tel. 202.783.3238.

Vacation Work, 9 Park End Street, Oxford OX1 1HJ, England.

Viking Penguin Inc., 40 West 23rd Street, New York, NY 19919.

Volunteers for Peace, 43 Tiffany Road, Belmont, VT 05730; tel. 802.259.2759.

Volunteers in Asia, Box 4543, Stanford, CA 94309; tel. 415.723.3228.

Williamson Publishing, P.O. Box 185, Charlotte, VT 05445.

World Trade Academy Press, 50 E 42nd Street, New York, N.Y. 10017; tel. 212.697.4999.

Worldwise Books, P.O. Box 3030, Oakton VA 22124.

Writers Digest Books, 1507 Dana Avenue, Cincinnati, OH 45207; tel. 800.289.0963, fax 513.531.4744.

**W.W. Norton & Co., Inc., 500 Fifth Avenue, New York, NY 10110; tel. 800.233.4830, 800.458.6515.

Note: the consulates, embassies, and/or information offices of many countries in addition to those governmental organizations listed above can furnish free information on study, work, and travel in the countries they represent.

Appendix 2

Getting on with the Task
A National Mandate for
Education Abroad

Report of the National Task Force on
Undergraduate Education Abroad, 1990

In June 1989 NAFSA invited the Institute of International Education and the Council on International Educational Exchange to join in forming a National Task Force on Undergraduate Education. This report and its recommendations are the result of the task force's work.

The role of the United States as a leader among nations is changing rapidly. Despite our position of international leadership for almost fifty years, we are ill-prepared for the changes in business, manufacturing, diplomacy, science and technology that have come with an intensely interdependent world. Effectiveness in such a world requires a citizenry whose knowledge is sufficiently international in scope to cope with global interdependence.

—Advisory Council for International Educational
Exchange, *Educating for Global Competence.* p.1.

Task Force Purpose and Focus

At the very moment when dramatic changes in the world cause our nation to re-evaluate priorities and to search for policies and alignments which will serve our people in the new century, our position of international leadership among nations is rapidly shifting. The extraordinary events of 1989 rank as markers of human history comparable to those of 1848, 1914, and 1945. Without warning, the comfortable dimensions of the present convulsed and the world transformed itself in unimagined ways. Many of the goals of more than forty years of American foreign policy were realized in a matter of months. The United States, the Soviet Union, Europe, indeed the entire world, grapple with fundamental role changes as we all enter this new period in history, one that is full of possibility and hope.

Yet, in the United States, optimism about this new world is tempered by anxiety created not only by uncertainty about events still to unfold but also by our ability to rise to these new challenges. There is abundant evidence that our citizens are not well prepared for the international realities ahead. By any measure, whether it be comparisons of foreign language proficiency, tests of geographic literacy, or availability of specialists to advise government or business regarding eastern Europe or other distant but important parts of the world, the level of international knowledge and understanding in our country is wanting. In comparison with others, we as a people are poorly educated to deal with the political, economic and social issues which we will face in a new global era that will not measure strength primarily in terms of military preparedness.

In fact, for the past several years, there has been growing acknowledgement that education must provide more international content and lead to greater sensitivity and understanding. For undergraduates at our universities and colleges, a serious educational experience in another country brings cross-cultural understanding and international learning not achievable through almost any other approach. Opportunities for such experience abroad are still confined to a small fraction of American undergraduates, mainly upper middle class, and still focus predominantly on western Europe and on study of the humanities and social sciences. Study-abroad opportunities largely neglect the rest of the world and internationally important professional fields. At a time when American citizens and professionals in most fields require much more international knowledge, the narrow scope of undergraduate education abroad constitutes a grave neglect of extremely important needs and limits opportunities to a select few.

It was to address this situation that the National Association for Foreign Student Affairs (NAFSA) invited the Council on International Educational Exchange (CIEE), and the Institute of International Education (IIE) to join it in forming the National Task Force on Undergraduate Education Abroad. The Task Force was established in June 1989 and adopted the following mandate:

• To make undergraduate study and other academically related experiences abroad a higher national priority, with particular reference to such specific needs as increasing financial support, greater diversity of opportunity and program participation, and the assurance of program quality.

• To initiate and introduce language in existing legislation that will facilitate and expand undergraduate study abroad, develop new legislation at the state and federal levels, and explore and support nonlegislative/governmental avenues of funding.

• To develop an action agenda for the exchange field and the broader higher education community and involve these constituencies in the advocacy and implementation of the Task Force's recommendations.

Crucial to the work of the Task Force were the accomplishments of the "Bartlett Committee," a nationally distinguished group appointed by CIEE and named for its chair, Thomas A. Bartlett, to review and make recommendations on future priorities for study abroad. We, the members of the Task Force, fully support the priorities set forth by that committee in its 1988 report, "Educating for Global Competence," and have defined as our own agenda advocating and facilitating their implementation. Chief among them are: a major expansion of undergraduate education abroad, greatly increased access for minority and other underrepresented students, and correction of the grossly disproportionate involvement of Western European program sites compared to all the rest of the world.

Although the Task Force expects to function actively for only a year, making undergraduate education abroad a higher national priority will require the ongoing support of many. Crucial to this effort will be the followup activities of the sponsoring organizations: CIEE, IIE, and NAFSA as well as others involved in the process. If such efforts are catalyzed by the Task Force and some progress achieved before its work is done, the substantial commitment of our sponsors will have been well justified.

The establishment of the National Task Force reflects and should strengthen the mounting awareness that study abroad is one of the most effective means to achieve international education for undergraduates and the internationalization of colleges and universities. Although in the past undergraduate study abroad may have in some instances been deficient in academic substance and lacked institutional and national support, its importance is now beginning to be more widely recognized in the United States. Some recent events and trends reenforce this development.

In reaching its conclusions the Task Force benefitted and drew on a large number of recent studies and reports which have targeted the need to strengthen international education and exchange. Our primary inspiration came from the earlier mentioned CIEE report, "Educating for Global Competence." The more significant recent studies and reports which represent the mounting awareness of the value of an international educational experience are listed in the reference section.

One of these studies, however, should be mentioned here because of its findings on the results of study abroad. A five-country, five-year study, for which the U.S. report was published in summer 1990, compellingly documents the major impacts of study abroad in terms of students' international learning, interests, and career aims: the U.S. students substantially increased foreign language proficiency; after their sojourn abroad their knowledge of their host country increased dramatically, as did their interest in and knowledge of international affairs; a majority of the American study-abroad returnees planned on careers that would benefit from the knowledge and perspectives gained from their period abroad. [Ed. note: This report was published in two volumes by the European Cultural Foundation as *Higher Education Policy Series #11: Study Abroad Programmes*, vol.1, ed. by Barbara B. Burn, Ladislav Cerych, and Alan Smith; and *Impacts of Study Abroad Programmes on Students and Undergraduates*, vol.2, by Susan Opper, Ulrich Teichler, and Jerry Carlson. It is available from Jessica Kingsley Publishers, 118 Pentonville Road, London, N1 9JN.]

An additional and important point of further reference for the Task Force was its understanding of the impressive educational goals of ERASMUS, the European Community program aimed at ensuring that by 1992, 10 percent of EC university students can afford and will have a significant study-abroad experience in another EC country. ERASMUS will prepare European students not only for the professional, commercial, technical, linguistic, academic, and diplomatic needs of a united Europe, but also for performing effectively in the world market of ideas and trade. According to the most recent data available, hardly two percent of American undergraduates study abroad for academic credit, a percentage far below the ERASMUS goal of 10 percent by 1992. In the view of the Task Force, American higher education must also vigorously meet this latter challenge.

The Task Force Focus. While focussing on the undergraduate level, the Task Force explicitly recognizes the importance of opportunities for study and other experiences abroad at all levels of American education, from secondary school to graduate school and postgraduate research; for students, teachers, and scholars. But we believe that it is the internationalization of the undergraduate experience which can have the greatest impact on American society in terms of lifelong interests and values. Moreover, while the main emphasis of this report concerns formal study-abroad programming organized and overseen by colleges and universities or by consortia of higher education institutions, the Task Force is convinced that international work or service experiences, as well as other forms of immersion in the daily life of a foreign culture, can contribute greatly to a student's formal academic and/or preprofessional education and understanding of the world, even if this educational gain is not measured in terms of academic credit.

Summary of Recommendations

The work of the Task Force has resulted in five major recommendations. Each recommendation is treated in more detail in one of the following five chapters, and they are presented here in summary form. Taken together, they will greatly enhance the contribution of overseas study-abroad programs to the internationalization of the higher education experience of undergraduates.

Expansion of Education Abroad. By the year 1995, 10 percent of

American college and university students should have a significant educational experience abroad during their undergraduate years. Achieving this will require substantial growth in the number and type of opportunities provided and a more pervasive integration of education abroad into institutional strategies aimed at strengthening the international dimension in U.S. higher education.

Increased Diversity. As numbers and opportunities are expanded we urge that greater diversity be a major goal for all aspects of education abroad: greater diversity in participating students, in foreign locations, and in types of programs.

Curricular Connections. The study-abroad experience must be integrated into regular degree programs in many different fields including professional schools. In some fields, study abroad should become a requirement, for example, for future foreign language teachers in elementary and secondary schools.

Major Inhibitors. A variety of factors inhibit expansion of numbers and diversity in undergraduate education abroad. Some are historical; others are tied to negative perceptions. We urge that all be vigorously addressed. They include:

- Insufficient institutional commitment to international education.
- Negative views of some faculty members.
- Restrictive curricular requirements.
- Foreign language deficiencies.
- Inadequate study-abroad support services on campus and abroad.
- Inadequate information about education-abroad opportunities and their relative quality.
- Financial regulations and shortfalls.

Financial Options. While lack of money is not always the main obstacle to program development or student participation, expanded funding from both private and public sources will be essential if the academic community is to diversify the types of institutions, students, and experiences involved in study abroad in the years ahead.

I
Expansion of Education Abroad

In order to enhance the impact of study abroad on the internationalization of U.S. colleges and universities, the goals set forth in "Educating for Global Competence" must be implemented. Chief among them is: participation in study abroad by 10 percent of all undergraduates by 1995, and, for the longer term, 20 to 25 percent by the year 2008, two decades after the CIEE committee completed its report. The rationale for these goals merits repeating:

It is absolutely essential that college students cultivate an informed and sensitive awareness of those parts of the world in which more than half the global population lives....

The intensely interdependent nature of the world community and the challenges to American competitiveness mean that we need to increase the competence of students in their knowledge of other countries and their abilities with foreign languages.

An educational experience in a foreign setting certainly contributes significantly to this increased knowledge and competency, and yet, according to IIE figures, the number of students receiving credit for studying abroad in 1987–88 was only 62,341. Although this figure omits data from some non-responding institutions, it nevertheless documents that only a tiny fraction of America's more than 12.5 million college and university students have a study-abroad experience.

The expansion of education abroad is urgent for the following reasons:

• The impact of study abroad is far greater if substantial numbers of students rather than the occasional few participate. Only then does the experience produce important multiplier effects on home campus curricula and teaching and on students' academic and personal goals and achievements.

• Americans must, like their European and Japanese student counterparts, learn to function professionally across national boundaries. The United States cannot afford to lag in preparing future professionals for the internationally involved careers that await them.

The National Task Force strongly urges American colleges and universities to integrate study abroad into their institutional strategies for strengthening not only international education but also the quality of their overall academic programs. Study and other educational experiences abroad, as part of the internationalization of undergraduates programs, should play a much more central role in what colleges and universities are all about: in their missions and goals, in their institutional structures and policies, in their educational programming and planning, and in their allocations of staff and other resources.

II
Increasing Diversity

Ensuring that at least 10 percent of U.S. students have an educational experience abroad requires more than mere linear increases in what now exists. Recruiting more undergraduates must involve a wider spectrum of students studying in a wider range of geographic destinations and new and different program models.

Geographic Locations. The overwhelming dominance of western Europe in U.S. study-abroad programming, while historically understandable, is no longer compatible with the nation's needs in international education. To function as citizens and professionals in a shrinking world, American students should learn about all of it, not just the Anglo-European countries. At the same time it must be recognized that study abroad in many countries and regions outside of western Europe can present American students with a variety of difficult challenges: unfamiliarity with the host country's culture and language(s); enormous competition among host country students; a limited number of places in higher education; major differences in accommodations, student services; different approaches to teaching and learning; smaller libraries and fewer academic facilities; and unfamiliar student social interaction. These kinds of differences make it especially important to revise program models for study abroad and to develop new ones, especially for Third World country sites.

The National Task Force urges as a short-term target that undergraduate study outside of western Europe be expanded to at least one-third of all study-abroad students. At present more American undergraduates study in the United Kingdom alone than the total of all in Asia, Africa, the Middle East, and Latin America. To reach this new goal, these major world regions must see a doubling of American undergraduates pursuing education abroad.

Minority Student Participation. Efforts to expand the number of undergraduates who study abroad must address the lack of diversity among them. Traditionally American study-abroad students have come from affluent, middle or upper class, white, professional families rather than from the broad spectrum of American society. Even though minority enrollments in American colleges and universities have increased overall by 8 percent in 1984-86, and in 1986 represented 10 percent of all four-year college students, minority participation in study abroad has increased little, representing only a tiny fraction of all undergraduate study-abroad students.

Because, as stated in "Educating for Global Competence," "it is clearly in the national interest to have internationally skilled students from the widest possible range of backgrounds," recruiting the underrepresented minorities, especially blacks and Hispanics, to study abroad calls for special measures, not least of which may be special funding.

III
Developing Program Approaches

Forging Curricular Connections. The existence of few or no connections between home campus curricula and what students study abroad is an important deterrent to study abroad for American students. Students who do not study abroad give as reasons their perception that it did not fit with or was not required by their major, might prolong their degree period, and was not encouraged or was even explicitly discouraged by their faculty advisers.

Study abroad can enroll substantially more undergraduates only if it is clear that their studies abroad will both earn them academic credit and will be treated as an integral part of their degree program and an asset to it. In particular, a study-abroad period should be treated as part of, rather than apart from, their studies for their major. It is ironic that in the United States where the academic credit system facilitates the recognition of studies done elsewhere, students in many disciplines find this difficult or impossible with respect to requirements for their major. In western Europe, even with only an incipient system of academic credit, ERASMUS enables many EC students who study in another EC country to have their work treated as an integral part of their home campus degree.

In order to strengthen study-abroad's connections with home campus curricula, the following steps are needed:

• Students should have greater access to information on study-abroad opportunities, including specific courses, in order to plan their study abroad far enough in advance so that it can be incorporated into and not extend their degree period.

• American faculty members and undergraduate advisers should have sufficient information on courses their students wish to take abroad to counsel them on courses that will count towards the degree and to encourage them to study abroad.

• To integrate study abroad more closely into home campus curricula and reduce the sense of alienation many returnees experience on returning to campus, faculty should attempt to build on students' international learning, developing or modifying courses in which such students tend to enroll.

• Colleges and universities should encourage an academically related experience abroad as an option in all degree programs.

Subjects Throughout the Curriculum. If more students are to have educational experiences abroad, program opportunities must become much more varied in subject or discipline focus. Rather than being primarily in humanities and social sciences fields, education-abroad opportunities must be targeted across disciplines. Obvious fields are public health, education (including practice teaching abroad), architecture, environmental studies, and hotel and travel administration, but business and engineering, because of their large enrollments and the rapid internationalization of careers in these fields, must also be priorities.

Major constraints to including study abroad in such fields as engineering and business are the tight curricular requirements, including sequencing, which leave little flexibility for students. The Task Force believes, however, that early and careful planning should, given faculty encouragement, enable more of these students to study abroad. The fact that some professional schools in the United States not only make it possible but encourage their majors to study abroad suggests that this is indeed a realistic goal.

New Models. In expanding study abroad to encompass 10 percent of all undergraduates and diversify both participants and destinations, merely replicating and multiplying current program models is unrealistic and inappropriate. For students who are older, of minority background, employed (46.5 percent of full-time students under 25 years are employed at least part-time), are disabled, or have limited funds, study abroad often is not perceived to be an option. The needs of such students are mostly ignored by the more typical study-abroad models and structures. The Task Force cannot prescribe the new models for greatly expanded and diversified education abroad. These must be developed pragmatically by individual institutions, consortia, or other appropriate organizations. However, features to consider include more short-term stays, flexible language requirements, "no-fee swapping" of students between U.S. and foreign institutions, and built-in student work or service components that reduce costs.

An important model for diversifying education abroad is work experience in another country which puts students in close contact with the local people and culture. Undergraduate student interest in work experiences abroad is increasing rapidly and certainly at a faster rate than study-abroad program participation. Nevertheless, little interest in support for these students has been shown by much of the international education and academic communities, who confine their attention to academic programs and may wrongly dismiss experiential learning as of little educational value. Internships, various types of cooperative education arrangements, voluntary service and independent study/research projects are among approaches which could either generate academic credit or be academically or professionally relevant to degree programs at the home institution.

For students preferring to work abroad rather than pursue formal courses, whether for reasons of finance or other motivation, the many opportunities now available, for example through CIEE and the various other organizations which facilitate work abroad, should be brought to students' attention, and be further expanded. Other possible models would be service in an undergraduate Peace Corps, working as undergraduate teaching assistants in schools or colleges abroad, or participating in workcamps and other kinds of volunteer activities.

IV
Attacking Major Inhibitors

The Task Force identified seven factors which stand in the way of expansion of and improved quality in undergraduate study abroad. While there is some overlap among them, each impediment is sufficiently separate from the others to call for a different treatment and strategy, either at the institutional level or more broadly. They must be addressed.

First, the lack of institutional commitment to a strong international dimension in undergraduate education is a serious impediment at some colleges and universities. Without such a commitment—that is, a determination to adjust and tune undergraduate learning to the multicultural and global realities of the decade ahead—there will be little institutional encouragement for students to study abroad and for faculty members to organize new programs.

National associations and organizations are helping to build commitment, reinforced by an impressive array of national commission pronouncements, state governors' recommendations and the general search for excellence in education. Many institutions, in spite of strained financial circumstances, are studying their international educational needs, often in the context of a review of the core undergraduate curriculum.

Substantial momentum now exists toward attaining a greater international dimension in higher education. For example, a recent national initiative, the Coalition for the Advancement of Foreign Languages and International Studies (CAFLIS), consists of 160 regional and national organizations, both large and small, seeking to improve international education and enhance the nation's competence to deal with global issues. Yet, there are still some colleges and universities which have not embraced such commitments and others which have done so superficially. The Task Force encourages the faculty and students at these institutions to push hard for a more vigorous international commitment, one which includes undergraduate study abroad as a means to accomplish curricular and educational ends.

The strategy will vary among colleges and universities, faculties, departments, and disciplines. The authors of a report which canvassed a cross-section of institutions in four selected states note the following:

We were struck repeatedly by the importance of a charismatic leader in galvanizing a campus to focus on and undertake study abroad. Usually the key person is the president, but it also may be a provost, dean, state governor, system chancellor, or even some dynamic senior faculty member. Enormous resources are not required to make study-abroad work; what are usually lacking where such a program does not exist are vision, a sense of commitment, and a clarion call to action.

We urge persistence on the part of those who are already committed, but whose institution may be laggard. Persistence, enlisting internal and external allies, pushing for creation of a review committee and strategic planning to take advantage of opportunities and normal information flow are all important. These endeavors must be taken with a thorough knowledge of and sensitivity to the institution's governance structure.

Even with general institutional commitment, attitudes of individual faculty and those prevailing in some departments can be a problem, sometimes even a severe obstacle to forming new programs or encouraging student participation. The explanation for lack of faculty support includes such inglorious reasons as inertia and the egocentric "what's in it for me?" Less crass but equally parochial—and more prevalent—is the attitude among some faculty, even those who ought to be among the strongest proponents of study abroad, that study abroad deprives them of their best students, actually taking students out of their classrooms and reducing their full time equivalent statistics. But, by far the most frequent cause of lack of faculty interest in or opposition to study-abroad programs is that they are not perceived to be relevant to or supportive of what faculty do. Faculty often do not recognize the academic legitimacy of the students' activities abroad. In support of their position, faculty members cite student reports selectively, for example, those asserting that students' experience abroad was not as rigorous academically as their experience on the campus.

One approach to winning the support of faculty is to design study-abroad programs with particular faculty in mind and to begin to plan new programs with them. For example, professional-school faculty who typically are suspicious of study-abroad opportunities because they perceive them as detracting from preprofessional training should be asked to identify the off-campus experience that might enhance the preparation of students in his or her field. Responses that point toward greater knowledge of Japanese culture or business practices, or the implications of the European Community in 1992 for U.S. society should become the starting point for planning a new course or a program in Japan or Europe. Faculty should participate in program planning, course design, and site selection, and then help fit the program into the curriculum and form part of an advisory committee to the program. Faculty can be similarly involved in programs calling for direct enrollment in foreign institutions or the design of appropriate internships. Quite naturally they will become advocates for such study-abroad experiences in their classrooms and potential future resident directors, as well as academic advisers to students returning from abroad. Most important, they will become the legitimizers of the program on campus to their more parochial colleagues, to hesitant administrators and to doubting parents.

A more interesting challenge and one that requires more imagination is to involve the faculty who teach international subjects but who have not traditionally been associated with study-abroad programs, for example, a professor of international relations or security studies. Again, the key is to begin with the faculty member's professional interests and concerns. The result might be a program designed around a theme—e.g., the European Economic Community, NATO, international security in a world of declining great power competition—at a site identified by the professor where colleagues are doing quality work on the subject and where broad opportunities may exist for students' exposure to key officials and participants.

In short, faculty members must become convinced that some learning of their subject matter may well take place in a foreign setting. Not all will become convinced; nor should they, since much subject matter is indeed better taught at home. But getting them involved at a formative stage is an important step.

Curricular issues in various forms comprise a third inhibitor and were addressed in the preceding chapter.

A fourth inhibiting factor, closely related to curricular issues, is the national problem of language deficiencies. Study abroad is an important tool for attacking this serious national deficiency. New program development in other than English, Spanish or French speaking locations is not always easy but should be undertaken. This is especially true because the overseas study program has tended to be viewed from a traditional liberal arts viewpoint, i.e., overseas study as the domain and mainly serving the needs of Eurocentered language, literature and arts majors. Creative thinking and planning will result in broader curricular focus for study abroad and include a language and culture component.

The point is that higher education must break out of its inhibiting mold. The benefits of study abroad to other fields and situations must be seen; for example, programs in China can provide excellent learning situations for English-speaking American undergraduate students even if their introduction to the Chinese language is modest. There is much to be learned in China from English-speaking Chinese lecturers and English texts about Chinese subjects, and through an accompanying U.S. faculty member. The same is true in Japan, the Middle East and the USSR. There are also many sites outside Europe where French and Spanish language can profitably be explored in other cultural contexts, specifically those of Africa and Latin America. In general, much more can be done to structure programs which are not so dependent on language skills and the needs of language and literature programs. Faculty in architecture, history, business, government, social work, engineering and many other fields can develop sound programs for students who do not speak the local languages.

In fact, properly structured, an experience can serve to introduce students to language study.

At some universities, mainly those with little tradition of encouraging study abroad, there is a serious deficiency of support services to facilitate recruitment and flow of students. The Task Force considers this to be the fifth substantial inhibitor of faculty and student initiative. This deficiency may also extend beyond the U.S. campus to the situation abroad where facilities may be weak and support service minimal.

There should be an office available on campus to assist, advise, and encourage both faculty and students. Professional study-abroad personnel should be included in any initiatives to strengthen involvement in study abroad. Such an office can provide the leadership, working with departments, to expand and diversify undergraduate study abroad. The study-abroad professional can assure full consideration of options and encourage adequate coverage of language and culture studies in new programs. The absence of such a unit, and the resultant lack of attention to professional and support services, slows down growth of quality programs locally and participation of students in externally sponsored programs.

Even with adequate support services on campus, weak support arrangements in some areas abroad prevent expansion of program sites. This is particularly true in Third World locations where suitable living facilities may be in very short supply, where health problems may exist or personal security may be a concern. Obviously, there are locations which are still inaccessible to U.S. undergraduate students and may be so for some years to come. But there are many which are suitable and can become available through proper planning, cooperation among U.S. institutions and organizations and with colleagues in the foreign setting.

In some cases, reciprocity—such as interinstitutional exchanges of students—is the key. In others, the presence of U.S. students and faculty will be seen as especially welcome. A combination of initiative and persistence will overcome the problems in many locations abroad. In some cases new investment in facilities may be needed; in others, elaboration of potential benefits in both directions and patient negotiation will be sufficient. If study-abroad locations are to be diversified, such patience combined with healthy persistence will certainly be needed. Consortia and networking schemes are part of the solution to this inhibitor, and ways must be found to put them in place.

Lack of accurate and adequate information about the opportunities and realities of undergraduate study-abroad opportunities can serve as another significant inhibitor. There is so much incomplete or misleading information available that those concerned with providing a good flow of accurate information on all aspects of undergraduate education abroad must be particularly alert and active. Unfortunately, there are some programs in existence which deserve criticism; but these are the great exception. They are easily offset by examples of learning experiences abroad which surpass the experience of those who study only on campus. Frequently, the value of study abroad can be seen both in the academic learning that takes place, and also in an enhanced self-confidence and sense of personal direction which serves the individual student better than, perhaps, any other single undergraduate experience.

Lack of timely, accurate information can affect the judgment of faculty at the departmental level as well as that of those in the administration of the university. Therefore, both must be targets of any information campaign. The best instigators of such campaigns are those on campus who are committed to the expansion of the international dimension, and particularly, overseas study-abroad opportunities. Their allies are the similarly committed, national organizations armed with data.

The study-abroad support unit on campus should be the main force in spreading the good word about opportunities available. If no such office exists, it remains to others who are committed within the faculty or the administration and in national organizations to be sure that program information is widely available and that the distortions of the past are corrected.

Another target of accurate information flow must certainly be the "consumer"—the undergraduate student. Undergraduate study abroad is serious academic business and it must be portrayed that way, not as an academic holiday. Furthermore, the student who seeks information about opportunities offered by national consortia or by other universities should have ready and adequate information. A support services office on campus should be the source for such information.

It is also important that parents as well as students understand the plus and minus factors related to any specific program of study abroad. There are certain costs, but there are certainly overwhelming benefits in most such study situations, and these must be communicated effectively to families and supporting individuals. Outreach beyond the confines of the institution is essential. The insecurity caused by reports of terrorist activity, or a sense of hostility toward Americans abroad, can be easily overstated and parents can draw the wrong conclusion from newspaper headlines. Those concerned about accurate portrayal of the foreign situation must certainly be alert to problems, but also find ways to counter them with timely and realistic appraisals.

The seventh inhibitor is the shortage of funds for exploring and establishing new programs and for supporting some students. The chapter which follows deals directly with available options and recommends actions.

V
Addressing Financial Options

The problems of finance should be considered from several perspectives and levels.

Institutional Issues. Fortunately, most colleges and universities allow their students who participate in study-abroad programs organized by their home campus to receive financial aid. However, it is still common to find institutions which do not allow financial aid for programs sponsored by other institutions, to find private institutions where students cannot use institutional aid for study away from the home campus, or to find that only some kinds of federal aid are allowed for support of study abroad.

These situations clearly deter undergraduates from study abroad. Colleges and universities that are fully committed to undergraduate education abroad will take action to ensure that their study-abroad students are entitled to and receive at least the same level of financial support abroad—federal, states or private—as at the home campus (institutional commitment is also reflected in the faculty reward system and in support services and program funding relating to study abroad).

We applaud the approach of the University of California system and some other institutions which assume that just as costs for study at UC are supported by the university, so should they be when UC students study abroad. Furthermore, the UC system funds much of the cost of hosting "reciprocity students" from partner institutions abroad in order to assure UC student access to classrooms abroad. This UC approach contrasts with that of other institutions which expect study abroad to be self-funded by students or even revenue-generating for the U.S. institutions. Where the latter viewpoint prevails, it is a painful indicator of the low priority accorded to study abroad. If study abroad is to gain more priority, colleges and universities ideally should invest institutional resources in the activity.

The wide range of financial models suggests that where there is a will, there is a way. The task may be more difficult at low tuition public universities in contrast with higher tuition institutions. But if study abroad ranks as a high enough priority, no institution for financial reasons should have to deny its undergraduate students an opportunity to study abroad for credit either in a university-managed program, or through a well-planned and managed consortium program, or independently. Any institution can design affordable programs, assure that support services are sufficient, that exploratory funding is available, and that student aid funds are useable if needed.

Government Support at State and National Levels. State and federal support for undergraduate study abroad has been limited and, when available, over-regulated. At the federal level there are several issues. Statutory and regulatory limits prevent students who study abroad from receiving aid without major delays, bureaucratic obstacles, or other disincentives. Federal aid does not normally take into account that study abroad may involve extra costs compared to study at the home campus, just as laboratory studies for the science student may require extra expenditures. Even though it is in the national interest that study abroad involve more diverse students and sites abroad, almost no public funding now is targeted to that need.

In light of these and related circumstances, the Task Force recommends a careful review and modification of regulations, specifically:

• Existing statutory and regulatory limits which discourage or prevent undergraduate study abroad should be revised to facilitate undergraduate education in other countries and reflect sensitivity to the special needs of students participating in it;

• Federal law and regulations relating to student financial aid should ensure that the extra costs of study abroad, when applicable, are taken into account in determining students' awards;

• Federal eligibility requirements should be revised to allow more aid to

275

study-abroad students because most cannot work while studying abroad;

• Federal appropriations to institutions which do not allow students to use the aid for which they are eligible for study abroad should be restricted or made conditional on the institution's assuring the availability of this aid.

Moving beyond federally-funded financial aid regulations, at the federal level, the National Task Force has reviewed existing legislation and programs which involve or are pertinent to undergraduate education abroad in order to identify what might best advance the field. As part of this we were concerned whether at a time of budget deficits nationally, we should focus on including a larger or new undergraduate study-abroad dimension within existing programs, or advocate new federal legislation and funding in support of this field. The Task Force decided to do both, as is set forth below.

• The Fulbright Student Program, almost entirely graduate, should be expanded to provide a few highly targeted awards for undergraduate study abroad, with priority to diversifying student participation, nonwestern destinations, and underrepresented disciplines. Another important target group are graduating seniors, for whom Fulbright awards can serve to attract and facilitate a talented and more diverse study-abroad pool.

• The International Student Exchange Program (ISEP) which provides an excellent study-abroad model offering cost-effectiveness, reciprocity, and diversity, should be continued and expanded, especially in the developing, nonwestern world.

• The Group Projects Abroad program of the U.S. Department of Education, which encourages international and foreign language education for current and future teachers and emphasizes sites outside of western Europe should encourage the inclusion of undergraduates as program participants, especially the underrepresented minorities.

• There are a number of provisions of the Higher Education Act, Title VI, which deserve attention, especially in the months leading up to its reauthorization in 1991. The Foreign Language and Area Studies (FLAS) Fellowship Program under the Department of Education (Title VI) should give more opportunities to undergraduates for study abroad, especially for study of "critical" languages and in nonWestern countries (though allowable under the program, very few awards have been made for undergraduate study abroad). Title VI, Section 604, the Undergraduate International Studies and Foreign Language Program, should be revised to authorize support for study abroad, especially that which is closely related to on-campus foreign language and international studies curricula funded under this program. Title VI, Section 605, authorized but not yet funded, in granting funds to higher education institutions for intensive summer language courses, should include among eligible participants advanced foreign language students as well as teachers. Title VI, Sections 612 and 613, of the Higher Education Act, in encouraging more internationalization in business studies and programs, should give strong encouragement to internships abroad for undergraduates in business/foreign language fields.

• PL 480 legislation, which authorizes a percent of sales of American commodities abroad and paid for in local currency to be used towards the costs of U.S. programs abroad, should make support of undergraduate study abroad a priority.

• A variety of federally-funded programs, mostly administered by the U.S. Information Agency to support undergraduate education abroad, such as the Youth Exchange Initiative, the Bundestag Program with the Federal Republic of Germany, the Samantha Smith Program, and so on, should be reassessed in order to ensure adequate participation by minority and other underrepresented students.

• The University Affiliation Program of USIA should include, as a consideration in funding applications, the U.S. university's intention to make study abroad or student exchange an element in the interinstitutional relationship.

In addition to the above measures, the Task Force views as essential and urgent a new federal initiative to implement the objectives described above, including:

• Providing a substitute or work/study option for income earned while working in the United States (at present, students rarely can be approved for work abroad while studying);

• Supporting nontraditional, minority and other underrepresented students to study abroad, and among them students aspiring to programs focused in the Third World/developing countries.

The Coalition for Advancement of Foreign Language and International Studies (CAFLIS) has issued its action plan, which calls for expanded study abroad and urges creation of a new entity to help orchestrate and support major improvements in international education over the next decade. As this new national initiative takes shape and funding becomes available, we urge attention to study-abroad needs.

Corporate Role. Prompted by concerns for international competence, developments such as Europe 1992, and the accelerating internationalization of business and industry, the interest of U.S. corporations in promoting greater awareness among their staff of the cultures, languages, and ways of doing business of other countries has sharply increased in recent years. Even though the subsidiaries of many U.S.-based firms hire host country nationals as local managers, more and more U.S. corporations are acknowledging needs for internationally trained recruits.

In seeking more support for undergraduate study abroad, colleges and universities should take the above trends and concerns into account and seek more assistance from the private sector. This should apply especially for programs which enable business students to become competent in other languages and knowledgeable about other cultures. Such assistance might take the form of financial contributions by U.S. firms to such programs or providing funded internships or other practical experience opportunities with their operations abroad. Such assistance should also be sought for programs abroad for engineering undergraduates because of the rapid internationalization of this field.

Third World Debt. The huge debts which some countries now owe to banks in the United States and other developed countries must be considered a possible source of funding for new overseas study programs. The "debt-for-development" or "debt-for-environment" programs which have been studied, planned, and in a few cases, actually launched, suggest to those of us concerned with building new study programs in diverse areas that a "debt-for-study" theme would also be appropriate. In fact, the U.S. Department of Commerce issued a report on just such a possibility as part of the department's desire to increase U.S. competitiveness, in this case through educating American students in a foreign setting.

These large debts are found in countries which offer great potential for diverse new educational programs—for example Brazil, Mexico, Argentina, and some countries of Africa. The existence of these multibillion-dollar funds are a real problem but they also pose a challenge. Can we find a way to use them for educational purposes, namely the establishment of new opportunities for U.S. students to study in these countries? And can such programs offer some benefit to other concerned parties as well? We believe that if properly designed they offer such possibilities and are clearly worth the effort.

At this time, most transfers of debt to serve development, environment, or educational purposes are not being offered as gifts. The debt funds must be negotiated and purchased, presumably at a greatly discounted rate. The currency must be used in the country of origin, not converted to U.S. dollars or other hard currency. But that is precisely where study-abroad programs encounter most operating expenses—in the foreign setting—so the restriction should be manageable.

Since students pay hard currency for undergraduate study, they provide a source of funds to buy discounted debt currency. Their payments make it feasible to use debt funds to underpin study-abroad programs. Of course, an outright gift of such funds to create an endowment fund locally would be better, but is probably unrealistic at the present time. Use of purchased debt funds could result in lower costs to the students, reduced debt totals, and improved educational opportunity.

Without providing detail here, we recommend that those involved in discussions of debt usage for worthwhile purposes keep U.S. undergraduate study in mind. The Task Force has already started to discuss such possibilities with relevant persons and believes it to be feasible and certainly desirable.

VI
Towards Action

We have recommended two broad goals—significant expansion of and greater diversity in education-abroad programs—and three routes towards realizing them. These three are to align study-abroad programs more closely with the undergraduate curriculum, to attack the identifiable, widespread inhibitors to growth and diversity, and to refine and improve the financial base for study abroad.

These five recommendations, as elaborated in this report, lend themselves to concerted, organized effort at the national, state, and institutional levels. We urge that at each level the community concerned with undergraduate study abroad work through existing organizations to move strategically on these goals. Where organizations do not exist, they must be created or the task absorbed within some other entity. We urge a direct approach to these goals as an important part of the broad effort to internationalize higher education and to produce well-educated leadership for the twenty-first century.

At the national level, this will mean that existing organizations concerned with education abroad must ally with others to see that it is incorporated in all initiatives to educate for global competence. Education abroad must be placed on the agendas of national association meetings, including college and university presidents, area studies and discipline-based organizations, professional education associations, and others. Included in this effort might be the entity proposed by the Coalition for Advancement of Foreign Languages and International Studies. All of these groups and organizations should, in concert and individually, seek to bring a better understanding of the importance of study abroad in a quality program of international education.

These alliances should be a part of a broader and more activist strategy to advance study abroad than has been present in the past. As the Higher Education Act moves towards reauthorization in 1991, education abroad as a component of Title VI should be prominent. It should be promoted within each of the varied strands of financial support for higher education, for example, as a part of broader minority student participation. An activist stance, one allied with other groups, will bring higher visibility for the study-abroad field as its leaders increasingly work with legislative and executive branch leaders on issues related to expansion and diversity goals.

At the state level, action is critical because most public institutions of higher learning derive a large share of their revenues from state governments and because private corporations frequently link their political activities and their philanthropic work to the communities in which they are located. Action at the state level by those committed to the goals of this report should focus on those organizations that comprise the political environment in which educational policy decisions are made. Obviously, this in-cludes the official bodies that formulate educational policy for the state and establish the budgets for public institutions.

The objective must be to convince officials at the state level that study abroad is an integral and valuable part of higher education. study-abroad ad-vocates should seek to place study abroad in all state processes such as higher-education legislation, budgets, or university support arrangements that deal with international education. The report of the National Governors Association should be viewed as a foundation—and justification—for bold actions.

Equally important, action should be directed at civic groups and corpora-tions. Together these constitute the largest portion of the constituency for international education in the private sector at the state level. Without their support, it will be difficult to convince state governments to make study abroad a matter of priority in the policy process. The goal is to create a grass-roots mandate for study abroad. Many corporate leaders are already on record nationally as favoring international education. The state level ac-tion plan should focus on winning the explicit support of corporate leaders for study abroad. Local corporations and civic groups can play an important role in convincing state officials and institutional administrators that study abroad is integral to our efforts to prepare the coming generation for the challenges they will confront. Fortunately, state and regional level organiza-tions which support international education are generally well-positioned to lead these study abroad efforts.

Much of what we are recommending must become part of the action agenda at the institutional level. We urge that leaders of colleges and uni-versities where international education, including study abroad, is not yet a priority appoint a task force to develop strategy to accomplish this goal. In pursuing the goal, academic leadership should forge alliances with appro-priate interest groups and individuals within and beyond their institutions in order to maximize the effectiveness and impact of their efforts.

While there is no single model for strengthening study abroad, among the many possible strategies for action at the institutional level are the fol-lowing.

• Allocate institutional funds to study abroad as a legitimate and signifi-cant instructional offering, and make it an important target for institutional fund-raising.

• Encourage and accord appropriate recognition to faculty involvement with and contributions to study abroad, including student advising, pro-gram development, and the integration of study abroad into the home cam-pus curricula.

• Take such measures as may be required to assure that students who study abroad are not penalized with respect to financial aid, and endeavor to provide special assistance to minority and other students underrepresented in study abroad so that they have equal access to it.

• Establish/strengthen a central office to develop, monitor, and coordinate international education, including study abroad, with appropriate staffing and other resources. The nature of the central office will vary, but the essential need for such leadership is increasingly apparent.

These national, state, and institutional activities and strategies fall in various ways within our five recommendations. Each of the five calls for specific actions, including the formation of political alliances, direct debate, and other tactics at each level. These actions will take different form and substance from one institution and locality to another. But we have suggested the ways they can be approached, recognizing the need to vary the pattern and strategy within our diverse system.

Whatever the variation, those committed to internationalizing higher education and, specifically, expanding and improving study abroad, must now get on with the task. Never before has the need been so apparent, nor the opportunity greater.

REFERENCES

A partial list of recent reports and publications on the value of educational experiences abroad appears here, as well as those references footnoted in the text of this report.

America in Transition: The International Frontier. Report of the Task Force on International Education, Washington, D.C.: National Governors' Association, 1989.

Boyer, Ernest. *College.* New York: Harper & Row, 1987.

Burn, Barbara B., Jerry S. Carlson, John Useem, and David Yachimowicz. *Study Abroad: The Experience of American Undergradu*ates. Greenwood Press, 1990.

Educating for Global Competence: The Report of the Advisory Council for International Educational Exchange. New York: Council on International Educational Exchange, 1988.

"Exchange 2000: International Leadership for the Next Century." Washington D.C.: The Liaison Group for International Educational Exchange, 1990.

Financial Aid for Study Abroad: A Manual for Advisers and Administrators. Edited by Stephen Cooper, William Cressey, and Nancy Stubbs. Washington, D.C.: National Association for Foreign Student Affairs, 1989.

Goodwin, Craufurd D. and Michael Nacht. *Abroad & Beyond: Patterns in*

American Overseas Education. Institute of International Education Research Report. Cambridge: Cambridge University Press, 1988.

"Improving U.S. Competitiveness: Swapping Debt for Education." A Report to the Secretary of Commerce, U.S. Department of Commerce, International Trade Administration, Washington, D.C.: U.S. Department of Commerce, 1988.

"International Competence: A Key to America's Future." A Plan of Action of the Coalition for the Advancement of Foreign Languages and International Studies, Washington, D.C.: CAFLIS, 1989.

"International Cooperation in Business Education." A Wingspread Conference Report. Edited by Stephen J. Kobin. New York: Council on International Educational Exchange, 1989.

Lambert, Richard D. *International Studies and the Undergraduate.* Washington, D.C.: American Council on Education, 1989.

Nation at Risk. Washington, D.C.: National Committee on Excellence in Education, 1983.

Open Doors: 1988-89: Report on International Educational Exchange. Edited by M. Zikopoulos, New York: Institute of International Education, 1989.

"Renewing the National Commitment to International Understanding through Educational and Cultural Diplomacy." Washington, D.C.: National Association for Foreign Student Affairs, 1989.

"Study, Work and Travel Abroad: A Bibliography." Washington, D.C.: National Association for Foreign Student Affairs, 1989.

MEMBERS OF THE NATATIONAL TASK FORCE ON UNDERGRADUATE EDUCATION ABROAD

Peggy Blumenthal
Vice-President, Educational Services
Institute of International Education—New York
809 United Nations Plaza
New York, NY 10017

Barbara B. Burn, Associate Provost
Director, William S. Clark International Center
Clark Hill Road
University of Massachusetts—Amherst
Amherst, MA 01003

Jack Egle
President and Executive Director,
Council on International Educational Exchange
205 East 42nd Street
New York, NY 10017

Mary Anne Grant
Executive Director,
International Student Exchange Program
1242 35th Street, N.W.
Washington, D.C. 20057

Ralph H. Smuckler
Dean and Assistant to the President
International Studies and Programs
Michigan State University
211 Center for International Programs
East Lansing, MI 48824-1035

Joseph Tulchin
Director
Office of International Programs
University of North Carolina—Chapel Hill
Chapel Hill, NC 27514

Appendix 3

Evaluation Guide

In spring 1986 the NAFSA Field Service, with support from USIA, funded a SECUSSA seminar at Penn State University to develop a survey instrument for collecting information from returning study-abroad participants. Included here is Penn State's adaptation of the survey for use in collecting information about other institutions' programs.

PENNSTATE

EDUCATION ABROAD PROGRAMS

PROGRAM EVALUATION QUESTIONNAIRE

The main purpose of this questionnaire is to learn more about your impressions of your study abroad experience. The information you provide is important: It can help us to improve the program.

Your responses will be shared only with the persons at Penn State University directly responsible for the academic oversight and administration of the Education Abroad Programs. What we want are your honest and frank responses.

The questions in this survey employ a number of formats. Most questions involve a scale on which you can circle the number that best represents how you feel. Other questions are "open-ended," asking you to write out an answer. On these, write only as much as you need to answer the question. Please try to answer all the questions, though you are of course free to skip any questions that you would like.

In addition, please feel free to comment on any of the questions, or on the questionnaire as a whole. This is a new questionnaire, and we would be happy to have your feedback on it.

Thank you in advance for your cooperation in completing this survey. Its usefulness — and our ability to improve future program offerings — depends solely on your cooperation.

PLEASE RETURN YOUR COMPLETED QUESTIONNAIRE TO THE

OFFICE OF EDUCATION ABROAD PROGRAMS
222 Boucke Building
The Pennsylvania State University
University Park, PA 16802

Name: _____ (Optional)

Sex: Female _____   Male _____

Age: _____   Semester standing while abroad _____

EAP PROGRAM: _____

Dates attended: _____

Date questionnaire completed _____

286

1. PERSONAL BACKGROUND

College Major: Pre-departure _____ Current _____

College Minor (if any): Pre-departure _____ Current _____

What have you done since the program ended (check all that apply)?   Ethnic Category (optional)

    traveled abroad _____   _____ Asian

    worked abroad _____   _____ Black

    returned to school _____   _____ Hispanic

    worked at a temporary job in the U.S. _____   _____ Native American

    taken a permanent job in the U.S. _____   _____ White

    Other (please specify) _____   _____ Other (please specify) _____

2. PRIOR EXPERIENCE ABROAD

Had you participated in a study abroad program before (including high school)?
    Yes _____   No _____
If yes, where, when, for how long, and in what program?

Had you traveled/lived in the host country before?
    Yes _____   No _____
If yes, where, when, for how long, and with whom (e.g., parents, friends, host family)?

Had you traveled/lived in other foreign countries before?
    Yes _____   No _____
If yes, where, when, for how long, and with whom (e.g., parents, friends, host family)?

3. ON-SITE SUPPORT SERVICES

Please indicate, on the left side, the extent to which each of the following resources was available and used by you. Then indicate, on the right side, your level of satisfaction with each resource. (If a resource was available, but you didn't use it, please circle "Not Applicable.")

	Not Available	Available But Not Used	Available And Used	Not Applicable	Extremely Dissatisfied				Extremely Satisfied
Program administrator	_____	_____	_____	0	1	2	3	4	5
On-site academic advising	_____	_____	_____	0	1	2	3	4	5
On-site personal advising and informal support	_____	_____	_____	0	1	2	3	4	5
Orientation	_____	_____	_____	0	1	2	3	4	5
Instructional resources (e.g., libraries, bookstores)	_____	_____	_____	0	1	2	3	4	5

	Not Available	Available But Not Used	Available And Used	Not Applicable	Extremely Dissatisfied				Extremely Satisfied
Instructional facilities	_____	_____	_____	0	1	2	3	4	5
Medical/dental services	_____	_____	_____	0	1	2	3	4	5
Recreational facilities	_____	_____	_____	0	1	2	3	4	5
Coordination between sponsoring institution and host institution	_____	_____	_____	0	1	2	3	4	5
Communication from home institution	_____	_____	_____	0	1	2	3	4	5

4. FOOD AND HOUSING

In what type of setting did you live? Rate your level of satisfaction with each setting.

	Not Applicable	Extremely Dissatisfied			Extremely Satisfied
_____ host family	0	1	2	3	4	5
_____ University housing	0	1	2	3	4	5
_____ rooming house	0	1	2	3	4	5
_____ an apartment	0	1	2	3	4	5
_____ room in private home	0	1	2	3	4	5
_____ other (specify): _____	0	1	2	3	4	5

How did you get your meals? Check all sources. Indicate your level of satisfaction with each source.

	Not Applicable	Extremely Dissatisfied			Extremely Satisfied
_____ host family	0	1	2	3	4	5
_____ University dining hall	0	1	2	3	4	5
_____ restaurant or cafeteria	0	1	2	3	4	5
_____ cooked own meals	0	1	2	3	4	5
_____ other (specify): _____	0	1	2	3	4	5

Did you have a choice?   Yes _____   No _____

5. ACADEMIC PROGRAM

Indicate the extent to which each of the following formats characterized your program.

	Not At All			Extremely
Course lectures	1	2	3	4	5
Course discussions	1	2	3	4	5
Individual or small group tutorials	1	2	3	4	5
Field trips	1	2	3	4	5
Other (describe): _____

288

By what means was your academic performance evaluated? (check all that apply)

_____ written exams

_____ oral exams

_____ papers

_____ class discussion

_____ field reports

_____ projects

_____ other (specify): _____

Was assessment of your academic performance:

_____ continuous or repeated

_____ once at the end of course

_____ both, depending on course

Courses abroad were:

_____ less demanding

_____ as demanding

_____ more demanding than those at Penn State

Please indicate your level of agreement with each statement by circling the appropriate response.

	Strongly Disagree			Strongly Agree
The program prerequisites (if any) were relevant.	1	2	3	4	5
The program prerequisites (if any) were reasonable.	1	2	3	4	5
This was the wrong academic program for me.	1	2	3	4	5
The instructors were effective.	1	2	3	4	5
The criteria for student evaluation (e.g., grading) were fair.	1	2	3	4	5
The program was intellectually challenging.	1	2	3	4	5
I could have learned the same material at my home institution.	1	2	3	4	5
Creative work/ideas were adequately recognized.	1	2	3	4	5
Instructors were stimulating.	1	2	3	4	5
Students were stimulating.	1	2	3	4	5
You were free to work at your own pace.	1	2	3	4	5
The mode of assessment (i.e., grading) was adequately explained at the beginning.	1	2	3	4	5
The resources of the host country (e.g., museums, community organizations, and activities) were well used.	1	2	3	4	5
Field trips were an important part of this program of study.	1	2	3	4	5

Please provide the following information about your courses and professors

Using 1 = Poor; 2 = Fair; 3 = Good; 4 = Excellent; 0 = Not applicable

Course Title	Professor	**COURSES** Clarity of Objectives	Pace	Class Content	Suitability of texts/materials	Appropriateness of Exams/Written Materials	Overall rating	**PROFESSORS** Knowledge of subject	Attitude toward students	Fairness of Grading	Availability outside of class	Feedback on academic progress	Communication skills	Quality of Instruction

Was the course load: _____ too light _____ just right _____ too heavy?

The amount of self-discipline required was: _____ too little _____ just right _____ too much.

PLEASE FEEL FREE TO PROVIDE ADDITIONAL COMMENTS ON THE BACK

6. COST

How did you finance your study abroad? Please indicate about what percentage was provided by each of the sources below.

_____ scholarships and grants from Penn State

_____ scholarships and grants from other sources (please specify: _____

_____

_____ loans

_____ family

_____ personal savings

_____ on-site employment

Exclusive of tuition, fees, room and board, about how much did you spend? _____

7. INDIVIDUAL DEVELOPMENT

Please indicate your level of agreement with each statement by circling the appropriate response.

	Strongly Disagree			Strongly Agree	
a. I have gained better insight into myself as a result of study abroad.	1	2	3	4	5
b. Study abroad has made me more receptive to different ideas and ways of seeing the world.	1	2	3	4	5
c. I have a greater sense of independence or self-confidence due to living and studying abroad.	1	2	3	4	5
d. Study abroad has increased my interest in social issues.	1	2	3	4	5
e. My interest in world events has increased.	1	2	3	4	5
f. My interest in the arts has increased through my study abroad.	1	2	3	4	5
g. My experience abroad has changed my career plans.	1	2	3	4	5
h. My career plans are now more uncertain.	1	2	3	4	5
i. My interest in language learning has increased.	1	2	3	4	5
j. My tolerance of other people and customs has increased.	1	2	3	4	5
k. I understand the U.S. better.	1	2	3	4	5
l. I like the U.S. better.	1	2	3	4	5
m. My ability to adapt to new situations has increased.	1	2	3	4	5
n. I became more interested in academic study.	1	2	3	4	5
o. My major has changed, or probably will change, as a result of this program.	1	2	3	4	5

Language skills (if applicable):	Excellent	Good	Fair	Poor
Your proficiency before the program:	_____	_____	_____	_____
Language training on the program:	_____	_____	_____	_____
Your proficiency after the program:	_____	_____	_____	_____
The level of proficiency you would recommend for beginning the program:	_____	_____	_____	_____

How much difference do you think language proficiency made in what you got from your total experience abroad?

_____ a) tremendous difference

_____ b) quite a bit of difference

_____ c) some difference

_____ d) little difference

_____ e) no difference

8. SOCIAL AND CULTURAL EXPERIENCE

Please indicate your level of agreement with each statement by circling the appropriate response.

	Strongly Disagree			Strongly Agree	
a. I was satisfied with the amount of contact with host country nationals.	1	2	3	4	5
b. There was sufficient contact with other internationals.	1	2	3	4	5
c. There was too much contact with U.S. citizens.	1	2	3	4	5
d. I was able to form close friendships with internationals.	1	2	3	4	5
e. I was able to see how a wide variety of people (e.g., professionals, laborers) lived in the host culture.	1	2	3	4	5
f. The staff helped me to take part in, and understand, the local culture.	1	2	3	4	5
g. The program structure facilitated interaction with the local culture.	1	2	3	4	5

9. OVERALL EVALUATION

Please indicate your level of agreement with each statement by circling the appropriate response.

	Strongly Disagree			Strongly Agree	
I would recommend this program to a friend.	1	2	3	4	5
I look forward to another international experience.	1	2	3	4	5
Overall, I rate my study abroad experience as excellent.	1	2	3	4	5

Overall, how would you compare what you gained abroad with what you would have gained in a comparable time at your home institution?

_____ much more valuable

_____ more valuable

_____ about the same

_____ less valuable

_____ much less valuable

10. <u>FORMATIVE FEEDBACK</u>

1. What do you consider the *most desirable* characteristic of the program?

What do you consider the *least desirable* characteristic of the program?

What are the *primary benefits* that you feel you derived from participation in the program?

2. Different students have different sorts of objectives in study abroad, as well as different levels of preparation, and no one program is right for everyone. For what sorts of students, if any, would you recommend this program?

What sorts of students, if any, would you especially recommend <u>not</u> enroll in this program?

3. If you were responsible for planning and implementing the program in which you participated, what changes would you make?

4. Before studying abroad, what didn't you know that you wish you had known?

5. Did you have any problems after returning? Please describe.

Appendix 4

Code of Ethics

NAFSA: Association of International Educators

Institutional and individual members of NAFSA: Association of International Educators are dedicated to providing high-quality education and services to participants in international educational exchange. They represent a wide variety of institutions, disciplines, and services. A code of ethics which proposes to set standards for the professional preparation and conduct of all NAFSA members must accommodate this diversity. This document sets forth a number of general guidelines for ethical conduct applicable to all NAFSA members and then details principles pertaining to many of the various activities members undertake.

Whether paid or unpaid for their work in international educational exchange, all NAFSA members are expected to uphold professional standards.

International educators operate in complex environments, with many legitimate and sometimes competing interests to satisfy. Ultimately, their allegiance must be to the long-term health of international educational exchange programs and participants.

1. NAFSA Members Have a Responsibility to:

a. Maintain high standards of professional conduct.

b. Balance the wants, needs, and requirements of program participants, institutional policies, laws, and sponsors, having as their ultimate concern the long-term well-being of international educational exchange programs and participants.

c. Resist pressures (personal, social, organizational, financial, and political) to use their influence inappropriately. Refuse to allow considerations of self-aggrandizement or personal gain to influence their professional judgments.

Sorting through ethical dilemmas is often best done with help from others, either one's superiors in the organization or experts in one's subject-matter area.

Since they work in an area affected by rapid social, political and economic changes, members must make constant efforts to keep current in order to be professionally competent.

One of the most challenging aspects of work in the field of educational exchange is balancing among the dictates of various cultures and value systems. Members need to be well aware of the influence that culture has had on their own values and habits, and on the interpretations and judgments they make of the thoughts and habits of others.

d. Seek appropriate guidance and direction when faced with ethical dilemmas. Make every effort to ensure that their services are offered only to individuals and organizations with a legitimate claim on those services.

2. In Their Professional Preparation and Development, Members Shall:

a. Accurately represent their areas of competence, education, training, and experience.

b. Recognize the limits of their expertise and confine themselves to the performance of duties for which they are properly trained and qualified, making referrals when situations are outside their area of competence.

c. Be informed of current developments in their fields, and ensure their continuing development and competence.

d. Stay abreast of developments in laws and regulations that affect their clients.

e. Actively uphold the Association's code of ethics when practices that contravene it become evident.

3. In Relationships with Students and Scholars, Members Shall:

a. Understand and protect the civil and human rights of all individuals. Not discriminate with regard to race, national origin, color, gender, religion, sexual orientation, age, political opinion, immigration status, or disability.

b. Recognize their own cultural and value orientations and be aware of how those orientations affect their interactions with people from other cultures.

c. Demonstrate awareness of, sensitivity to and respect for other educational systems, values and cultures .

d Not exploit, threaten, coerce, or sexually harass students or scholars.

e. Refrain from invoking immigration regulations in order to intimidate students or scholars in matters not related to their immigration status.

f. Maintain the confidentiality, integrity, and security of student records and of all communications with students. Secure permission of the student or scholar before sharing information with others inside or outside the organization, unless disclosure is authorized by law or institutional policy, or mandated by previous arrangement.

g. Refrain from becoming involved in personal relationships with particular students and scholars when such relationships might result in either the appearance or the fact of undue influence being exercised on the making of professional judgments.

h. Respond to inquiries fairly, equitably, and professionally.

i. Seek qualified assistance for students or scholars who appear to be experiencing unusual levels of emotional difficulty.

j. Accept only those gifts which are of nominal value and which do not seem intended to influence the manner in which professional responsibilities are exercised, while remaining sensitive to the varying significance and implications of gifts in different cultures.

k. Assure the provision of information and support services needed to facilitate participants' adaptation to a new educational and cultural environment.

While enjoying interpersonal dealings with people from other cultures, members need to avoid situations in which their judgments may be or appear to be clouded as a result of personal relationships—either positive or negatives ones—with particular exchange participants.

Although a categorical ban on accepting gifts would be inappropriate for members who work with individuals representing cultures where the giving of gifts is important, members need to exercise caution in accepting gifts that might be intended to influence them as they carry out their duties.

Being tolerant and respectful of differences in behavior and values among culturally-similar others is often more difficult than being tolerant of those differences when they are manifested by people from other cultures. Nevertheless, members should make every effort to show their same-culture colleagues the respect they show their different-culture clients.

Just as they have duties to their clients, members have duties to their professional colleagues. When members accept responsibilities through the Association, they should carry them out with dispatch.

In the press of daily business, it is often tempting to overlook the long-term need for professional development. Members need to remain cognizant of the need for continuing professional development.

4. In Professional Relationships, Members Shall:

a. Show respect for the diversity of viewpoints found among colleagues, just as they show respect for the diversity of viewpoints among their clients.

b. Refrain from unjustified or unseemly criticism of fellow members, other programs, and other organizations.

c. Use their office, title, and professional associations only for the conduct of official business.

d. Make certain when participating in joint activities that collaborators receive due credit for their contributions.

e. Carry out, in a timely and professional manner, any Association responsibilities they agree to accept.

5. When Administering Programs, Members Shall:

a. Clearly and accurately represent the goals, capabilities, and costs of the programs.

b. Recruit individuals who are qualified to offer the instruction or services promised, train and supervise them responsibly, and assure by means of regular evaluation that they are performing acceptably and that the overall program is meeting its professed goals.

c. Strive to establish standards, activities, and fee structures which are appropriate and responsive to participant needs.

d. Encourage and support participation in professional development activities.

6. In Making Public Statements, Members Shall:

a. Clearly distinguish, in both written and oral public statements, between personal opinions and opinions representing the Association, their own institutions, or other organizations.

b. Provide accurate, complete, current, and unbiased information.

7. Members with Admissions Responsibilities Shall:

a. Consider the welfare of both potential and actual applicants as their primary responsibility.

b. Adhere to the following guidelines for the ethical recruitment of foreign students::

(1) Provide enough candid and pertinent information that a foreign student unfamiliar with United States practices in higher education may make informed academic judgments.

(2) Develop an admissions policy for foreign students which requires that admissions judgments be made by institutional personnel who rule on other admissions, is based on a system of written criteria, and is applied in competition with other applicants.

(3) Seek a match between the needs and aspirations of the prospective student and the educational opportunities the institution affords.

(4) Accept the commitment to provide effective educational opportunity for foreign students and establish appropriate institutional policies governing foreign student recruitment, admissions, support activities, specialized programs and curricula.

(5) Provide realistic estimates of costs for tuition, educational expenses, subsistence and related fees and of the extent to which financial aid or scholarships are available to foreign students.

(6) Restrict evaluation of foreign academic records to personnel who

are trained and competent in interpretation of foreign educational records.

(7) State clearly to students admitted to English language programs the extent of commitment made for their further education in the United States.

(8) Contract only with individuals or organizations whose practice conforms to the NAFSA Code of Ethics.

c. Make certain they are well versed in the art of evaluating educational credentials from abroad, employing a thorough knowledge of foreign educational systems.

d. Provide complete, accurate, and current information about their institutions' admissions criteria, educational costs, financial support opportunities, academic programs, and student services, in order to give students who are unfamiliar with local educational practices the basis for an informed choice. Encourage prospective students to make realistic assessments of their prospects for achieving their educational objectives at the member's particular institution.

Irrelevant criteria, such as an applicant's immigration status, should not be applied in making admission decisions.

Members with admission responsibilities sometimes come under pressure to admit applicants whose qualifications do not appear to prepare them for success. Those pressures ought to be resisted.

e. Employ only criteria relevant to a candidate's academic potential, level of language proficiency, educationally relevant special abilities and characteristics, and availability of financial support, in determining admissibility.

f. Resist pressure from institutional officers to admit unqualified applicants.

8. Members with Responsibility for Teaching English as a Second Language Shall:

a. Employ fair and accurate English proficiency tests in admissions and placement, and then use the test results in the student's best interest, evaluating students based on their individual merits and accomplishments.

Members making English language placement recommendations ought to base them on evidence of the applicant's linguistic proficiency, not on assumptions based on the applicant's national origin or other irrelevant factors.

b. Use up-to-date methods and materials appropriate to the needs of the specific populations and individuals being instructed.

c. Assure that the instruction they offer concerns not just the linguistic aspects of English, but also cultural aspects, the understanding of which will aid students in achieving their academic goals.

9. Members Who Advise Foreign Students and Scholars Shall:

a. Clarify the adviser's role to all parties and limit advice to matters within that mandate, making appropriate referrals when necessary.

Members should keep in mind that policies on the confidentiality of information apply to law-enforcement organizations as much as they do to any other type of organization.

b. Fully inform students, at appropriate times, of the types of information the institution is required to furnish to governmental agencies, and furnish those agencies with only that information required by law and regulation.

c. Decline to reveal confidential information about foreign students and scholars even if requests for such information come from law enforcement agencies or organizations appearing to have thoroughly benevolent motives.

Members ought not seek to influence their advisees' decisions by withholding information that might help the advisees thoroughly consider alternatives open to them.

d. Assist students and scholars in making prudent decisions, not withholding information that might widen their range of choices and not encouraging illegal actions.

10. Members with Responsibilities in Community Organizations Working with Foreign Students and Scholars Shall:

a. Make certain that organizations providing programs for foreign students and scholars have clear statements of purpose and responsibility, so that all parties can know what is expected of them.

People who are visiting another country may have no reliable way of knowing about the goals of organizations seeking their participation or affiliation. To assist these visitors, organizations have a responsibility to make their objectives clear.

b. Accurately portray their services

In their efforts to attract an adequate number of domestic participants in such activities as spouse and host family programs, members ought to resist pressures to accept as participants individuals whose motives are less than benevolent.

and programs, making clear the identity, the intent, and the nature of the sponsoring organization and of each particular event or service.

c. Provide appropriate opportunities to observe and to join in mutual inquiry into cultural differences.

d. Provide adequate orientation for volunteers and participants in community programs so they may understand each other and may interact constructively. The organization should make clear that surreptitious, deceptive or coercive proselytizing is unacceptable.

11. Members with Responsibilities in Students Abroad Shall:

Members in the study-abroad area sometimes face pressures to meet enrollment goals by accepting or encouraging the participation of students whose potential for benefitting from the program seems limited. These pressures should be resisted.

a. Provide complete and accurate information to students they advise, in order for students to make informed choices. Seek to ensure that students select overseas opportunities that seem suitable in terms of academic content, location, language preparation, emotional maturity, and cultural variation.

With the plethora of study-abroad programs available, members need to remain mindful that their clients rely upon them for judgments about program quality.

b. Ensure that any promotional materials they make available concern well-documented programs with reputable sponsors.

c. Assure appropriate educational guidance of students bound abroad through orientation and reentry programs and materials.

—Original text approved by the NAFSA Board of Directors on May 28, 1989.

—Revisions approved by the NAFSA Board of Directors on October 5, 1992.

Appendix 5

How to Read
Study-Abroad Literature

by Lily von Klemperer

Originally published in the NAFSA Newsletter, *December 1976.
The following version reprinted here was taken from IIE's* Academic
Year Abroad.

This is a sample advertisement for a summer program abroad:

TWA
Spend Your Summer in Sunny Spain
Live in a Medieval Castle
Learn Spanish at a Famous University
College Credit Available
Outstanding Faculty
International Student Body
Limited Enrollment—All Ages Eligible
Inclusive Charge
Write for Fully Illustrated Brochure
Director of Admissions
P.O. Box 000, Grand Central Station
New York, NY 10017

This advertisement probably never existed in its entirety. Its components,
however, appear in many advertisements, posters, and brochures. Advertisements and poster may have to be somewhat flashy and overstated to
catch the eye. Brochures, on the other hand, should be factual, realistic,
and totally honest.

Let us analyze the components of the sample ad, line by line, in order to
remind ourselves (1) how to read, interpret, and write descriptive literature
on study programs abroad, and (2) what questions to ask ourselves and others before enrolling in a program.

TWA. If the advertisement or brochure is "crowned" by TWA, a travel agency, or a similar commercial organization, while the name of the sponsoring U.S. college or university appears in small print elsewhere, whose program is it? And who is responsible for the program's academic standards, if any?

Spend Your Summer in Sunny Spain. A pleasant prospect! But look carefully at the prominence of this statement and ask what the real purpose of this program is: A summer in the sun—or a summer spent studying a foreign language and culture? How many hours will be spent in class and how many on the beach? What is the curriculum? Who teaches what, where, and when?

Live in a Medieval Castle. How romantic! But where is that castle? Is it near that "famous university" or will you have to commute to classes each day? Are the rooms shared or single? Are study facilities available? Are there inexpensive eating places nearby?

If family living is suggested, is it a family that has experience with U.S. students? Will they converse with you in the language you are studying? Is there public transportation after 6 p.m. or do students have to rely on expensive taxis?

Learn Spanish at a Famous University. Why isn't the name of the host institution given? Foreign universities generally suspend regular operations during the summer months, when their facilities may be available to anyone willing to pay the rent. The "famous university" may not actually be involved in the curriculum at all. The ad may refer to courses arranged by the sponsoring organization or to a special program for foreigners, which may or may not be organized by the host institution.

Some ads refer to "accredited" institutions or programs. To check the U.S. accreditation of a college or university, consult *Accredited Institutions of Postsecondary Education*, published annually by the American Council of Education for the Council on Postsecondary Accreditation. Information on foreign universities is available in *The World of Learning* (Europa Publications), the *International Handbook of Universities* (de Gruyter), and the *Commonwealth Universities Yearbook* (Association of Commonwealth Universities).

College Credit Available. The crucial questions here are (1) who makes this credit available? and (2) does the student's home institution accept credit offered by this program?

If receiving academic credit for your studies abroad is important to you, check the brochure to see if your school is listed as a participating institution or as a school that has accepted program credits in the past. Then consult your academic or study-abroad adviser before you enroll in the program to see whether the credits offered can be applied to your degree program.

Outstanding Faculty. Who are they? Where do they teach? What are their credentials? And, are they accessible to the students outside class?

International Student Body. Look closely at the roster of students in the back of the brochure. Are they swelling the ranks of "international students" by listing the children of U.S. parents residing abroad? Or will you in fact be mixing with bona fide representatives of other cultures?

Limited Enrollment—All Ages Eligible. Does this statement "limited enrollment" presuppose selectivity when all ages are eligible? How homogeneous is a program open to everybody, unless it includes classes specifically geared to the various academic levels?

It would be more helpful to know the type of student for whom the program is designed—his academic level, educational or professional background, motivation, and goals.

Inclusive Charge. There are almost as many variations to this term as there are programs. Is there an estimate of total expenses? Read the small print. Find out exactly what is covered and, more importantly, what is not covered. For example, are there periods of time abroad not covered by the inclusive fee? Will you have to pay for transportation to and from classes each day?

Ask about refund policies: Is there a nonrefundable application fee? Will tuition and program fees be refunded if circumstances force you to drop out of the program?

Write for Fully Illustrated Brochure. Even organizers of high-quality programs love to publicize them with attractive photographs of breathtaking scenery, lively cafe scenes, marble columns, and gothic spires. Unless the brochure devotes equal space to academic facilities, however, one may well question whether there is any provision at all for serious study.

Director of Admissions. Is there a name of a responsible person or just a title—or not even that? If you search the "fully illustrated brochure" and find no board of advisers, no trustees listed—no names whatsoever—what conclusions would you reach?

P.O. Box 000, Grand Central Station. Is there a street address or just a postal box number? Is there a phone number? How can one get hold of the program director in an emergency? And does a box number or street address in Ann Arbor necessarily imply University of Michigan sponsorship?

All these remarks—negative and positive—are a bid for honesty. Descriptive literature on foreign study should reflect the serious intent of the organizers. It should reflect quality, selectivity, and effective academic control. A meaningful and solid program cannot accommodate all tastes, all needs, all levels of maturity. But whatever it is meant to represent should be stated clearly and honestly.

Contributors

ARCHER BROWN has worked in the educational exchange field for more than thirty years, currently as deputy executive vice president of NAFSA: Association of International Educators. Prior to 1978, she was assistant executive director of the Council on International Educational Exchange in New York.

CYNTHIA FELBECK CHALOU is the coordinator of study abroad at North Carolina State University. She served as NAFSA's Region VII SECUSSA representative from 1988–1990, and now serves on the SECUSSA national team. She also serves on the International Student Exchange Program (ISEP) advisory board and the SECUSSA Task Force on Financial Aid. She coauthored an adviser's guide entitled, "Staying Healthy While Studying Abroad." Since serving as a Peace Corps volunteer in Swaziland, 1980–82, she has traveled professionally and personally though Europe, Africa, and Latin America.

STEPHEN COOPER is director of academic programs abroad at Louisiana State University, where he also teaches speech communication. He has chaired the CIEE editorial board and served on CIEE's board of directors and executive committee. He is a frequent presenter and panel chair at NAFSA and CIEE conferences. Among his publications is NAFSA's *Financial Aid for Study Abroad: A Manual for Advisers and Administrators*, which he co-edited with Nancy Stubbs and Bill Cressey. He has served on the SECUSSA Task Force on Financial Aid since its founding in the mid-1980s.

PAUL DEYOUNG is the director of international programs at Reed College. During his fifteen years at Reed, he has developed a comprehensive international framework (Reed is a member of the International 50 Liberal Arts Colleges), including overseas study, on-campus international programs and international student and scholar services united within one office. He holds undergraduate and graduate degrees from Stanford University and a Ph.D. from the University of Oregon. He is a long-standing member of IIE, NAFSA, and CIEE. He has been a Fulbright grantee to Germany, and he has most recently been researching the impact of reunification on higher education exchanges between the United States and the former GDR.

307

JANEEN FELSING is associate director for overseas study at the University of Oregon. She has a master's degree from the University of Iowa, where she also worked for several years as assistant director in the Office of International Education and Services. She has held a variety of NAFSA positions, including SECUSSA chair of Region IV (1984–86); SECUSSA national team member (1986–89); program coordinator, national conference in Minneapolis (1989); and member, SECUSSA Task Force on Financial Aid.

CATHERINE GAMON is vice president, of the College Division of the American Institute for Foreign Study (eastern region). Formerly, she was the coordinator in the Opportunities Abroad Office at the University of California-San Diego International Center (1989–91); the opportunities abroad adviser at UCSD International Center (1984–89); and assistant director for overseas resources, Bechtel International Center, Stanford University. She was the editor of *NAFSA's Study, Work, and Travel Abroad: A Bibliography*, and author of the AIFS *Advisors' Guide.*

MARGERY A. GANZ is a tenured associate professor of history at Spelman College and has served as the college's official coordinator of study abroad for the last four years. She has given several talks at NAFSA, CIEE, and IES annual conferences on the subject of minority students and study abroad. Her last talk, "The Spelman Experience: Encouraging and Supporting Minority Students Abroad," appears in *Black Students and Overseas Programs: Broadening the Base of Participation* published by CIEE. Currently she serves on Beaver College's Center for Education Abroad national advisory board, Butler University's national advisory council, and CIEE's board of directors.

JAMES GEHLHAR has been active in NAFSA and SECUSSA since 1979. He directs the Center for International Education at the University of Tennessee-Knoxville. Having been an international student in Lebanon and in Scotland, his academic area of interest is the Middle East. He currently represents NAFSA on the International Education Data Collection Committee and is on the SECUSSA Task Force on Financial Aid.

JOAN ELIAS GORE is field director for the middle atlantic and southeastern United States for the Council on International Educational Exchange. She has worked with agencies that have developed and managed programs worldwide; functioned as resident director for overseas programs; and worked as a study-abroad adviser and administrator at a university. She has written, published, and presented on a wide variety of topics in the field of study abroad, including study-abroad fairs, financial aid, professional development, the historical development of American undergraduate study abroad, and health issues critical to the American student abroad.

MARY ANNE GRANT is executive director of the International Student Exchange Program in Washington, D.C.

JACK HENDERSON is director of off-campus studies and an associate professor of French at Dickinson College, where he directs the operation of twenty overseas study programs. He has been active in international education and study abroad for more than twenty-five years. A member of NAFSA since 1973, he has participated in regional and national conferences and has served on numerous national academic advisory boards, committees, and task forces. He was a contributor to the 1975 *SECUSSA Sourcebook*.

WILLIAM HOFFA, presently the field director, university programs, for CIEE, holds a doctorate in English and American studies. He has eighteen years of teaching experience at Vanderbilt University and Hamilton College. For nine years, Mr. Hoffa was executive director of Scandinavian Seminar. He is a regular contributor to NAFSA national and regional conferences, and currently serves as chair of the SECUSSA national team.

ELEANOR KRAWUTSCHKE is currently completing a law degree at the University of Toledo College of Law with an emphasis on international law. She has been the coordinator of the Foreign Student Services Department at Western Michigan University, and has also taught foreign languages. She coauthored three NAFSA publications: *Transcripts from Study Abroad Programs: A Workbook, Study Abroad Programs: An Evaluation Guide*, and *Students Abroad: A Guide for Selecting a Foreign Education.*

DAVID LARSEN is vice president of Beaver College in Pennsylvania, where he directs the Beaver College Center for Education Abroad, one of the oldest and largest study-abroad programs in the United States. He has been involved in international education since 1969 and has recently served as a director of the Fulbright Association of CIEE and of the Association for International Practical Training. He is a frequent consultant and writes and speaks on topics related to the field.

MICHAEL LAUBSCHER, director of the Office of Education Abroad Programs at the Pennsylvania State University, has had over twenty years of experience in the field of international education. After four years of active duty as an officer in the U.S. Air Force, he joined Penn State in October 1971. He has been a presenter on panels at NAFSA's national and regional conferences and CIEE's national conferences. He holds a B.A. and an M.A. from Penn State, and recently completed his D.Ed. in higher education, also at Penn State. His primary area of scholarly interest is in the role of experiential education in promoting an appreciation for cultural diversity.

JOSEPH NAVARI has been the director of the Office of International Programs and adjunct professor of history at the University of Akron since 1987. He was formerly the director of the Center for International Studies at St. Cloud University in Minnesota. He has been a Fulbright scholar in Germany and a Peace Corps instructor in Tunisia. He has also presented a numerous NAFSA national and regional conferences.

WILLIAM NOLTING has been the director of overseas opportunities at the University of Michigan International Center since 1989. This office has received commendation from CIEE almost annually as the national leader in work-abroad programs. He was previously coordinator of international programs at Colgate University, where he also served as assistant director of the Yugoslav Study Group. A member of NAFSA since 1985, he has been the SECUSSA representative for Region X (1988–89), has presented in and chaired numerous conference sessions, and is currently a member of the SECUSSA Task Force on Financial Aid. His own overseas experience includes graduate study in philosophy and sociology at the Universitaet Freiburg and the Technische Universitaet Berlin in Germany, where he supported himself by working as a cabinetmaker, metalworker, technical translator, and interpreter.

JACK OSBORN was until 1992 the director of off-campus study at Scripps College in California, where he directed programs abroad in Zimbabwe, Quito, Paris, and Heidelberg. He has been a frequent contributor at NAFSA meetings, and has been on the advisory boards of Beaver College's Center for Education Abroad and Butler University's Institute for Study Abroad.

MARGARET BROWN PAVIOUR is currently a health educator in the Thomas Jefferson Health District in Charlottesville, Virginia. She was perviously the director of health education in the Department of Student Health at the University of Virginia. She holds a bachelor's from Oberlin College and a master's in community health education from CUNY-Hunter College.

JOHN PEARSON is the director of the Bechtel International Center and assistant dean of students at Stanford University. Formerly, he was the assistant director for international education at the University of Tennessee-Knoxville. He was a SECUSSA team member, (1989–92); chair of AACRAO Study Abroad Committee, 1991–92; and a member of the UK PIER workshop team (group leader for the study-abroad chapter) in 1990. He is presently SECUSSA liaison to NAFSA's ANSWER project; and a member of the advisory boards of Beaver College's Center for Education Abroad, Scandinavian Seminar, and *Transitions Abroad* magazine. He has a bachelor's in American studies from the University College of Wales, Swansea (1970), and a master's in American studies from the University of London (1971).

RONALD PIROG is associate director of off-campus studies and assistant professor of German at Dickinson College in Carlisle, Pennsylvania. He has been a NAFSA member since 1987 and a SECUSSA Region VIII representative (1990–92). He has chaired and presented at workshops and sessions at the NAFSA VIII conference. On the Dickinson College campus, he is the coordinator for the Institute of European/Asian Studies, the Appalachian Semester Program, and the Central Pennsylvania Consortium for Student Exchange.

PAUL PRIMAK coordinates programs in Denmark, Ecuador, Japan, and Korea for the Oregon state system of higher education. He is currently developing new programs in Mexico and Thailand. Previously, he served as assistant director of the Office of International Education and Exchange at the University of Oregon (1980–91). He has traveled throughout western Europe and in Mexico, Ecuador, Japan, Korea, and Thailand. His bachelor's is in political science, and he has done graduate work in international studies and educational policy at the University of Oregon.

TOM ROBERTS is the director of the Institute for Study Abroad at Butler University. Formerly vice president and director of program development for the Institute for European Studies, he has served NAFSA as chair of the Lily von Klemperer Awards Committee, as founder and first chair of the SECUSSA Old Timers, as co-editor of *Transcripts from Study Abroad Programs: A Workbook* and *Recording the Performance of U.S. Undergraduates at British Institutions*, chair of SECUSSA (1986–87).

KATHLEEN SIDELI is associate director for academic affairs at the Office of Overseas Study at Indiana University-Bloomington, where she designed a campus information center based on a self-help system. She has been active in the field of computer applications for study abroad since the mid-1980s. She is also a part-time assistant professor in the Department of Spanish and Portuguese, teaching grammar, culture, and literature. She is a co-author of a textbook of advanced Spanish grammar that is currently being used at Indiana University.

MARVIN SLIND is currently a visiting assistant professor of history at Washington State University (since 1989); prior to that he was associate director of the Office of International Education at Washington State University. He served as SECUSSA chair in 1990–91. He has a B.A. in history from Pacific Lutheran University (1969), and a M.A. and Ph.D. in history from Washington State University (1972 and 1978, respectively). He attended the University of Heidelberg as a Fulbright scholar in 1975–76.

HEIDI SONESON is the program director for European programs in the

311

Global Campus at the University of Minnesota. In this position, she coordinates group programs in Austria, England, France, Poland, and Russia. In addition, she has initiated programs for nontraditional students and for underrepresented disciplines in study abroad.

PAULA SPIER is the retired dean of Antioch College's international programs. She continues to be active as a consultant, panelist, writer, and reviewer. She has served as executive coordinator for the CIEE Advisory Council on International Educational Exchange (which produced the 1988 *Educating for Global Competence*), as chair of the Fulbright Selection committee for the German exchange project, on the SECUSSA team, and NAFSA's board of directors, as well as on numerous committees for Antioch and the Great Lakes Colleges Association. She has been honored with CIEE's Award for Service, NAFSA Region VI's Leo Dowling Award, and NAFSA's Life Membership Award. She is currently working on a manuscript tentatively titled *Mother Spier's Guide to the World*.

NANCY STUBBS is currently the acting director of study abroad programs at the University of Colorado-Boulder (1992–present), where she served as the associate director 1988, and was the finance officer for international education (1979–88). She has a B.A. in music education and M.A. in public administration from the University of Colorado-Boulder. She has presented at NAFSA, CIEE, and AACRAO conferences, and chairs SECUSSA's Committee on Financial Aid and Study Abroad (1989–present). She co-edited NAFSA's *Financial Aid for Study Abroad*.

ELLEN SUMMERFIELD is director of international programs and a professor of German at Linfield College, Oregon. Prior to coming to Linfield, she taught at Middlebury College and directed Middlebury's graduate school in Mainz, Germany. She also served as assistant director of foreign study at Kalamazoo College. She holds a doctorate in German language and literature from the University of Connecticut and has published in the fields of German literature and international education. Her third book, *Crossing Cultures through Film*, will be published by Intercultural Press in summer 1993.

HENRY WEAVER is emeritus professor of chemistry and provost of Goshen College in Indiana. From 1979 to 1991 he served as the deputy director of the University of California system's Education Abroad Program. He is the co-author of *Students Abroad: Strangers at Home*.

MY YARABINEC studied as a junior in Italy and did graduate research at the British Museum in London, England. He served in the U.S. Peace Corps in Morocco, and worked for the French cultural services for five years in Paris

312

and three years for the French consulate in San Francisco. He has worked as an international student adviser at the University of Southern California and as the campus relations officer for California State University International Programs, where he was in charge of recruitment, publicity, and promotion for the CSU system's study-abroad program. He is currently the executive director of the Northern California Careers Consortium, which is based at the University of California-Berkeley.